Payroll Management

2017 Edition

Steven M. Bragg

For more information about AccountingTools® products, visit our Web site at www.accountingtools.com.

ISBN-13: 978-1-938910-77-7

Printed in the United States of America

Table of Contents

Table of Contents

Table of Contents

Table of Contents

Table of Contents

Table of Contents

Table of Contents

Preface

The payroll department has one of the most difficult jobs in business – it must comply with a maze of payroll regulations, volumes of paperwork, and an array of disjointed systems to somehow pay employees the correct amounts, remit taxes to the government on time, and issue accurate and timely reports to the government and management.

Payroll Management makes the payroll department's job easier by clearly defining the most efficient and effective means for running the department, while also addressing the following topics:

- Whether an individual is an employee
- How to track employee time worked
- How to calculate all types of employee earnings
- How to process tax withholdings and other deductions
- How and when to remit taxes to the government
- How to select the best method for paying employees
- How to complete and submit government forms
- How to set up a payroll recordkeeping system
- Which procedures, forms, and controls to install for payroll processes
- How to measure the performance of the department

An appendix contains the due dates for key filings and remittances to the federal government.

Payroll Management is designed for both professional accountants and students, since both can benefit from its detailed descriptions of payroll systems, controls, procedures, and regulations.

Payroll Management provides the basis for operating a payroll department. It is also updated annually to incorporate the latest payroll regulations. As such, it may earn a place on your book shelf as a reference tool for years to come.

Centennial, Colorado
November, 2016

About the Author

Steven Bragg, CPA, has been the chief financial officer or controller of four companies, as well as a consulting manager at Ernst & Young. He received a master's degree in finance from Bentley College, an MBA from Babson College, and a Bachelor's degree in Economics from the University of Maine. He has been a two-time president of the Colorado Mountain Club, and is an avid alpine skier, mountain biker, and certified master diver. Mr. Bragg resides in Centennial, Colorado. He has written the following books and courses:

7 Habits of Effective CFOs
7 Habits of Effective Controllers
Accountants' Guidebook
Accounting Changes and Error Corrections
Accounting Controls Guidebook
Accounting for Casinos and Gaming
Accounting for Derivatives and Hedges
Accounting for Earnings per Share
Accounting for Inventory
Accounting for Investments
Accounting for Intangible Assets
Accounting for Leases
Accounting for Managers
Accounting for Stock-Based Compensation
Accounting Procedures Guidebook
Agricultural Accounting
Behavioral Ethics
Bookkeeping Guidebook
Budgeting
Business Combinations and Consolidations
Business Insurance Fundamentals
Business Ratios
Business Valuation
Capital Budgeting
CFO Guidebook
Change Management
Closing the Books
Coaching and Mentoring
Constraint Management
Construction Accounting
Corporate Cash Management
Corporate Finance
Cost Accounting (college textbook)
Cost Accounting Fundamentals
Cost Management Guidebook
Credit & Collection Guidebook
Developing and Managing Teams
Employee Onboarding

Enterprise Risk Management
Fair Value Accounting
Financial Analysis
Financial Forecasting and Modeling
Fixed Asset Accounting
Foreign Currency Accounting
Fraud Examination
GAAP Guidebook
Hospitality Accounting
How to Run a Meeting
Human Resources Guidebook
IFRS Guidebook
Interpretation of Financial Statements
Inventory Management
Investor Relations Guidebook
Lean Accounting Guidebook
Mergers & Acquisitions
Negotiation
New Controller Guidebook
Nonprofit Accounting
Partnership Accounting
Payables Management
Payroll Management
Project Accounting
Project Management
Public Company Accounting
Purchasing Guidebook
Real Estate Accounting
Records Management
Recruiting and Hiring
Revenue Recognition
The MBA Guidebook
The Soft Close
The Statement of Cash Flows
The Year-End Close
Treasurer's Guidebook
Working Capital Management

On-Line Resources by Steven Bragg

Steven maintains the accountingtools.com web site, which contains continuing professional education courses, the Accounting Best Practices podcast, and hundreds of articles on accounting subjects.

Payroll Management is also available as a continuing professional education (CPE) course. You can purchase the course (and many other courses) and take an on-line exam at:

www.accountingtools.com/cpe

Chapter 1
Payroll Management

Introduction

In a traditional payroll department that is indifferently managed, the payroll staff spends most of its time on payroll data entry for the next scheduled payroll, and cleaning up errors and mistakes from the last payroll. The nature of this work has two ramifications:

- The payroll staff works on nothing but data entry-level tasks; and
- The department is so inundated with the high volume of transactions that it never has any time to spare for systemic improvements.

This chapter describes a fundamental change in the responsibilities and work flow of the payroll department, which ultimately transforms it into a smaller group of well-trained employees who monitor transactions being entered into the payroll system by people outside of the department, and who are process specialists who are committed to continually enhancing the efficiency and effectiveness of the department.

Related podcast episodes: Episodes 126 through 129 of the Accounting Best Practices Podcast discuss the streamlining of payroll. They are available at: **www.accountingtools.com/podcasts** or **iTunes**

Payroll Cycle Duration

One of the more important payroll management decisions is how long to set the payroll cycle. Each payroll requires a great deal of effort by the payroll staff to collect information about time worked, locate and correct errors, process wage rate and deduction changes, calculate pay, and issue payments. Consequently, it makes a great deal of sense to extend the duration of payroll cycles.

If payrolls are spaced at short intervals, such as weekly, the payroll staff has to prepare 52 payrolls per year. Conversely, paying employees once a month reduces the payroll staff's payroll preparation activities by approximately three-quarters. Since paying employees just once a month can be a burden on the employees, companies frequently adopt a half-way measure, paying employees either twice a month (the *semimonthly* payroll) or once every two weeks (the *biweekly* payroll). The semimonthly payroll cycle results in processing 24 payrolls per year, while the biweekly payroll cycle requires the processing of 26 payrolls per year.

An example of a weekly payroll cycle is shown below, where employees are paid every Tuesday for the hours they worked in the preceding week.

Weekly Payroll Cycle

January						
S	M	T	W	T	F	S
	1	2	3	4	5	6
7	8	9	10	11	12	13
14	15	16	17	18	19	20
21	22	23	24	25	26	27
28	29	30	31			

An example of a biweekly payroll cycle is shown below, where employees are paid every other Tuesday for the hours worked in the preceding two weeks:

Biweekly Payroll Cycle

January						
S	M	T	W	T	F	S
	1	2	3	4	5	6
7	8	9	10	11	12	13
14	15	16	17	18	19	20
21	22	23	24	25	26	27
28	29	30	31			

An example of a semimonthly payroll cycle is shown below, where employees are paid on the 15th and last days of the month.

Semimonthly Payroll Cycle

January						
S	M	T	W	T	F	S
	1	2	3	4	5	6
7	8	9	10	11	12	13
14	15	16	17	18	19	20
21	22	23	24	25	26	27
28	29	30	31			

An example of a monthly payroll cycle is shown below, where employees are paid on the last day of the month.

Monthly Payroll Cycle

January						
S	M	T	W	T	F	S
	1	2	3	4	5	6
7	8	9	10	11	12	13
14	15	16	17	18	19	20
21	22	23	24	25	26	27
28	29	30	31			

An argument in favor of the biweekly payroll is that employees become accustomed to receiving two paychecks per month, plus two "free" paychecks during the year, which has a somewhat more positive impact on employee morale. Nonetheless, the semimonthly payroll represents a slight improvement over the biweekly payroll from the perspective of payroll department efficiency, and is therefore recommended.

If employees are accustomed to a weekly payroll cycle and they are switched to one of a longer duration, expect to have some employees complain about not having enough cash to see them through the initial increased payroll cycle. This problem can be mitigated by extending pay advances to employees during the initial conversion to the longer payroll cycle. Once employees receive their larger paychecks under the new payroll cycle, they should be able to support themselves and will no longer need an advance.

A further issue is when a company operates a different payroll cycle for different groups of employees. For example, hourly employees may be paid on a weekly cycle and salaried employees on a semimonthly cycle. To complicate matters further, a company may have acquired other businesses and retained the payroll cycles used for their employees. Retaining all of these payroll cycles places the payroll staff in the position of perpetually preparing payrolls, so that it never has time for other activities. To avoid this problem, convert all of the different payroll cycles to a single one that applies to all employees. This may take a large amount of effort, but is mandatory if the payroll staff is to be unburdened from base-level data entry activities.

In short, paying employees at roughly half-month intervals and not allowing any additional payroll cycles can greatly reduce the work load of the payroll department. Once achieved, the staff will have more time available to address the improvement possibilities described in the following sections.

Streamlined Timekeeping

It is entirely common for the payroll department to be mired in the accumulation of timekeeping information; this encompasses the error-laden steps of coaxing timesheets from employees, correcting their submissions, and cajoling supervisors to approve the timesheets – followed by manually entering the information into the payroll software.

Several issues must be addressed in order to break free of the timekeeping data entry trap. These issues are:

1. *Who submits information.* There is no need to collect hours-worked information from salaried employees, so they should not submit timesheets for payroll purposes. Further, if those employees who are paid on an hourly basis nearly always work a standard 40-hour work week, they should only be reporting on an exception basis, when their hours worked vary from this baseline amount.

2. *How much information to collect.* The main protest against the last point is that employees must submit information irrespective of their salary or wage status, because the company is also tracking hours billed to customers or hours worked on specific jobs. This brings up two sub-issues:

    - *Is the information needed at all?* In many cases, the information collected through the payroll system was originally needed for a specific project or report. The data collection continues, though the project has long since been completed or the report is no longer used. Thus, consider periodically questioning the need for any information being collected through the payroll system.

    - *Can the information be separated from the payroll system?* In those cases where the information *must* be collected (such as hours worked that will be billed to customers), does the payroll staff need to collect it? For example, if a company has a large number of salaried consultants whose hours are billed to customers, the payroll staff can pay them without any timekeeping data collection at all – the collection of billed hours is more appropriately a function of the billing staff.

3. *How to automate timekeeping.* The automation of timekeeping involves two sub-issues, which are:

    - *How to automate data collection.* There are a number of solutions available that allow employees to directly enter their hours worked and a selection of additional data into a timekeeping database, thereby eliminating the traditional timesheet or time card and the need for the payroll staff to manually collect and enter this information. Technologies to choose from include the online timekeeping system, computerized time clocks, and timekeeping by smart phone. See the Employee Time Tracking chapter for more information.

    - *How to create an interface to the payroll system.* The automation of data collection only means that the information is stored in a computer database – it must still be shifted into the correct fields within the payroll system, so that payroll can be processed. This calls for a custom interface that automatically shifts the data, with no manual intervention.

Note that the automation of timekeeping is presented as the *last* action to take when streamlining timekeeping. That is because it is better to explore the *need* for timekeeping first, so that the timekeeping requirement can be whittled down to the bare minimum before investing any funds in an automated timekeeping solution.

The impact of streamlined timekeeping on the payroll department can be extraordinary - there may be no data entry work for the payroll staff at all. Instead, the department is more concerned with operating the timekeeping systems and monitoring entered information for discrepancies, missing fields, and errors. Ultimately, this means that the type of knowledge required of the payroll staff will shift away from data entry skills and toward data analysis and computer systems.

Tip: The cost of the equipment, software, and training related to an automated timekeeping solution may appear excessive for a company with a small number of employees, since the cost of manually collecting timekeeping information is not large for them. If this is the case, consider outsourcing payroll to a supplier that also provides an online timekeeping service. This solution is not expensive, and still provides the benefit of shifting timekeeping data entry away from the payroll staff.

Electronic Payments

After timekeeping, the next largest use of payroll staff time is paying employees. There are a number of controls and processing steps associated with payments using paychecks, and an even greater number if employees are paid with cash. This labor can be greatly reduced by shifting employees to either direct deposit or pay cards. In both cases, funds are shifted electronically to employees, so there is no paycheck distribution. See the Payments to Employees chapter for more information.

Some state governments do not allow employers to switch to electronic payments without the consent of their employees. This problem can be resolved by requiring new employees to opt out of electronic payments, by issuing reminders to those still receiving paychecks, and by having educational meetings to show the benefits of electronic payments. While the target should be 100% electronic payments, even a smaller percentage results in less work for the payroll staff.

To fully implement electronic payments, send remittance advices to employees by e-mail, or send them an e-mail notification of where they can access this information in a secure online data repository. Similarly, issue the annual Form W-2 to employees by storing the forms in an online data repository that employees can access.

By using online systems to pay employees and issue reports, the payroll department can completely avoid the time-consuming steps of printing checks, having them approved, and handing them out to employees.

Employee Self-Service

Employees sometimes need to change the information used to compile their net pay, such as benefits that require pay deductions, or their marriage status, or withholding allowances. Traditionally, employees fill out a form in which they authorize these changes to their payroll records, and the payroll staff enters the information into the payroll system. This is not a large chore in a smaller company, but can involve full-time staff in a larger company where the sheer volume of employees results in a great many changes.

This data entry task can be eliminated by having employees enter the information directly into the payroll system themselves, using an online portal. The types of information they can enter includes the items just noted, as well as changes to their addresses and bank account information. The self-service portal is a common feature if payroll processing is outsourced to a major payroll supplier, though there is usually an extra fee charged to use it.

The payroll staff should still monitor the information being entered by employees for errors. This can be done by reviewing a change log or by creating custom reports that only report changes that exceed predetermined "normal" entries (such as entering a withholding allowance that is inordinately high).

Manager Self-Service

Department managers are the source of a different set of payroll information. They submit changes to employee pay rates, department codes, and shift differentials, as well as start and termination dates. As was the case with employee self-service, it is possible to construct an online portal through which managers can make these changes themselves. And as was the case for employee self-service, the payroll staff should monitor these changes.

It is critical for the payroll staff to monitor changes made by managers, since these alterations will impact the company's compensation and payroll tax expenses. Monitoring may include comparing pay changes to the authorized pay change percentages assigned to each manager, and verifying pay rates with senior management if the rates exceed authorized levels.

Manager self-service is not as easy a feature to find in many payroll systems, since it is considered to have a smaller cost-benefit than employee self-service. Nonetheless, if the improvement steps noted in the preceding sections have been completed, this is the next logical step to pursue.

Transaction Error Analysis

It requires far more time to track down a payroll error and correct it than it does to initially enter the transaction correctly. Further, the more experienced (and expensive) staff are typically assigned to investigate and correct errors. Thus, the cost of transaction errors is high, and is worthy of detailed analysis to find the causes of errors and prevent them from occurring again.

Transaction error analysis begins with the summarization of all payroll errors into a single document, so that they can be classified and prioritized. This may call for an informal system where the payroll staff forwards any complaints received regarding pay problems, which are then translated into a standard format. Then

6

select a single error type to pursue, and investigate it with the goal of isolating the specific issue that caused the error to occur. Then fix the issue, and monitor it to see if the error has now been eliminated. Examples of errors and their causes and possible corrections are shown in the following table:

Sample Payroll Errors and Corrections

Error	Source of Error	Error Correction
Timesheet not recorded	Employee did not submit timesheet	Send automated e-mail notification
Incorrect timesheet total	Clerk incorrectly added hours	Switch to computerized time clock
Overtime not approved	Supervisor did not sign card	Switch to computerized time clock
No benefits deduction	Clerk did not add deduction	Use standard deductions checklist
Allowance not updated	Clerk did not enter allowance change	Install employee self-service
Paycheck not signed	Checks stuck together	Use signature stamp
Paycheck issued for terminated employee	Clerk did not update pay status to terminated	Install manager self-service

Tip: Do not turn transaction error analysis into a witch hunt, where blame for an error is assigned to a specific person. If this approach is taken, the payroll staff will not forward any errors. Instead, make it clear that changes to the underlying systems are being pursued that will keep errors from arising again.

Staff Training Program

An employee in the payroll department needs a broad skill set in order to work at an optimal level of efficiency. These skills become more broad-ranging over time, as the department moves away from data entry tasks and into data analysis and system installations. Also, the legal requirements associated with payroll are considerable, and are increasing in complexity every year. Further, as the department rolls out a variety of payroll tools for employees to use throughout the company, the payroll staff must enter into a training role, where they show employees how to use these tools. Clearly, there is a need for a comprehensive and ongoing training program for the entire payroll staff.

In a modern, thoroughly computerized payroll department, the staff should receive training in the following areas:

- *Payroll software.* Every payroll software package has a different set of commands, modules, file structures, and so forth, and employees must be fully aware of how to handle transactions through the software. This usually involves a separate training class for each module of the software. Even if payroll is outsourced, the supplier's online software must still be accessed, so training in its software is required.

- *Payroll processes.* There is a particular flow to payroll processes that is driven by the level of automation, the type of software, and payroll regulations. Employees must be thoroughly familiar with these processes.
- *Regulatory changes.* There are regulatory changes every year that impact the payroll department. While the payroll manager could simply send everyone to a conference to learn about the most recent changes, a more cost-effective approach is to have a consultant monitor the changes and create a custom in-house training class to convey these changes to the staff. The latter approach requires a significant consulting fee, but keeps the staff in-house for the training, thereby avoiding travel and conference fees. It also results in a seminar that is expressly designed for the needs of the company and the locations where it has employees.
- *Data analysis.* As the department shifts away from data entry, there is a greater need for the payroll staff to review data entered by others, to verify that it is correct. This calls for training in report writing software, so that they can create a set of standard analysis reports that highlight possible data entry issues.
- *Training skills.* When the payroll department pushes software and hardware out from the department for use by other employees to enter information, it must also take on the task of training employees in their use. Consequently, several members of the department should be taught how to train others.

It is difficult to standardize payroll training for everyone in the payroll department, since some people are specialized on specific tasks, and their skill sets do not need to extend beyond those areas. Also, some people have more experience than others. Consequently, ascertain the skill set required by each person, and the specific areas in which extra training is needed to bring them up to the required standard. Then create a training plan for everyone in the department, and go over it with them on a regular basis to review their progress in meeting their training goals.

The Payroll Calendar

The payroll department's activities are driven by a large number of deadlines – for paying employees, depositing taxes, issuing reports, and so forth. Without a proper amount of documentation, it would be impossible to go through a year without missing some deadlines, and likely incurring both the wrath of employees and government-imposed penalties.

The solution to these problems is the departmental payroll calendar. This is a full-year schedule, on which is recorded all due dates and who is responsible for them. The payroll manager retains this full schedule, and may issue a subset of the calendar to his employees, so that each one has a calendar containing only those activities for which he or she is responsible. An example of a master department payroll calendar for a single month is shown next.

Sample Payroll Calendar

Monday	Tuesday	Wednesday	Thursday	Friday
1 Issue metrics Process payroll Fund bank acct Journal entry	2 State deposit	3 Forward garnishments	4	5 Timesheets EFTPS deposit
8 Process payroll Fund bank acct Journal entry	9 Issue checks State deposit	10 Forward garnishments Form 4070	11	12 Timesheets EFTPS deposit
15 Process payroll Fund bank acct Journal entry Jones vacation	16 Issue checks State deposit Jones vacation	17 Forward garnishments Jones vacation	18 Jones vacation	19 Timesheets EFTPS deposit Jones vacation
22 Process payroll Fund bank acct Journal entry	23 Issue checks State deposit	24 Forward garnishments	25	26 Timesheets EFTPS deposit
29 Process payroll Fund bank acct Journal entry	30 Issue checks State deposit	31 Forms W-2 Forms 1099 Form 940 Form 941 Form 945 FUTA deposit		

Note that the calendar also includes a scheduled week of vacation for one employee. This information provides the staff with notice of a capacity reduction during that week, which it will need to plan around.

The payroll calendar is particularly important if there are new employees in the department who do not yet have experience with those deadlines pertaining to the operations of the department – it is a useful reminder for these individuals.

Ideally, the payroll manager should consult the payroll calendar for the following day, and verify that the staff is aware of the deadlines for that day, and how any issues will be addressed. If a specific date is likely to require a larger amount of work than usual (such as the final day of January in the preceding example), the manager can use the calendar to plan well in advance for how to handle the work load.

Information Confidentiality

A major issue for any payroll department is to ensure that a large part of the information it processes remains confidential. Most employees would consider it disastrous if information about their wages, pension plans, garnishments, social security numbers, and so forth were to be made public. This information is located in the payroll register and employee files, and may be scattered among other payroll reports, as well. The following are recommended methods for improving the confidentiality of payroll information:

- *Locked storage.* Clearly, the best single action to take is to enhance confidentiality is to keep payroll documents in a locked storage area. This can be a locked storage cabinet, or locked room with a door that automatically closes and locks.
- *Password protection.* Anyone using the payroll software must input a password to access the system. Further, set the software to require a new password at frequent intervals.
- *Limit authorization.* Even within the payroll department, it is not necessary for every employee to have full access to payroll information. For example, if there is a clerk who only handles employee timesheets, do not give that person access to other types of payroll information.
- *Shred documents.* Once the company is no longer required to continue archiving old payroll files, do not just throw them in the trash; instead, shred them. There are shredding services in most major cities that can handle this task.
- *Dissemination policy.* Have a department policy that no one ever gives out confidential information without specific authorization. In all cases, this should involve the approval of the payroll manager.

Summary

This chapter has addressed a number of general management concepts that are designed to improve the efficiency and effectiveness of the payroll department. Ultimately, this can result in a department that has shifted almost entirely away from data entry activities, and instead spends most of its time monitoring payroll transactions, installing new systems, and issuing reports related to payroll expenses. This sweeping change will also result in a department whose employees have a much higher knowledge of payroll regulations, controls, and systems.

The sections presented near the beginning of this chapter were sorted in order by the importance of their impact on the payroll department. Thus, consider implementing changes in the following order:

1. *Reduce and consolidate the number of payrolls.* This can substantially reduce the work load of the department, giving it more time to implement additional changes.
2. *Streamline timekeeping.* The time savings from eliminating data entry tasks is potentially enormous.
3. *Shift to electronic payments.* The payroll staff can avoid printing and distributing paychecks if it can persuade employees to switch to direct deposit or pay cards.

4. *Install employee self-service.* Employees can enter information directly into the payroll system related to their withholding allowances, benefits, bank accounts, mailing information, and so forth.
5. *Install manager self-service.* Managers can enter information directly into the payroll system related to employee pay rates, department codes, shift differentials, and so forth.

A comprehensive staff training program should be implemented as the preceding steps are gradually completed, because the nature of the employees' work will diverge more and more from their original data entry-oriented tasks and into areas that require more knowledge. They will also need training skills, since they must show employees throughout the company how to use the new timekeeping and self-service systems to enter information into the payroll system. Thus, the training program may begin as a relatively small effort, and gradually change into a major undertaking that involves all of the payroll staff on an ongoing basis.

In the following chapters, we move on from the management concepts espoused in this chapter to address the multitude of issues surrounding timekeeping, payroll processing, tax remittances, and so forth that form the day-to-day concerns of the payroll department.

Chapter 2
Definition of an Employee

Introduction

The key factor in deducting payroll taxes or withholding income taxes from a person's wages is whether or not to classify that person as an employee. There are also significant liabilities for a company that incorrectly designates a person as an independent contractor who is actually an employee. Thus, it is important to understand the circumstances under which an individual is classified as an employee.

The Employee Defined

A person who performs services for a business may be categorized in one of the following ways:

- *Common-law employee*. Under common-law rules, someone is an employee if the employer has the right to control what will be done and how it will be done, even if the individual has a considerable degree of freedom of action. A person who meets these criteria is considered an employee, irrespective of all other considerations. For example, a person is still an employee if he works on a full-time or part-time basis, and irrespective of any job title, such as being called an agent or an independent contractor.
- *Independent contractor*. This includes people who follow an independent trade in which they offer services to the public, such as doctors, locksmiths, and plumbers. These people are not considered employees, especially if they have control over the means and methods of producing their work.
- *Statutory employee*. A worker is considered an employee if he or she falls into one of the following categories:
  - A driver who delivers food, beverages (other than milk), laundry, or dry cleaning for someone else. This person may be on a commission form of compensation.
  - A full-time life insurance salesperson who sells primarily on behalf of one company.
  - Someone who works at home under guidelines issued by the entity for which the work is done, with materials furnished by and returned to that entity.
  - A traveling salesperson who works full-time for one entity to obtain orders from customers. These orders must be for items for either resale or use as supplies in the customer's business. The customers must either be contractors, retailers, wholesalers, or operators of ho-

tels, restaurants, or any other businesses dealing with food or lodgings.

In addition, the service contract must state or imply that substantially all of the services are to be performed personally by the worker, the worker does not have a substantial investment in the assets used to perform the service, and the service is performed on a continuing basis for the same payer.

- *Statutory nonemployee.* By statute, there are three categories of workers who are *not* considered to be employees. They are:
    - *Companion sitters.* Includes individuals who provide personal attendance, companionship, or household care services to children, the elderly, or the disabled.
    - *Direct sellers.* Includes individuals selling consumer products other than in a retail establishment, and those delivering newspapers. This classification applies if payments to the person are directly related to sales or other output, rather than the number of hours worked, and their services are performed under a written contract stating that they will not be classified as employees for federal tax deduction and withholding purposes.
    - *Qualified real estate agents.* Includes real estate agents as well as those people engaged in appraisal activities where they earn income based on sales. This classification applies if payments to the person are directly related to sales or other output, rather than the number of hours worked, and their services are performed under a written contract stating that they will not be classified as employees for federal tax deduction and withholding purposes.

The definition of a statutory employee is of particular significance, because payroll taxes are only deducted from the wages of statutory employees; federal income taxes are not withheld from their wages.

If the employer wants to request a determination from the IRS regarding whether a worker is to be classified as an employee, file Form SS-8, Determination of Worker Status for Purposes of Federal Employment Taxes and Income Tax Withholding.

Employee Withholding Liability

If a person is designated as an employee, deduct social security and Medicare taxes from that person's pay, as well as withhold income taxes. If a company does not do so for a designated employee, the company is liable for these items. Further, the company is responsible for the full employer share of all social security and Medicare taxes.

If there is a reasonable basis for not classifying a worker as an employee, it is possible to gain relief from this liability. However, relief is only possible if the company has filed all required federal tax returns in a manner consistent with how it has treated the worker.

The Independent Contractor Designation

Perhaps the single most critical issue in the definition of an employee is whether an individual should instead be classified as an independent contractor. The point is a major one, since a company can avoid a significant liability for deducting payroll taxes and withholding income taxes, as well as for avoiding the payment of matching amounts of social security and Medicare taxes.

To determine whether a person can be classified as an independent contractor, review the entire working relationship between the company and the person, and arrive at a decision based on the complete body of evidence. There are three categories of facts to consider, which are:

- *Behavioral control.* A person is an employee if the business has the right to direct and control how the person does the task for which he was hired. The amount of control is based on the level of instruction regarding such issues as when and where to work, what equipment to use, which employees to use, where to buy supplies, what sequence of tasks to follow, and so forth. Behavioral control can include training by the company to perform services in a particular way.
- *Financial control.* Facts indicative of financial control by the company are the extent to which a worker is reimbursed for business expenses, the amount of investment by the worker in the business, the extent to which the worker sells his services to other parties, whether the amount paid to the person is based on time worked rather than for a work product, and whether the worker can participate in a profit or loss.
- *Type of relationship.* A person is more likely to be considered an independent contractor if there is a written contract describing the relationship of the parties, the business does not provide benefits to the person, the relationship is not permanent, and the services performed are not a key aspect of the regular business of the company.

EXAMPLE

Mr. David Stringer is a securities attorney who specializes in the issuance of bonds. He has been paid on an hourly basis for the last ten years by his sole client, Heavy Lift Corporation (HLC), and is reimbursed by HLC for expenses incurred. The CFO of HLC does not attempt to control the work habits of Mr. Stringer. There is no contract between the two parties; instead, Mr. Stringer simply issues an invoice to HLC at the end of each month, and the company pays it. HLC does not pay any benefits to Mr. Stringer. HLC is not in the business of selling bonds – it only does so periodically in order to raise capital.

The cumulative evidence in this situation is in favor of Mr. Stringer being an independent contractor. HLC does not exercise behavioral control, though there is some evidence of financial control that would be reduced if Mr. Stringer had any additional clients. The type of relationship is more firmly in favor of independent contractor status, since HLC does not pay benefits and Mr. Stringer's area of specialization is outside of the regular business of the company.

EXAMPLE

Myron Sotherby hires Ames Whitmore to supervise the construction of his new garage. Mr. Sotherby pays suppliers directly, carries workers' compensation coverage for Mr. Whitmore, supervises the work on a daily basis, and pays Mr. Whitmore on an hourly basis, irrespective of the status of the project. Mr. Whitmore cannot work on other projects until the garage has been completed. Mr. Whitmore is an employee of Mr. Sotherby.

EXAMPLE

Waylon Price has signed a contract with Milford Sound to provide concrete pouring services for several of Milford's public stadium projects. Under the terms of the contract, Mr. Price's firm will be paid a flat fee once specific tasks have been completed, and is liable for any subsequent issues with the concrete through a one-year warranty period. Mr. Price carries workers' compensation insurance for his business, and he employs several people. Mr. Price is an independent contractor.

EXAMPLE

Hubble Corporation lays off Red Miller, and then agrees to pay him a flat fee to design trajectory tracking software for one of Hubble's telescopes. Hubble does not provide Mr. Miller with any specific work instructions, and only sets a target date for delivery of the software. He is not required to attend any meetings of the programming department. He has signed an agreement with Hubble, which specifically states that he is an independent contractor, and will receive no benefits from the company. Mr. Miller is an independent contractor.

EXAMPLE

Vern Tucker is a paint specialist who works in the auto repair shop of a large auto sales company. He works a 40-hour week and is paid 40% of the amount billed to each customer. The auto sales company provides all of his equipment and paint supplies, and also monitors the time he takes in comparison to the estimates given to customers. Mr. Tucker is an employee.

EXAMPLE

Gene Brooks is a taxi cab driver. He pays Ultimate Cab Company $150 per day to rent a cab from it, which includes a sophisticated on-line dispatching service. Ultimate Cab also advertises its vehicles to the general public. Mr. Brooks pays for the ongoing servicing of the cab, as well as fuel. He keeps all fares that he receives from customers. Mr. Brooks is an independent contractor.

The W-2 Contractor

In the work environment, a person can be an employee or a contractor. An employee is a person who is supervised within a business and is subject to its work rules; the employer deducts taxes from the employee's pay, matches them in some cases, and remits them to the government. Payments made to an employee are reported on the Form W-2 following the end of each calendar year. An example of an employee is an accounting clerk.

A contractor works independently, and is not subject to the work rules of an employer. This person pays his or her own payroll taxes. Payments made to a contractor are reported on the Form 1099 following the end of each calendar year. An example of a contractor is an independent consultant.

Given these two definitions, it appears impossible to be a W-2 contractor, since the Form W-2 applies to employees, not contractors. However, if a person were employed by a temporary work agency, the agency would be in the role of employer, and so would deduct taxes and issue a Form W-2 to the person. Meanwhile, the person would be working for the business that is paying the temporary work agency for his or her services. Thus, the person can be considered a contractor from the perspective of the business paying the temporary work agency, and an employee from the perspective of the work agency. Consequently, the term *W-2 contractor* is an amalgamation of two different concepts.

The Salesperson Designation

Depending upon the situation, it is possible that a salesperson may not meet the definition of a common-law employee, as defined earlier. If so, the employer is not required to withhold federal income taxes from his pay. However, his pay may still be subject to social security, Medicare, and FUTA taxes if his work situation meets *all eight* of the following criteria:

- Works full-time for one entity, except incidental activities on the side; and
- Sells on behalf of the entity; and
- Sells to wholesalers, retailers, contractors, or operators of hotels, restaurants, or similar entities; and
- Sells merchandise for resale, or supplies for use in a customer's business; and
- Does substantially all work personally; and
- Has no substantial investment in facilities (not including transportation); and
- Maintains an ongoing relationship with the entity for which he works; and
- Is not an employee under common-law rules.

Employees of Exempt Organizations

An exempt organization is one that is exempt from paying the federal income tax under section 501(c)(3) of the Internal Revenue Code. An organization must apply to the IRS for exempt status, which will only be granted if the entity conducts the bulk of its activities in one or more of the following areas:

- Charitable activities
- Fostering national or international amateur sports competition
- Literary or educational activities
- Prevention of cruelty to children or animals

- Religion
- Scientific endeavors
- Testing for public safety

The following rules apply to payroll taxes and income tax withholding for these organizations:

- *Federal income tax.* Must withhold federal income taxes from employee pay in the normal manner.
- *Social security and Medicare taxes.* Must deduct the normal amount of these taxes, unless the organization pays an employee less than $100 per calendar year or it is a church opposed to the payment of these taxes for religious reasons that has filed Form 8274, Certification by Churches and Qualified Church-Controlled Organizations Electing Exemption from Employer Social Security and Medicare Taxes. In the latter case, employees must pay the self-employment tax instead.
- *Federal unemployment tax.* Is exempt from this tax, which also means that the organization does not have to file Form 940, Employer's Annual Federal Unemployment Tax Return.

Ministers

A minister is a person who is ordained, commissioned, or licensed by a church, and who is given authority to conduct religious worship and related functions. Define a minister as an employee if he or she performs services in the exercise of ministry and is subject to the control of the church entity.

The earnings of a minister are not subject to federal income tax withholding, nor are social security and Medicare deductions made by the employer. However, the minister must pay the self-employment tax and federal income tax. Though the employer is not responsible for these items, it can reach an agreement with the minister to voluntarily withhold taxes to cover the minister's liability for the self-employment tax and federal income tax.

Employee Scenarios

This section contains several specific situations where employee status is defined.

Classes of employees. There is no distinction between classes of employees. A production worker, administrative assistant, manager, and vice president are all likely to be considered employees. Thus, job titles have no impact on the employee designation.

Director of a corporation. A director is not an employee with respect to any services performed in his or her role as a director. We refer in this case to a member of the board of directors.

Leased employees. A company furnishing workers to other firms, such as a temporary staffing agency, is the designated employer for tax deduction and withholding purposes.

Officer of a corporation. An officer is usually considered an employee. However, if the person performs no services or only minor ones, and does not receive any pay, do not classify this individual as an employee.

People in Business for Themselves

Individuals who are in business for themselves are not defined as employees. These people are commonly in an independent trade where they offer their services to the public. Examples are:

Authors	Locksmiths
Doctors	Plumbers
Lawyers	Veterinarians

However, if a business has been incorporated, anyone working for the corporate entity is considered an employee. Thus, corporate officers are considered employees of the corporation.

Family Employees

There are special considerations in regard to payroll taxes and income tax withholdings for family employees, which are:

- *Federal income tax withholding.* Irrespective of the age of a child, if that person works for a parent, he or she is subject to income tax withholding unless the child is engaged in domestic work in the parent's home, or the payments are for less than $50 in the quarter, or the child is not regularly employed to do the work.
- *Social Security and Medicare taxes.* Any payments made to a child under the age of 18 who works for his or her parent are not subject to social security or Medicare taxes, as long as the business is a sole proprietorship or a partnership in which each partner is a parent of the child.
- *FUTA taxes.* Payments to a child under the age of 21 who works for his or her parent, even if not in a business, are not subject to the federal unemployment tax.

Working off the Books

The concept of working off the books means that a person is being compensated in cash for services performed, but the payments are not recorded on the books of the employing business. The business offers this sort of arrangement in order to avoid paying any payroll taxes, as well as to avoid paying for workers' compensation insurance and any of the benefits normally offered to its employees, including medical insurance and vacation pay.

The person accepting a "working off the books" arrangement may do so out of desperation, since there is no other work available. Alternatively, the individual may not have a work permit, or may be trying to avoid any record of earnings in order to avoid child support obligations.

There are a number of issues with working off the books that both the employing business and the person being paid should be aware of. Consider the following:

- *Payroll tax liability.* The employer now has a liability for the payroll taxes that it did not withhold and remit to the government. Also, the person being paid still has an obligation to report the earnings and pay income tax on the earnings; if not reported, the person is liable for both the related income tax and penalties.
- *Social security credit.* Since no payroll taxes were remitted to the government, the person being paid does not receive social security credit for the payments, which translates into reduced social security payments (if any) upon retirement.
- *Injury compensation.* The person being paid is not covered by workers' compensation insurance, and so must personally pay for any medical care received if there is an injury resulting from work for the employing business.
- *Unemployment income.* If a person receiving cash from an off the books situation is also receiving unemployment payments, it is possible that the unemployment payments must be paid back, with interest.

A working off the books arrangement is not the same as treating the recipient of payments as a contractor. Under a contractor arrangement, the employing business is formally recording the payments made, and reports this information to the government following the end of each calendar year on a Form 1099.

Intern Rules

An intern is a person engaged in temporary employment, with an emphasis on on-the-job training. Some employers consider interns to be a source of free labor, and so enter into arrangements where interns agree to work for no pay. The Department of Labor has issued a set of criteria for the situations in which interns may work for free. The criteria are:

- *Advantage gained.* The employer of the intern does not gain an immediate advantage by employing the intern. If anything, such employment may hinder the operations of the employer.
- *Benefit.* The experience of the internship is for the benefit of the intern, not the employer.
- *Displacement.* The intern is not displacing a regular employee.
- *Education basis.* The internship is designed to provide training similar to what would be provided in an education environment.

- *Job entitlement.* The intern is not entitled to a full-time position with the employer once the internship period has ended.
- *Pay understanding.* Both the intern and the employer understand that no wages will be paid as part of the internship.

These criteria severely limit the number of situations in which an intern will not be paid. In most cases, an intern is entitled to be paid wages and overtime.

Summary

The classification of an individual as an employee (or not) is critical to whether a business should withhold federal income taxes or deduct payroll taxes from his or her pay. If a company classifies a person incorrectly as an independent contractor, the business is liable for employment taxes for that person. Though there is a relief provision where there is a reasonable basis for not treating a worker as an employee, this still represents a potentially large liability. Thus, it is critical to properly understand the circumstances under which a company is compensating its employees, and to apply the rules noted in this chapter to determine the correct designation for every individual.

It may be tempting to simply designate everyone as an employee when there is any doubt about the proper classification. However, doing so means that a company is incurring the cost of matching a person's social security and Medicare taxes. Consequently, the best decision method is to err on the side of designating a person as an employee, but only after a proper review of the situation and the corresponding IRS guidelines.

Chapter 3
Employee Time Tracking

Introduction

The primary input to the payroll process is the collection of data about hours worked by those employees who are paid on an hourly basis. There are several factors to consider when developing the best way to collect this information. Consider the following:

- *Collection cost.* There are several aspects to the cost of collecting employee time information. There is the cost required for employees to record information, the cost required by the payroll staff to review, correct, and summarize it, and the cost of any equipment needed to collect it.
- *Data errors.* Some types of data collection are highly prone to errors, while one would have to try very hard to create an error in other types of data collection systems. This does not mean that a high-error system should not be considered, since it may have other characteristics that would otherwise make it an ideal solution under certain circumstances.
- *Employee effort.* Some data entry systems require manual input from employees, which can involve a notable effort, depending upon the frequency and amount of data recorded.
- *Interface to payroll system.* More automated time tracking solutions interface perfectly into a company's payroll computer system, while others require the manual rekeying of information. Rekeying is a major cause of payroll errors, so the existence of an automated interface is a positive consideration when selecting a time tracking system.
- *Payroll staff effort.* Some time tracking systems require the payroll staff to carefully review, correct, and rekey payroll information in varying degrees, which can potentially absorb the bulk of the payroll department's available time during payroll processing periods.
- *Security.* Some companies have problems with fraudulent time tracking by employees. There are time keeping solutions available that can mitigate (though not eliminate) this security concern.

As will be discussed in this chapter, there are a variety of factors that will vary the optimum time tracking technique selected for any company, which can include such factors as employee dispersion, the total number of employees, and the level of integration with the payroll computer system.

But before selecting a time tracking solution, consider the type of payroll data to be collected, which is addressed in the next few sections. If the amount of data collection can be limited, this reduces costs and increases employee efficiency.

> **Related podcast episodes:** Episodes 126 through 129 of the Accounting Best Practices Podcast discuss the streamlining of payroll. They are available at: **www.accountingtools.com/podcasts** or **iTunes**

Time Tracking Scope

The first step in developing a time tracking system is to determine the extent of the time tracking that is *really* required. An overly conservative controller may feel that it is necessary to have every employee submit a time report for every day worked, detailing the time spent on every activity. If so, ask *why* this is necessary. Are management decisions being made that are based on this information? Is the information required by law? Does a customer want to see the information as part of the periodic billings that the company sends it? In most cases, the answer is no. And even if the answer is yes, there are ways to mitigate the amount of information collected. Consider the following example:

EXAMPLE

Luminescence Corporation operates an LED manufacturing facility. Management is concerned about employee productivity, and wants to have all employees fill out a time sheet each day, detailing their activities. The payroll manager of Luminescence points out that the time required to fill out these timesheets will surely contribute to a further decline in productivity, and suggests the following set of alternatives:

- Limit the timesheets to the engineering and production departments, where the productivity issue appears to be worst;
- Use standardized activity codes, in order to reduce the time required to fill out the time sheets; and
- Limit this time keeping requirement to one month per year.

In the preceding example, the last alternative (to limit the time tracking period) was the most crucial. When management demands that employees report more information through the time tracking system, it may take action on the resulting information for a short period of time, but will likely stop doing so fairly soon, once it achieves whatever goal it initially set. From that point onward, the only valid reason for continuing to collect the information is to verify that employees are not deviating from the current use of their time; this is a control point, and can be easily reviewed by sampling employee activities at fairly lengthy intervals. Thus, continuing to require *all* employees to record a large set of data in perpetuity is highly inefficient.

What about a requirement by a customer to report certain information to it that requires employee time keeping? This requirement arises occasionally in consulting projects, where customers want to know exactly what activities billable employees are engaged in. The scope of such customer-imposed requirements can be reduced by comparing customer demands to the current set of information already being tracked by the timekeeping system, and negotiating with the customer to modify their requirements to match the company's system. This is most effectively done before the contract is signed with the customer, so the controller should be involved in a review of any upcoming customer contracts where the customer is demanding such information.

The most difficult situation arises when certain information is required by law – specifically, the Federal Acquisition Regulation (FAR) of the United States government. In this case, the organization is required to collect certain information if its contract with the government meets FAR criteria. If the company has the misfortune of being required to comply with the FAR, hire a FAR consultant before the contract begins, in order to set up a data collection system that meets the FAR requirements. In this case, it is not a matter of reducing the scope of data collection – it cannot be done – but rather of ensuring that the business is collecting exactly the right information at the start of the project, so that it does not have to spend much more time later on, trying to retroactively collect the information.

Employee Exclusions

Whenever possible, try to exclude employees from the time tracking system. Instead, create a standard amount of hours worked, and only have them record their time worked if it varies from the predetermined amount. This is time tracking by exception, and works well for many positions where employees engage in essentially the same activities every day, and for the same period of time. Time tracking by exception is an excellent solution when employees do not see the need to continually submit time reports that document the same activities; in this situation, employees are much less likely to submit their time sheets on a timely basis, so the payroll staff must spend extra time reminding them to do so.

Another form of employee exclusion is to switch employees from being paid on an hourly basis to being paid on a salaried basis. By doing so, the need to track their time at all is eliminated, at least for the purpose of computing their pay. However, if an employee is salaried but his time is billed to customers (as is the case for a consultant), his time must still be tracked; in this situation, it makes no difference if the person is classified as hourly or salaried.

Converting an employee to salaried status will likely only apply to a very small proportion of all employees, since this status is governed by federal regulations. The key guidelines for designating a person as being eligible for a salary are as follows:

- *Administrative.* Those in charge of an administrative department, even if they supervise no one, and anyone assisting management with long-term strategy decisions.
- *Executive.* Those who manage more than 50% of the time and supervise at least two employees.
- *Professional.* Those who spend at least 50% of their time on tasks requiring knowledge obtained through a four-year college degree (including systems analysis, design, and programming work on computer systems, even if a four-year degree was not obtained). The position must also allow for continued independent decision making and minimal close supervision.

Even if an employee has been identified as being potentially convertible from an hourly to a salaried position, the employee may perceive this as an attempt to deny him overtime pay. If so, it may be necessary to offer a higher salary in order to mollify the employee, which may be a sufficiently large pay raise to negate any possible efficiency improvement from having to no longer track the person's hours worked. Thus, converting employees from hourly to salaried pay is an interesting concept, but is only applicable in a minority of situations.

Data Collection Scope

An employee time tracking system may be used to collect more information than hours worked. A time tracking system is a data collection system, and so can be used to collect information about anything. However, do not be tempted to overuse this capability, since collecting additional data requires more data entry time by employees. Instead, question the need for any additional data collection above the bare minimum amount. Ideally, this means the business is collecting the identification number of each employee and his time worked – and nothing else.

Above the baseline data collection level just noted, the next most common item to be collected is the pay code, which identifies hours worked as falling into a pay category, such as holidays, bereavement leave, jury duty, and vacation time. If pay codes are used, do not overwhelm employees with a multitude of these codes, since they will be more likely to record the wrong codes.

In the production area and materials management departments, it may be necessary to use activity codes for such tasks as receiving, putaways to stock, picking from stock, inventory counting, manufacturing, rework, and shipping. Resist the urge to use activity codes, because employees tend to spend their time in the same proportions on the same activities over time – collecting information to confirm that nothing has changed is a waste of time. Ideally, only require hourly production workers to clock in and clock out, and do not waste their time recording any additional time tracking information – with the possible exception of the next item.

If the cost of production jobs is being accumulated, employees may record the time they spend on individual jobs. These systems can be quite elaborate, with every conceivable cost being assigned to jobs. Such detailed record keeping may be required by customers, but if it is not, is it really necessary to record the information? In a custom production environment, the answer may very well be yes, since it is necessary to know how well the company is setting prices and controlling its production process. However, if the company is largely selling standardized products, consider strictly limiting the job tracking system to just those jobs that truly require custom work, and for which management regularly compares the budgeted to actual cost and takes action on this information.

EXAMPLE

Grubstake Brothers manufactures backhoes that are moderately customized to fit the needs of its customers. Management is considering whether to have the production staff track their time on specific jobs. The production manager asserts that the average employee works on three jobs per day, and so would need to track his time against each of the three jobs. There are 500 production employees, and they work an average of 20 days per month. Thus, timekeeping would change from two transactions per day per employee (clocking in and clocking out) to eight transactions per day (clocking in and out for each job). This translates into the following volumes per month:

<u>Current</u>: 500 employees × 20 days × 2 transactions = **20,000** time tracking transactions

<u>With job tracking</u>: 500 employees × 20 days × 8 transactions = **80,000** time keeping transactions

In addition, the payroll staff must collect and correct the increased volume of time keeping transactions, which may require it to hire an additional payroll clerk.

One way to deal with job costing is to split it away from the time tracking system, so that only those employees actively involved with custom jobs are required to track their time on a job-specific basis. This approach also means that job information can be collected at different intervals from when payroll-specific information is being collected, which reduces the amount of time-critical information that the payroll staff must deal with as part of its payroll processing activities.

Having reviewed the need for various types of information that could potentially be collected through a payroll time tracking system, we now turn to a review of the various types of time tracking systems that are available, and consider the strengths and weaknesses of each one.

Handwritten Time Sheets

Despite the broad range of automated solutions available, there is still a place for the handwritten timesheet. This is a simple form on which an employee lists his time worked per day. It requires more work to complete than a time card (see next), but is not an especially inefficient form of time keeping if it is also being used to record the work performed on specific jobs. The circumstances under which a time sheet is still practical should encompass the following:

- *Few employees.* This is the lowest-cost of all time tracking solutions, but only if there are very few employees. Once the headcount increases, more automated solutions become more viable.
- *Job costing environment.* This is a stronger alternative if it is necessary to record free-form notes, so it is ideal in a job costing environment where extra data collection is called for. It is particularly useful when there are no standardized job costing activity codes that would otherwise be used to provide a concise explanation of job activities.

- *Dispersed employees.* Time sheets are a reasonable alternative when employees are spread out, so that more expensive, networked time keeping solutions are not a viable alternative.

Time sheets suffer from several failings that restrict their use to the circumstances just noted. Specifically, there is no way to verify the hours recorded on a time sheet, so there is a risk of fraud. Also, given the legibility of the handwriting of some employees, there is a risk that the payroll staff will misinterpret the information on the time sheets. Finally, any paper-based document can be misplaced or lost, so there is a risk of never receiving a time sheet from which an employee would normally be paid.

EXAMPLE

Twill Machinery is an extremely small manufacturer of custom-designed milling machines. The company extensively modifies a few baseline designs to the specifications of its customers. Given the customized nature of its products, Twill must be certain that its quoting system is issuing prices that generate a profit. To do so, the controller hires a cost accountant and tasks her with creating a time tracking system.

The cost accountant finds that the company has only a rudimentary accounting system, without any computer database of costs incurred for each job. The company has a very limited budget for acquiring any additional computer equipment. She estimates that roughly 50% of the cost of each job is comprised of the specialized labor of Twill's small group of machinists. The machinists are extremely reliable, long-term employees. She also notes that the tasks performed on each job vary widely. The cost accountant elects to use handwritten time sheets, since there is little risk of fraud, there is no funding for more advanced systems, and the time sheets have sufficient space to include detailed notes about work performed.

Time Cards

The classic method for time tracking has been to insert a time card into a slot in a time clock, which punches the date and time onto the card. The name of an employee is printed on the top of each card, and the employee is responsible for punching in and out using the time clock. At the end of the week, the payroll staff removes all time cards from where they are stored near the time clock, replaces them with new cards, and compiles the amount of time worked from the completed time cards. Though time cards may be beginning to appear somewhat old-fashioned, they still work well under the following circumstances:

- *No computer interface.* When there is no system in place for linking a time tracking system directly into the payroll computer system, time cards are a reasonable method for data accumulation.
- *Moderately concentrated employees.* Time cards and punch clocks are inexpensive, so a business can afford to buy quite a few of them. This allows an employer to use a time card system in multiple locations, though it

would be impractical for the payroll staff to maintain control over the time cards in an excessive number of widely dispersed locations.

- *Standardized environment.* There is only room on a time card to collect information about hours clocked in and out. This means that job costing information cannot be collected, so time cards should be restricted to a standardized production environment where custom jobs are not used.

Despite the broad use of time cards, there are also several issues to be aware of that can cause problems. The key issues are:

- *Buddy punching.* Unless there is video monitoring of the time card storage area, there is a significant possibility that some employees will punch in the time cards of their fellow employees, which is known as *buddy punching*.
- *Summarization labor.* The payroll staff has to manually calculate the amount of hours worked from the time cards. This can be a substantial amount of work, and the calculations are highly error-prone. These summarization issues tend to limit the size of the workforce for which time cards can be used. For larger companies, a more automated time tracking system is needed that automatically summarizes information (see next).
- *Pay period duration.* Time cards work best when employees are paid on a weekly basis. Over a longer period, there is a risk that the time cards will not have sufficient space to hold all of the time punches.

EXAMPLE

Hegemony Toy Company produces military games that re-enact famous battles. The company's manufacturing operation involves the use of plastic injection molding equipment to produce military figurines, the lamination of battle maps on cardboard backings, and the printing of instruction cards. These operations are highly standardized, and are incorporated into several small production lines. Hegemony employs 200 production workers in a single facility. All employees enter and depart the building through a single corridor that leads to the employee parking lot. The company's payroll department is somewhat overstaffed. The company pays its employees on a weekly basis, with a three-day lag time between the end of the work week and pay day.

Given these parameters, the company can safely set up a single time card and punch clock system in the corridor between the parking lot and the production facility. By doing so, the payroll department can maintain control over the card rack, while the excess amount of payroll staff allows Hegemony to calculate hours worked at the end of each pay period.

Computerized Time Clocks

The computerized time clock is a specialized computer terminal that is linked to the central payroll database, and which has an employee badge scanner attached to it. The scanner can accept a bar coded, magnetic stripe, or radio-frequency identification employee card. An employee swipes his badge through the scanner, and the terminal automatically records his time. The central payroll system periodically polls the terminal and downloads the recorded scans. Thus, the computerized time clock incorporates a very fast and error-free data entry system that requires no rekeying by the payroll staff.

The automated time clock has several additional features. It can be set up with specific time periods during which employees are authorized to swipe their badges; outside of that period, the system will not accept their entries, which eliminates unauthorized overtime. The system can also spot any cases where an employee did not clock in (or out), and send a report to that person's supervisor, who can resolve the situation. Further, some models have additional data entry modes, so that employees can enter job codes to which their hours are assigned. Thus, the automated time clock also offers a number of built-in controls and an expanded data collection capability.

The computerized time clock has been the time tracking device of choice for a number of years now, but do not automatically assume that it is the best time tracking solution. It is one of the higher-cost solutions available, and so is most cost-effective only under certain circumstances, which are as follows:

- *Highly concentrated employees.* Given the high cost of an automated time clock, most companies only budget for a small number of them, which means that they are most cost-effective when there are a large number of employees using each one. Thus, the best environment for such a clock is a facility with a large number of employees who pass through a choke point where the clock is located.

- *Computer interface.* There should be a payroll computer database which polls the various time clocks and downloads information from them. This may require the use of shielded network cables (for a heavy industrial environment), or a wireless connection, or even a cellular phone linkage.

- *Data rekeying reduction.* An automated time clock can eliminate a vast amount, if not all, of the rekeying of payroll data into the payroll system. This is a particular advantage where there are many employees, and when the time period between the end of a pay period and the pay date is very small.

- *Longer pay periods.* There is no theoretical limit to the duration of a pay period for which an automated time clock can accumulate information, so a company is not limited to the one-week pay period that is very nearly a requirement under a time sheet or time card system.

> **Tip:** Though the computerized time clock is certainly a high-speed data entry device, there is an upper limit to how many employees can use it at the start of a work shift. If the queue in front of the clock is too long, some employees will be late for work. Consequently, it may be necessary to install multiple clocks or stagger shift start times in order to reduce the queue in front of each clock.

The preceding list is based on a general view of a full-function automated time clock. Such clocks cost in excess of $1,000 each, and may require shielded network cabling to tie them back into the payroll computer system. However, there are many lower-cost variations on this basic concept. For example, there are wireless automated time clocks available that eliminate the cost of cabling, and which can work well in a light industrial environment. Similarly, there are touchpad systems that can be set up at individual workstations, so that employees can enter their time and related job information without moving from their assigned work areas. Further, there are automated time clocks with less functionality that can be acquired for much less than $1,000. These variations on the basic concept make automated time clocks workable within a relatively broad range of environments.

An additional advantage of an automated time clock is that it requires more forethought by employees to engage in buddy punching. An employee would have to bring another employee's badge to work in order to fraudulently engage in buddy punching. Thus, the more casual level of buddy punching would be eliminated.

Tip: If automated time clocks are used, there is a slightly reduced risk of fraud if badges are issued to employees that contain a magnetic stripe, rather than a bar code. The reason is that employees could photocopy the bar code from the back of a badge, and then use the copy to construct a fake badge which they could then use for buddy punching. An alternative is to use red laminate over the bar code, which impedes the ability of a photocopier to make a clean copy of the bar code.

EXAMPLE

Puller Corporation manufactures large quantities of both plastic and wooden door knobs. The company has concentrated all of its production in one massive facility, which can be accessed from parking lots on three sides of the building. The 1,000 employees can enter or exit from three sides of the building. There is no need for job costing, so the company is only interested in collecting each employee's start time and ending time.

The ideal solution for this situation is to issue employee badges to employees, and install a computerized time clock at each of the entrances. The employees can then swipe their badges as they enter and exit the building at the beginning and end of their shifts.

Biometric Time Clocks

A variation on the computerized time clock is the biometric time clock. This is essentially the same as a normal computerized time clock, except that the input mode is usually a hand scanner, rather than a badge scanner. For it to operate properly, employees must first have their hands scanned by the system to create a baseline record. Thereafter, an employee would place his hand on the scanner, and the system would match its database of authorized scans to the employee's hand.

The key advantage of a biometric scanner is that it completely eliminates any possibility of buddy punching. However, this anti-fraud feature comes at a higher per-unit cost. Also, the scanning time is several seconds longer than for a standard badge swipe, so a biometric time clock cannot handle the data entry of as large a group of employees as can a standard computerized time clock.

EXAMPLE

Micron Metallic uses stamping machines to manufacture parts for washing machines. The work is dull, and employee turnover is high. Micron's payroll manager has noticed a growing problem with buddy punching at the company's existing time card system, and needs an alternative solution.

A biometric time clock is ideal for Micron, since the work environment and high employee turnover has led to a situation where employees are willing to engage in a large amount of buddy punching. The higher cost of biometric time clocks is readily offset by the savings the company will realize from the elimination of buddy punching.

Web-Based Time Tracking

A web-based timekeeping system is a website which employees can access in order to enter their hours worked. These systems are routinely offered by the larger payroll outsourcing companies, and can also be custom-designed by any company with a knowledgeable web design staff. A web-based time tracking system can be configured to accept any type of information, such as task codes. These systems are also useful from an employee feedback perspective, because they can notify employees of any data entry errors, and may also allow them to view additional information, such as the time sheets from previous periods and their remaining unused vacation time. It is most useful under the following circumstances:

- *Dispersed staff.* Employees can access the system wherever there is Internet access, anywhere in the world.
- *Large staff.* Many of the available time tracking systems are massively scalable, so they can be used by very large numbers of employees.
- *Full integration.* If payroll is outsourced to a supplier and the company is also using the supplier's web-based time tracking system, there will be an interface between the two, so there is no need to rekey information into the payroll system.

There are also several issues with web-based time tracking that make it a less-than-optimum solution in some situations. They are:

- *Internet access.* If some employees do not have ready access to the Internet, this is not a viable solution for them.
- *Efficiency.* A web-based system requires more manual data entry than a more efficient computerized time clock.

The pros and cons noted here point toward the use of web-based time tracking in companies where employees are dispersed, and especially when they are traveling constantly. Conversely, this is a more problematic solution in the production area, where efficient timekeeping is at a premium. Web-based time tracking could work well in a professional environment, such as consulting or software development, where employees typically have Internet access and need to record some additional task information along with their hours worked.

EXAMPLE

Norrona Software develops a variety of personal productivity applications that it sells through the various smart phone operating systems. Norrona only hires the best programmers, no matter where they may live, so its small staff is spread across 11 countries, and they all work from home.

Given its widely distributed work force, all of whom have access to the Internet, Norrona creates a simplified web-based time tracking system, which it also markets outside the company as a product.

Smart Phone Time Tracking

It is quite easy to track employee time using smart phones. Apps are now available for the main smart phone operating systems, which allow employees to accumulate their hours worked, append a description of their activities, and then e-mail the results to the employer.

There are also time tracking systems available for non-smart phones that allow users to punch their time worked into the phone, which then sends a text message to a central server, itemizing the hours worked. If the phone is also GPS-enabled, the system can also track employee locations on a map. These systems are operated by a third party supplier, so there is a monthly charge for the service, as well as the usual monthly carrier fees for each phone.

Smart phone time tracking is enormously useful for very mobile employees, such as salespeople and field service personnel. These people may be in multiple locations per day, and so do not have time to access a more traditional fixed computer terminal to record their hours worked and tasks completed.

Time tracking with smart phones is constantly evolving, so one could reasonably treat a laptop or tablet computer with a wireless connection as a smart phone. These larger devices are more likely to be connected to a standard web-based time tracking system, and may also contain a great deal of information for mobile employees, such as product repair manuals, that make them a much more versatile option than a smart phone, with its inherently limited size.

Cell phone time tracking has several restrictions that limit its use to more mobile employees, such as:

- *Computer interface.* There is no interface between the time recorded in a timekeeping app on a smart phone and a company's payroll computer system. This means that either someone must rekey the transmitted information into the payroll system, or a custom interface is created to automatically port the information into the payroll system. The major payroll outsourcing suppliers have smart phone interfaces into their systems, so this is not an issue if payroll is outsourced to any of these suppliers.

- *Phone cost.* If employees are using their smart phones to submit time sheets, it is entirely possible that the company should be paying the monthly service charges for those phones. If so, this amounts to a hefty fee in exchange for giving each employee a portable data entry terminal.
- *Efficiency.* The small form factor of a cell phone represents an inherent limitation on the speed with which someone can enter information. This is a particular problem if employees are required to record descriptive information alongside their hours worked.

These constraints make smart phone time tracking an improbable choice for anyone working within a company location, where less expensive and more efficient alternatives are available.

EXAMPLE

Hammer Industries runs a nationwide field service operation that repairs the construction equipment that it has sold to customers. There are many types of construction equipment that the company has produced over the past twenty years, and they are all still in service. The field service staff needs access to the service manuals for all of these products, and also needs to be in contact with the service manager, who schedules their daily job routings.

The obvious time keeping solution is either a tablet or laptop computer with a wireless connection, so that they can submit hours worked, communicate with the service manager, and access service manuals.

Time Keeping Methods Usage Grid

The following table defines the circumstances under which a particular time tracking system will operate most effectively, as well as the levels of error and fraud risk associated with each system.

	Time Sheets	Time Cards	Computer Clocks	Biometric Clocks	Web Time Keeping	Smart Phones
Computer interface	None	None	Yes	Yes	Optional	Optional
Cost	Low	Low	High	High	Moderate	Moderate
Employee dispersion	Dispersed	Moderate	Concentrated	Concentrated	Dispersed	Dispersed
Error risk	High	Medium	Low	Low	Low	Low
Fraud risk	High	High	Moderate	Low	High	High
Number of employees	Few	Moderate	High	Moderate	High	High
Pay period	Short	Short	Any	Any	Any	Any
Production environment	Job cost	Standard	Any	Any	None	None
Summarization labor	High	High	Low	Low	Low	Low

Automated Time Tracking Reminders

Whenever a company adopts a web-based or smart phone time tracking system (or the less-advanced time sheet system), it will have an immediate and ongoing problem, getting its employees to remember to submit their hours worked in a timely manner. This can be a serious concern, especially when there are only a few days between the end of the pay period and the pay date in which to persuade employees to enter their time.

The traditional solution is to badger dilatory employees with phone calls, but a more advanced solution is to program the payroll software to automatically issue e-mails to employees at increasingly frequent intervals, and to copy their supervisors after the first one or two reminders. This approach keeps an annoying task away from the payroll staff, while ensuring that a proper amount of escalation will be followed at precisely defined intervals.

Summary

The broad array of time keeping issues and solutions noted in this chapter should make it clear that there is no single, ideal solution that will fit the needs of every company on the planet. Instead, consider a company's exact data collection needs, and tailor a data collection system to those needs. It is entirely possible that a company will require several entirely different time tracking systems for different functional areas. For example, a manufacturer of washing machines may find that a badge scanning system is perfect for its manufacturing operation, where many employees are concentrated into a small area, while using a time accumulation system on a smart phone or wireless tablet computer for its highly dispersed field service staff.

Periodically evaluate how the current time tracking system continues to meet the company's needs, and modify the system as necessary. This evaluation may be at long intervals, since most companies do not undergo massive changes to their operations with any frequency. A time tracking system review should be part of any acquisition, where the time tracking needs of the acquiree are evaluated, along with how they can be integrated into the acquiring entity's systems.

Chapter 4
Employee Compensation

Introduction

There can be great complexity involved in the calculation of employee wages, partially because they can be in so many forms – commissions, overtime pay, sick pay, vacation pay, and so forth. In this chapter, we discuss the various permutations of each type of compensation and how to calculate them.

A key part of the reporting of compensation is based on whether an individual is considered an employee. That issue is addressed separately in the Definition of an Employee chapter.

The Difference between Salaries and Wages

Someone who is paid a salary is paid a fixed amount in each pay period, with the total of these fixed payments over a full year summing to the amount of the salary. A person receiving a salary is not paid a smaller amount for working fewer hours, nor is he paid more for working overtime. This is considered an *exempt* position, since it is excluded from minimum wage and overtime regulations.

EXAMPLE

Henry Peabody has a $52,000 salary and he is paid once a week. Thus, the gross amount of each of the 52 pay checks he receives during the year is $1,000. This is calculated as $52,000 annual salary ÷ 52 weeks.

Someone who is paid wages receives a pay rate per hour, multiplied by the number of hours worked. A person who receives wages is also entitled to overtime pay of 1.5 times his normal rate of pay if he works more than 40 hours per week. This is considered a *non-exempt* position, since it is included in minimum wage and overtime regulations.

EXAMPLE

Catherine Arbowski is paid a wage of $20 per hour. She will receive gross pay of $800 ($20/hr × 40 hours) if she works a standard 40 hour week, but will only receive gross pay of $400 ($20/hr × 20 hours) if she works 20 hours in a week.

There is also a difference between salary and wages in regard to the speed of payment. If a person is paid a salary, he is paid through and including the pay date, because it is very simple for the payroll staff to calculate his salary, which is a fixed rate of pay. However, if a person is paid wages, he is usually paid through a date that is several days prior to the pay date; this is because his hours may vary, and the payroll staff needs several days to calculate his pay.

If a person is paid wages and there is a gap between the last day worked for which he is paid and his pay date, that gap is paid in his *next* paycheck. This gap does not exist for a salaried worker, since he is paid through the pay date.

The expression of a person's pay rate varies depending on whether that person receives a salary or wages. Thus, a person may receive a salary of $52,000, or wages of $25.00 per hour. Assuming a standard work year of 2,080 hours per year, the person receiving wages of $25.00 per hour is actually earning the same gross pay as the person receiving a salary of $52,000 (2,080 hours × $25/hour).

Salaries are usually expressed in terms of the amount paid per year, but they are sometimes stated in terms of a company's pay period, such as the salary per week, biweekly period, semimonthly period, or month.

EXAMPLE

Emily Burton is paid an annual salary of $80,000. This amount can be expressed in any of the following ways:

Period	Calculation	Amount/Period
Weekly	Annual salary divided by 52	$1,538.46
Biweekly	Annual salary divided by 26	3,076.92
Semimonthly	Annual salary divided by 24	3,333.33
Monthly	Annual salary divided by 12	6,666.67
Annual	Annual salary	80,000.00

It may also be necessary to convert a salary figure that is expressed in terms of a pay period into an hourly rate of pay. To do so, follow these steps:
1. Annualize the salary figure by multiplying it by the number of pay periods in the year.
2. Convert the annualized figure by dividing it by 2,080 hours.

EXAMPLE

Melissa Dunkirk earns a semimonthly salary of $3,750. We convert that rate of pay into an hourly figure as follows:
1. Multiply $3,750 by the 24 semimonthly payrolls in a year to arrive at an annual salary of $90,000.
2. Divide the annualized $90,000 salary by the 2,080 work hours in a year to arrive at the hourly rate of $43.27 per hour.

Unless stated otherwise, when we refer to "wages" in this chapter, we are referring to both salaries and wages.

The Work Week

An important concept in the calculation of employee compensation is the definition of a work week. A work week is any period of 168 consecutive hours that recurs consistently. Thus, management can set any start and ending dates and times as being the official corporate work week – but it must apply that work week consistently. To prevent confusion among employees, it is best to retain the same work week definition in perpetuity, barring a justifiable reason for changing it.

> **Tip:** List the beginning and ending dates and times for the company work week in the employee manual, so that everyone knows the time period over which they are being paid.

The definition of a work week is important for two reasons:
- *Pay day.* If a company lets a certain number of days pass from the end of a work week until the day on which paychecks are handed to employees, pay day is derived from the ending date of the work week.
- *Overtime.* If overtime is based on the number of hours worked in a work week, it is possible that the work week can impact the calculation of overtime pay.

> **Tip:** If a company buys another business, mandate the same work week for both entities. Otherwise, it will be inefficient to track differing work periods, probably with different payroll cycles.

Compensation Definition

For tax purposes, compensation is generally defined as all pay given to an employee for services performed, and it does not have to be in cash. Examples of compensation include:
- Bonuses
- Commissions
- Fringe benefits
- Salaries
- Vacation allowances
- Wages

All of these forms of compensation may be subject to various payroll taxes and income tax withholdings. There are a large number of instances under which fringe benefits are exempt from these taxes and withholdings, as described in the Employee Compensation chapter.

Supplemental Wages

The IRS treats supplemental wages somewhat differently than wages. Follow these rules for supplemental wages:

- If supplemental wages paid to an employee exceed $1 million per year, tax any incremental supplemental wages above the $1 million level at the highest income tax rate for that year. Withhold at this level, irrespective of the number of exemptions claimed by the employee in his Form W-4.

> **Tip:** It is not possible to avoid the maximum tax rate rule by paying an employee from multiple entities. If the entities are under common control, the payments must be aggregated to arrive at the total supplemental wages figure.

- If the supplemental wages paid to an employee are $1 million or less, follow these rules:
  - If supplemental and regular wages are combined, withhold federal taxes as though the total were a single payment.
  - If supplemental and regular wages are identified separately, and if income taxes are withheld from an employee's regular wages in the current or preceding calendar year, the employer can either a) withhold a flat 25% or b) add both types of wages together and calculate the income tax as though they are a single payment.
  - If supplemental and regular wages are identified separately, but income taxes were not withheld from an employee's regular wages in the current or preceding calendar year, add both types of wages together and calculate the income tax as though they are a single payment.

EXAMPLE

October Systems pays Ms. Andrea Canalone a base salary of $3,000 per month, in her role as a salesperson for the company. She is single and claims two withholding allowances. Using the 2016 wage bracket tables for income tax withholding, October withholds $285 from her pay in January. In February, the company pays her a commission of $1,500, which October combines with her regular wages and does not separately identify. October computes a withholding of $557 based on total compensation of $4,500.

In March, Ms. Canalone's base salary remains the same, while her commission is separately identified as $800. October uses the flat rate method to withhold 25% of the commission amount. The withholdings that October applies to her pay are $285 (as before) for her $3,000 base salary, and $200 to the commission payment, for a total withholding of $485.

Many types of supplemental wages are addressed in the following sections.

Commission Calculations

Commissions are commonly paid to any employee involved in the sale of a company's products and services. A commission payment is specifically tailored to generate actions that increase company sales, and are sometimes targeted at specific types of sales. Examples of different commission scenarios are:

- An increased commission rate for the sale of products with unusually high gross margins, in order to increase overall company profitability
- An increased commission rate for the sale of products that are about to be designated as obsolete, in order to eliminate remaining inventory
- An increased commission rate on sales in a new geographic region, in order to gain market share in that area
- An increased commission rate for sales near the end of the quarter, in order to meet the sales target for the quarter
- A retroactive commission booster, to give an incentive to meet a full-year sales goal
- A commission split, in order to encourage employees to work as teams to garner sales

> **Note:** If the company employs salespeople who travel constantly, they are normally paid on a salaried basis, with commissions added to their salaries. Conversely, if in-house salespeople are employed, such as in a retail environment, they may instead be paid hourly wages, in which case they may be entitled to overtime pay.

It is certainly laudable to configure a commission system that is fine-tuned to extract the maximum amount of sales activity and profitability out of a company. However, an excessively honed system can be a calculation nightmare for the payroll staff, which must work its way through a veritable blizzard of calculations to determine how much to pay, and to whom. Further, in a highly-complex commission system, it is not only likely that there will be commission errors, but actually unusual for there *not* to be errors.

EXAMPLE

Cromarty Consignment sells a variety of industrial supplies on a consignment basis on behalf of several dozen manufacturers. Cromarty uses a standard 2% commission for all sales, except for sales handled by the salaried in-house sales staff. Further, there are monthly special commissions funded by any manufacturer who wants to drive a special promotion for its products. There is also a regional override commission for two regions where Cromarty is attempting to increase market share. Further, each regional sales manager earns 0.25% on all sales generated in his or her region. In addition, all standard commissions are retroactively increased by 0.5% if a quarterly sales target is reached, and is retroactively increased another 0.5% if the annual sales target is reached. Finally, the company pays out a year-end bonus that is based on a percentage of all compensation earned, if a salesperson exceeds the annual sales target by at least 10%. Thus, there are seven elements in the Cromarty commission plan for the payroll department to track.

Tip: A key goal of the company controller at month-end is to close the books, so he will pester the payroll staff for the accrued commission expense for the month. If there is a complex commission structure, this may be difficult for the payroll staff to generate in a timely manner. The solution may be simple – use the historical percentage of commissions to sales for the accrued commission expense. If the actual expense is somewhat different from the historical percentage, record a journal entry in the following month to adjust for the difference.

The solution to the commission structure quagmire from the perspective of the payroll manager is to simplify the commission system to one or two basic rules. The problem is that the system is under the control of the sales manager, who is more concerned with motivating his sales staff than in reducing the work load of the payroll department. Here are some variations on how to deal with the situation:

- Push the issue up to a higher-level manager who can require changes to the commission plan.
- Ask that the commission plan only be altered by the management team as a group, and ensure that an accounting representative is included in that group.
- Charge the sales department for the time required by the payroll staff to process payroll.
- Move the commission calculation function to the sales department.

If the decision is made to move the commission calculation function to the sales department, this can interfere with closing the books each month, since the sales department has no particular incentive to rush through the commission calculations. A workaround is to accrue an approximate commission amount based on a percentage of sales, and adjust it in the next month, after the sales department forwards its completed calculations.

> **Tip:** If a company has a history of constantly changing its commission structure, work with senior management to enforce a policy that only allows a change to the commission plan once a year.

Under a moderately simple commission system, it may be possible to have even a fairly primitive accounting software package calculate commissions, or at least accumulate the relevant information. To do so, follow these steps:

1. Use a field on the invoice to identify each salesperson. This may be a simple numeric code, if there is not enough room to insert the name of a salesperson.
2. Set up the billing software to require data entry in the salesperson field. This ensures that the field is completed for every invoice.
3. Create a report in the accounting software that lists the salesperson name, invoice number, date, customer name, and sales total for each invoice.
4. At the end of each commission calculation period, export the report to an electronic spreadsheet, from which the information can be manipulated further to calculate commissions.

> **Tip:** If the company has an internal audit team, ask them to periodically review the commission calculations to see if there are any mistakes being made. This information can be used to revise the commission structure and calculation procedure to eliminate recurring errors.

In cases where the commission structure is extremely complex, the simple data export just noted may not be sufficient. Instead, if commissions involve an array of splits, bonuses, overrides, caps, hurdles, and so forth, consider buying an incentive compensation management software package. These packages operate independently from the accounting system, and so require a custom interface with the accounting system to import data. These systems not only calculate commissions under the most complex payment structures, but also print out statements for each salesperson and incorporate what-if modeling to see what happens under different commission scenarios. The downside of this software is its high cost, which includes not only the base price of the software but also the cost of customizing it to a company's needs and constructing an interface with the accounting system.

> **Tip:** Always match the frequency of commission payments to the company's payroll cycles. By doing so, commission payments can be incorporated into the standard calculation of payroll taxes and other withholdings. This is a particular problem when another company has been acquired, since the other entity may have different payroll cycles which will require a revised commission payment schedule when the payroll systems are consolidated into a single, standardized payroll cycle.

Commissions Based on Cash Receipts

In some organizations, commissions are based on cash received from customers, rather than initial sales. There are two predominant justifications for calculating commissions in this manner:

- Salespeople are more likely to be selective in selling to higher-quality customers, since they do not want to waste time making sales for which collections are problematic. The sales staff will also be more likely to work with the collections staff to collect payment on overdue invoices.
- This method works better for cash-strapped companies, since they only pay their salespeople when cash arrives from customers.

Despite these advantages, paying commissions based on cash receipts is uncommon, since it delays payments to salespeople. It can also cause problems for the payroll department, because the calculation of commissions requires a different source document. For commissions based on cash receipts, a report is needed that itemizes cash received during the commission period, sorted by customer. Further, the cash receipts clerk must be able to assign all cash receipts to unpaid invoices as soon as possible following the receipt of cash. Otherwise, unapplied cash effectively reduces the amount of commissions that salespeople are paid.

Final Commission Calculations

There is usually a clause in a salesperson's employment agreement which itemizes the method used to calculate that person's final commission payment. This calculation may include the following factors:

- The normal commission on orders shipped to customers
- A reduced commission on orders received but not yet shipped
- An allowance for sales work where no orders have yet been received

The level of precision declines as the calculation moves through the preceding three factors, from hard quantitative data to soft estimates. Given the difficulty of arriving at a final commission amount, this calculation tends to be a joint effort involving both the payroll department (for the first item) and the sales manager (for the second and third items). It is necessary to follow this admittedly judgmental approach to deriving a final commission for two reasons:

- If a company has fired a salesperson, state laws usually mandate that the business pay the former employee within a few days of termination. Thus, it is not possible to wait for sufficient time to pass for possible sales to resolve themselves into actual sales.
- As soon as a salesperson leaves, reassign his customers to a replacement salesperson in the computer system – so if the attempt is made to continue tracking sales for both the departed and incoming salespeople, the sales records may become intermingled.

Employee Business Expense Reimbursements

A business expense reimbursement arrangement is one under which employees incur expenses on behalf of a company, and are reimbursed by the company for those expenses. The tax reporting under such an arrangement is dependent upon whether the company has an *accountable plan* or a *nonaccountable plan.* The differences are:

- *Accountable plan.* Any amounts paid under an accountable plan are not classified as wages, and so are not subject to income tax withholding or payroll taxes. Under this plan, employees must do all of the following:
  - Have paid or otherwise incurred business expenses while performing services on behalf of the company; and
  - Have substantiated these expenses to the company; and
  - Returned any amounts in excess of substantiated expenses.

  Any amounts in excess of substantiated expenses that are not returned by employees are classified as taxable income to the employees.

> **Tip:** According to the IRS, amounts in excess of substantiated expenses must be returned within a "reasonable period of time," after which the company should classify them as taxable income. The IRS suggests that this period be within 120 days of when an employee incurs an expense on behalf of the company. In order to not surprise employees with this taxable income, adopt a practice of sending periodic notifications to employees, warning them of any remaining amounts to be substantiated or returned to the company.

- *Nonaccountable plan.* Any amounts paid under a nonaccountable plan are classified as wages. Payments are considered as having been paid under a nonaccountable plan under any of the following circumstances:
  - Employees are not required to substantiate their expenses, or do not do so in a timely manner.
  - Employees are not required to return the unused amount of an advance or do not do so in a timely manner.
  - Amounts are paid to employees even if the business does not reasonably expect them to have related business expenses.
  - Amounts paid are designated as reimbursements that would otherwise have been paid as wages.

If a company elects to reimburse its employees on a per diem or other type of fixed allowance system, the IRS considers employees to have made proper accounting to the company of their expenditures, as long as the reimbursement does not exceed the rates published by the federal government. The government publishes its per diem rates for meals and lodging in its Publication 1542, Per Diem Rates.

Any excess per diem reimbursement over the government rates is to be reported as taxable income to employees.

Golden Parachute Payments

A golden parachute payment is a payment made to an employee if there is a change in ownership or control of a company. If a company makes a golden parachute payment to an employee, record it as taxable income. The expense that a company would normally record for such a payment is not allowable for an excessive parachute payment. A payment is considered a golden parachute payment if all of the following conditions apply:

- The payment is compensation; and
- The payment is either to or for the benefit of a disqualified person, who is defined as anyone who was an employee or independent contractor in the 12 months prior to the change in ownership or control, and was a shareholder, officer, or highly compensated employee; and
- The payment is contingent on a change in ownership, control, or a substantial portion of the assets of the company; and
- The payment has a present value of at least three times the person's base pay. This base pay is the person's average annual compensation for the last five years.

EXAMPLE

David Binkley is the president of October Systems, which is acquired by a competitor. Under the terms of his employment agreement, Mr. Binkley receives a golden parachute payment of $800,000. This is more than three times greater than his average compensation of $200,000 over the previous five-year period. The excess parachute payment of $200,000 (calculated as $800,000 minus $600,000) is not a deductible expense for October Systems.

Hourly Rate Plan

The simplest and most commonly-used method for determining the compensation of an hourly employee is the hourly rate plan, under which hours worked are multiplied by an employee's hourly rate. This method can be more complicated if there is a shift differential or overtime. A shift differential is extra pay earned by employees who work a less than desirable shift, such as the evening, night, or weekend shifts. We address overtime calculations in a later section.

EXAMPLE

Arlo Montaigne works the night shift as a security guard at Electronic Inference Corporation. He earns a base wage of $13.50 per hour, plus a $0.50 shift differential. In the most recent work week, he logs 39 hours of work. The calculation of his wages earned under the hourly rate plan is:

$$(\$13.50 \text{ base wage} + \$0.50 \text{ shift differential}) \times 39 \text{ hours} = \$546.00$$

If there is a shift differential, add it to the base wage prior to calculating overtime.
What if an employee works a fraction of an hour? A computerized payroll system automatically converts this to a fraction of an hour. However, a payroll department that manually calculates wages may use a variety of simplification methods, such as rounding up to the nearest quarter-hour.

> **Tip:** If a calculation simplification method is being used for determining fractions of hours worked, be sure to state the method in the employee manual, preferably with a sample calculation. This reduces any employee uncertainty about how their pay is calculated.

EXAMPLE

The Crumb Cake Café calculates wages for its employees by hand. In the most recent week, pastry chef Mortimer Davis worked 39 hours and 41 minutes. The Café payroll clerk could use a calculator to determine that 41 minutes is 0.6833 hours (calculated as 41 minutes ÷ 60 minutes) and pay the chef on that basis. However, prior calculation errors have led to a company policy of rounding up to the next quarter hour. Accordingly, the clerk rounds the 41 minutes up to 45 minutes, and therefore records 39 ¾ hours for Mr. Davis.

Idle Time

If a company makes payments to its employees under a voluntary guarantee to pay them for idle time (any time during which an employee performs no services), classify these payments as taxable wages.

Overtime Pay

Overtime is a 50% multiplier that is added to an employee's base wage for hours worked over 40 hours in a work week. This calculation is subject to some variation by state, so review the local regulations to see if there is an overriding overtime calculation in place. Here are two rules to consider when calculating overtime pay:

- Do not include in the 40 base hours such special hours as holidays, jury duty, sick time, or vacations.
- Add the shift differential to the base wage, and then calculate overtime based on this combined figure.

EXAMPLE

Alfredo Montoya works the evening shift at Electronic Inference Corporation, which adds $1 of shift differential per hour to his base wage of $15 per hour. In the most recent work week, he worked 50 hours. The overtime premium he will be paid is based on the combined $16 wage that includes his shift differential. Thus, his overtime rate is $8 per hour. The calculation of his total compensation for that week is:

$$50 \text{ hours} \times \text{aggregate base pay of } \$16/\text{hour} = \$800$$
$$10 \text{ hours} \times \text{overtime premium of } \$8/\text{hour} = \underline{80}$$
$$\text{Total compensation} = \underline{\$880}$$

EXAMPLE

Alfredo Montoya works 35 hours during a week that includes Memorial Day. His employer, Electronic Inference Corporation, will pay him for a 43-hour work week, which adds the eight hours of the federal holiday to his hours worked. However, this will not include any overtime pay, since only 35 hours were actually worked.

There may be situations where an employee is paid different rates at different times during the work period. This situation may arise when the individual works on different jobs that have differing rates of pay associated with them. In these cases, there are three possible options for calculating overtime, which are:

- Base the overtime rate on the highest wage rate paid during the period
- Base the overtime rate on the average wage rate paid during the period
- Base the overtime rate on the wage rate paid after the 40th hour

The last alternative for calculating overtime requires the prior approval of the affected employee.

EXAMPLE

Marcel Moheko worked on two jobs during the past work week. He worked on Job A for 30 hours, and was paid $20.00 per hour while working on that job. He worked 15 hours on Job B and was paid $25.00 per hour for that job. The last job on which he worked was Job A. The calculation of his overtime pay under the three calculation methods is:

	Based on Highest Rate	Based on Average Rate	Based on Last Rate
Job A pay rate	$20.00	$20.00	$20.00
Job B pay rate	$25.00	$25.00	$25.00
Weighted average pay rate*	$21.25	$21.25	$21.25
Overtime rate	$12.50	$10.63	$10.00
Overtime hours	5	5	5
Total overtime paid	$62.50	$53.15	$50.00

* Calculated as ($20.00 × 75%) + ($25.00 × 25%)

Payments in Kind

If a company pays its employees in a medium other than cash, these are considered to be *in kind* payments. Examples of in kind payments are meals, lodging, and

45

clothes. Report the fair market value of in kind payments as taxable income to employees.

There are several types of in kind payment that are exempt from social security, Medicare, and federal unemployment taxes. They are:

- Noncash payments for household work
- Noncash payments for agricultural labor
- Noncash payments for services not in the employer's trade or business

Piece Rate Pay

A piece rate pay plan can be used by a business that wants to pay its employees based on the number of units of production that they complete. Use the following method to calculate wages under the piece rate method:

Rate paid per unit of production × Number of units completed in the pay period

If a company uses the piece rate method, it must still pay its employees for overtime hours worked. There are two methods available for calculating the amount of this overtime, which are:

- Multiply the regular piece rate by at least 1.5 to arrive at the overtime piece rate, and multiply it by the hours worked during an overtime period. Only use this method when both the company and the employee have agreed to use it prior to the overtime being worked.
- Divide hours worked into the total piece rate pay, and then add the overtime premium (if any) to the excess number of hours worked.

EXAMPLE

October Systems manufactures customized cellular phones, and pays its staff a piece rate of $1.50 for each phone completed. Employee Seth Jones completes 500 phones in a standard 40-hour work week, for which he is paid $750 (500 phones × $1.50 piece rate).

Mr. Jones works an additional 10 hours, and produces another 100 phones during that time. To determine his pay for this extra time period, October Systems first calculates his pay during the normal work week. This is $18.75 (calculated as $750 total regular pay, divided by 40 hours). This means that the overtime premium is 0.5 × $18.75, or $9.375 per hour. Consequently, the overtime portion of Mr. Jones' pay for the extra 10 hours worked is $93.75 (calculated as 10 hours × $9.375 overtime premium).

If October Systems had instead set the piece rate 50% higher for production work performed during the overtime period, this would have resulted in the overtime portion of his pay being $75 (calculated as $0.75 per unit × 100 phones produced).

The difference in the payout between the two overtime calculation methods was caused by the lower productivity level of Mr. Jones during the overtime period. He assembled 25 fewer phones during the overtime period than his average amount during the normal work week, and so would have earned $18.75 less ($0.75 overtime premium × 25 phones) under the second calculation method.

Tip: If there is a history of reduced employee productivity during overtime periods, pay overtime that is based on a premium over the standard piece rate. This reduces the cost to the employer. If the reverse is the case, pay overtime based on the average pay rate during the week.

Salaries Paid for Partial Periods

When a salaried person first starts work for a company or leaves it, or during unpaid leaves of absence, it is likely that his or her pay will cover a partial payroll period. In these cases, the payroll staff must calculate the reduced salary amount to pay the person for the partial period.

The calculation of an employee's salary for a partial period is to determine the person's hourly rate and then multiply this rate by the number of hours worked in the period. The most common method for calculating the hourly rate is to divide a person's annual salary by 2,080 hours. The 2,080-hour figure is the standard number of work hours in a year, which is derived by multiplying a 40-hour work week by 52 weeks.

EXAMPLE

Morgan Hanson has just been hired as the new marketing manager at Electronic Inference Corporation (EIC), at a salary of $85,000 per year. EIC pays its employees on a biweekly schedule, which is 26 pay periods per year. Mr. Hanson starts work on the 8th day of March, which leaves four business days remaining in the pay period that he will work.

To calculate Mr. Hanson's partial period compensation, the payroll staff first calculates his hourly rate of pay, which is:

$$\$85,000 \div 2{,}080 \text{ hours} = \$40.87/\text{hour}$$

The number of work hours left in the pay period is 32, which is calculated as eight hours per day, multiplied by the four remaining work days in the period. Thus, Mr. Hanson's partial period pay is $40.87 times 32 hours, or $1,307.84.

Tip: Use the same calculation method when an employee switches to a different pay level within a pay period; calculate the hourly rate at each pay level, and apply each rate based on the number of hours worked at each pay level.

Sick Pay

Sick pay is wages paid to an employee under a specific plan to an employee who is prevented from working due to injury or sickness. Either the company or a third-party insurer may make these payments to the employee. Sick pay may include both short-term and long-term benefits. Sick pay benefits are frequently paid out as a percentage of an employee's regular wages. Payments that are *not* sick pay include:

- Accident or health insurance payments unrelated to an absence from work
- Disability retirement payments
- Medical expense payments
- Workers' compensation payments

EXAMPLE

Ms. Donna Caruthers is severely injured in a car accident and has one arm amputated. Under a policy paid for by Ms. Caruthers' employer, a third-party insurance firm pays Ms. Caruthers $50,000 as compensation for the loss of her arm. Because the payment was based on the type of injury incurred and was unrelated to her absence from work, the payment is not defined as sick pay and is therefore not subject to federal employment taxes.

Sick pay is reported as taxable income to the employee. However, it is exempt from payroll taxes after the end of six calendar months after the calendar month in which the employee last worked for the business.

EXAMPLE

Mr. Ronald Natch became sick and left work on November 30. He then received sick pay for 10 months before he returned to work on October 1 of the following year. Sick pay paid to Mr. Natch after May 31 was not subject to social security, Medicare, or FUTA taxes, since the sick pay paid after that date exceeded the six-month limitation on such withholdings.

Mr. Natch became sick again on December 1 of the next year, and stayed out of work for another 10 months. However, this time he returned to work for one week at the end of March. By doing so, the six-month time limit was reset, so that all of his sick pay was subject to social security, Medicare, and FUTA taxes during the entire 10-month period.

Tips

In general, any tips that employees receive from customers are treated as taxable income. Employees are required to report cash tips to the company by the tenth day of the month after the month in which they received the tips, but not if the tips received were less than $20. This report should include:

- Tips forwarded by the company to employees that were paid with charge cards
- Tips employees received directly from customers

Tips distributed from a tip-sharing arrangement

Employees report tips to the company on Form 4070, Employee's Report of Tips to Employer. It is also allowable to create a similar form or an electronic system for employees to use. Such forms or systems must contain exactly the same information that would otherwise be reported on Form 4070, as well as the employee's signature (an electronic signature is acceptable if an electronic reporting system is used). Any electronic system must be capable of producing a hard copy, in case the IRS audits tip income.

The employer is responsible for collecting taxes from employee wages for reported tips, and for providing the employer-matched amounts for applicable taxes. If there are not enough employee funds available from which to deduct taxes by the tenth day of the month after the month for which tips are being reported, the company is no longer responsible for collecting any remaining taxes. Where there are not sufficient funds, the company should withhold taxes in the following order:

1. Withhold on regular wages (not tips); then
2. Withhold social security and Medicare taxes on tips; then
3. Withhold income taxes on tips.

If the company is unable to collect some taxes, report the uncollected amounts of social security and Medicare taxes in box 12 of Form W-2.

EXAMPLE

Andrew Malone is a waiter at the Crumb Cake Café. He reports $400 in tip income for the preceding month. In addition, Crumb Cake paid him $100 in hourly wages. His wage and tax withholding situation is:

	Wage Income	Tip Income	Total Income
Gross pay	$100.00	$400.00	$500.00
Federal income tax	(20.00)	(80.00)	(100.00)
Social security	(6.20)	(24.80)	(31.00)
Medicare	(1.45)	(5.80)	(7.25)
Total withholdings	$(27.65)	$(110.60)	$(138.25)
Net pay	$72.35	$289.40	$361.75

Crumb Cake's payroll clerk determines that the total withholdings required for Mr. Malone, according to the preceding table, amount to $138.25, and yet the company is only paying him $100 from which to withhold the funds. Thus, the payroll clerk uses the following progression of deductions to reach the $100 maximum withholding:

Priority	Items to Withhold	Withheld	Funds Remaining
1	Withholdings on wages	$(27.65)	$72.35
2	Social security and Medicare on tip income	(30.60)	41.75
3	Income taxes on tip income	41.75	0

The preceding table shows that only $41.75 of income taxes can be withheld from Mr. Malone's tip income, rather than the $80.00 that should be withheld. Mr. Malone is responsible for the $38.25 shortfall.

Vacation Pay

A company should treat employee vacation pay as reportable taxable income. When it is paid in addition to regular wages, treat it as supplemental wages.

Accrued vacation pay is the amount of vacation time that an employee has earned as per a company's employee benefit manual, but which he or she has not yet used or been paid. The calculation of accrued vacation pay for each employee is:

1. Calculate the amount of vacation time earned through the beginning of the accounting period. This should be a roll-forward balance from the preceding period.
2. Add the number of hours earned in the current accounting period.
3. Subtract the number of vacation hours used in the current period.
4. Multiply the ending number of accrued vacation hours by the employee's hourly wage to arrive at the correct accrual that should be on the company's books.
5. If the amount already accrued for the employee from the preceding period is lower than the correct accrual, record the difference as an addition to the accrued liability. If the amount already accrued from the preceding period is higher than the correct accrual, record the difference as a reduction of the accrued liability.

EXAMPLE

There is already an existing accrued balance of 40 hours of unused vacation time for Fred Smith on the books of October Systems. In the most recent month that has just ended, Fred accrued an additional five hours of vacation time (since he is entitled to 60 hours of accrued vacation time per year, and $60 \div 12 =$ five hours per month). He also used three hours of vacation time during the month. This means that, as of the end of the month, October should have accrued a total of 42 hours of vacation time for him (40 hours existing balance + 5 hours additional accrual - 3 hours used).

Fred is paid $30 per hour, so his total vacation accrual should be $1,260 (42 hours × $30/hour). The beginning balance for him is $1,200 (40 hours × $30/hour), so October accrues an additional $60 of vacation liability.

What if a company has a "use it or lose it" policy? This means that employees must use their vacation time by a certain date (such as the end of the year), and can only carry forward a small number of hours (if any) into the next year. One issue is that this policy may be illegal, since vacation is an earned benefit that cannot be taken away (which depends on the law in each state). If this policy is considered to be legal, it is acceptable to reduce the accrual as of the date when employees are supposed to have used their accrued vacation, thereby reflecting the reduced liability to the company as represented by the number of vacation hours that employees have lost.

What if an employee receives a pay raise? Then increase the amount of his entire vacation accrual by the incremental amount of the pay raise. This is necessary, because if the employee were to leave the company and be paid all of his unused vacation pay, he would be paid at his most recent pay rate.

The Minimum Wage

The minimum wage is a government-mandated pay rate that must be equaled or exceeded in payments to all employees, with exceptions in certain industries. The federal government periodically revises the minimum wage rate, though state governments occasionally override the federal minimum wage rate with a higher rate.

The simplest way to determine if a company is paying at least the minimum wage to an employee is to aggregate all compensation paid to that person during a work week, and divide by the number of hours worked in that week. If the calculation reveals a negative differential between the amount paid and the applicable minimum wage rate, the company must pay that person the wage shortfall.

EXAMPLE

Mr. Elmo Divens is a full-time trainee employee, and is paid a bonus of $30 per day if he can cut a minimum amount of meat for the Terminal Cow Company's slaughterhouse. He also receives base pay of $3.00 per hour. The current minimum wage is $7.25. In a recent week, Mr. Divens worked 40 hours and earned the daily bonus on three days. The minimum wage during that period would be $290 (calculated as 40 hours × $7.25). The amount Mr. Divens earned during that period was $210 (calculated as $120 of base pay, plus $90 in bonuses).

Mr. Divens' earnings are $80 less than the minimum wage, so Terminal Cow Company must pay him the difference in order to be in compliance with the minimum wage law.

Summary

This chapter has been primarily concerned with the various forms of payment to employees that are considered wages from a taxation perspective. Another form of compensation is fringe benefits, which are dealt with extensively in the Employee Benefits chapter. These two chapters address all forms of payment that employees receive. Then use the Payroll Taxes chapter to determine the amount of taxes to withhold from employee pay. Thus, this block of chapters comprises the core of the payroll calculation.

Chapter 5
Employee Benefits

Introduction

The management of employee fringe benefits originates in the human resources department, not the payroll department. Nonetheless, fringe benefits cause multiple issues in the payroll department, particularly in regard to the tax impact of those benefits and how they are reported to the Internal Revenue Service (IRS). This chapter addresses the payroll aspects of a number of employee benefits, including disability pay, flexible spending accounts, leaves of absence, life insurance, medical insurance, pension plans, stock options, vacation pay, and more. The Taxability of Benefits section near the end of the chapter notes the extent to which a fringe benefit should be reported as taxable income to an employee. The information in this chapter is based on IRS information available as of the writing of this book.

The Provider and Recipient of Benefits

A company is the provider of a benefit if it is issued in exchange for services performed for the company. The company does not have to be the direct provider of the benefit – it can be (and frequently is) performed by a third party who is paid by the company.

EXAMPLE

Nuance Corporation has 500 employees. Nuance pays a local supplier to provide dry cleaning service to its employees that is free to them. The provider of the benefit is Nuance, since it is receiving services performed by the employees, and it is hiring a third party to provide the benefit.

The person who provides services to a company is the designated recipient of the benefits provided by the company, even if the benefits are provided to a related person, such as a family member.

EXAMPLE

Ms. Allison Struthers has family medical insurance coverage with her employer, Nuance Corporation. Ms. Struthers is the recipient of benefits from Nuance, even though a portion of the medical insurance applies to other members of her family.

Adoption Assistance

A company may provide adoption assistance to its employees. If the company creates an adoption assistance plan that adheres to all of the following guidelines, the payments made by the company are considered nontaxable income to employees:

- Does not favor highly compensated employees or their dependents (which are employees who are at least 5% owners or who received more than $120,000 in compensation in the preceding year)
- Does not pay more than 5% of its payments during a year to shareholders or owners (which is anyone owning more than 5% of the stock or entitled to more than 5% of the profits generated by the business)
- Gives reasonable notice of the plan to employees
- Employees provide substantiation for their reimbursement claims

Though payments to employees under this plan are not subject to income tax withholding, they are still subject to social security, Medicare, and federal unemployment tax withholding.

Athletic Facilities

If a company operates a gym for its employees, the value of their use of the gym can be excluded from reported employee wages if the facility is substantially restricted to the use of employees and their families. For the purposes of this exemption, consider the following to be employees:

- Current employees
- Retired or disabled employees
- Widow or widower of a person who died, retired, or was disabled as an employee
- Leased employee who works for the company on a full-time basis for at least a year, and who is under the company's primary direction
- A partner who performs services for a partnership

Cell Phones Provided by Employer

If the employer provides a cell phone to an employee for business reasons, the value of the phone is excluded from the income of the employee. Examples of situations where cell phones are considered to be necessary for business reasons are:

- Need to speak with customers during times outside of normal company working hours.
- Need to contact the employee at any hour regarding work-related emergency situations.
- Need to speak with customers while away from the office.

Any personal use of a cell phone in such situations is considered to be a de minimis benefit (see next), and so is not included in the employee's income. However, if a cell phone is provided to promote goodwill with employees, boost employee morale, or attract recruits, the value of the cell phone must be included in employee wages.

De Minimis Benefits

It is acceptable to not report the fair value of a de minimis benefit that a company provides to its employees. A de minimis benefit is a benefit having so little value that tracking it would be unreasonable or administratively impractical. Examples of de minimis benefits are:

- Group-term life insurance whose payment is triggered by the death of an employee's spouse or dependent, where the face amount of the insurance does not exceed $2,000
- Holiday gifts having a low fair market value
- Occasional tickets to the theater or sports events
- Parties or picnics for employees and guests
- Personal use of a company–owned copier, as long as the machine is used by the business at least 85% of the time

Never categorize a cash or cash equivalent benefit as a de minimis benefit, with the exception of small amounts of meal money or transportation reimbursement. Examples of cash equivalent benefits are gift cards and credit cards.

Disability Insurance

Both short-term and long-term disability insurance coverage is available through third party insurance providers. There is an important tax rule that applies to such insurance: If the company pays for the cost of this insurance, any resulting proceeds to an employee are considered taxable income. However, if the employee pays the cost of the insurance, any proceeds are not taxable. If the company pays for only a portion of the insurance, any subsequent proceeds to the employee that are attributable to the employer-paid portion of the insurance are taxable income.

> **Tip:** The ramifications of who pays for disability insurance are significant, so consider allowing employees to pay for their disability insurance themselves. Also, fully inform employees of the ramifications of having the company pay for this insurance, and provide them with examples of what the impact would be on their net after-tax income if they were to be awarded disability payments.

EXAMPLE

Susan Turtledove is diagnosed with a severe case of arthritis, and qualifies for long-term disability pay. Her employer has been paying half of the cost of her long-term disability insurance. The insurance will pay her $3,000 per month. Of this amount, one half, or $1,500, will be recognized as taxable income.

If Ms. Turtledove had instead paid the entire premium for the long-term disability insurance, none of the $3,000 in monthly disability pay would have been recognized as taxable income.

A key issue with disability insurance is who is responsible for the reporting of taxable income to the government. The insurance carrier may attempt to shift this responsibility to the company. If so, the company must report the taxable portion of the amount of disability pay paid to an employee.

A small number of states have disability insurance programs, which provide benefits when an employee cannot work due to an illness or injury that is not related to work. Depending on the program, they are either financed entirely by employers, or jointly by employers and employee pay deductions, or only by employee pay deductions. The amount of these deductions is usually capped at a certain amount of employee annual pay.

Educational Assistance

If a company operates an educational assistance program, it can exclude from employees' taxable income the amount of educational assistance given to them, up to a limit per person of $5,250 per year. This exclusion only applies if the education has a reasonable relationship to the business of the company and is required as part of a degree program. The cost of courses or other education involving games, hobbies, or sports is specifically excluded from this exemption. Exempt costs include:

- Books
- Equipment
- Fees
- Supplies
- Tuition

Educational costs that are *not* exempt from reporting in employee taxable income include lodging, meals, transportation, and the cost of any supplies or tools that an employee is allowed to retain at the end of a course.

In order to have educational benefits be exempt for employees, there must be a separate written plan that specifically provides educational assistance only to company employees. The plan must provide for all of the following:

- It does not favor highly compensated employees. Such a person is one who is either a 5% owner during this year or the preceding year, or who was paid more than $120,000 in the preceding year. The later criterion can be ignored

56

if the person was not in the top 20% of employees in the preceding year when ranked by compensation.

- It does not provide more than 5% of its benefits during the year to share-holders or owners. Such persons own more than 5% of company stock on any day of the year, or are entitled to at least 5% of its profits.
- It does not allow employees to elect to receive cash or other benefits instead of educational assistance.
- The company gives reasonable notice of the program to eligible employees.

For the purposes of the educational assistance benefit, an employee is classified as:
- A current employee
- A former employer who retired, is on disability, or was laid off
- A leased employee working for the company on a substantially full-time basis for at least a year, and who is working under the company's direction
- A sole proprietor
- A partner who engages in services for a partnership

Employee Discounts

If a company gives its employees a price reduction on any property or services that it normally sells to its customers in the ordinary course of business, these price reductions are exempt from being reported as employee income. This exemption is limited to:
- A discount of 20% of the price the company would charge its customers for a service.
- A discount on merchandise of the gross profit percentage times the price the company would charge its customers. To calculate the gross profit percentage, subtract the merchandise cost from the total selling price and divide by the total selling price. This calculation is derived from all merchandise sold to customers and employees in the preceding tax year.

If a company is giving discounts to its highly compensated employees, the discounts are only exempt if the same discount is made available to all employees, or to a group of employees that does not favor highly compensated employees. A highly compensated employee is considered to be one who is either a 5% owner during this year or the preceding year, or who was paid more than $120,000 in the preceding year. The later criterion can be ignored if the person was not in the top 20% of employees in the preceding year when ranked by pay.

Flexible Spending Accounts

In a flexible spending account (FSA) arrangement, employees can sign up to have funds withheld from their pre-tax gross pay, which is stored in a fund for their subsequent use. The FSA is essentially a means by which the federal government makes it less expensive for employees to meet their medical and dependent care expenses.

If an FSA deduction is targeted at medical expenses, employees can apply actual expenditures for medical care against that fund. If an FSA deduction is targeted at dependent care expenses, employees can apply actual expenditures for dependent care against that fund. Employees are not allowed to mix the two funds for reimbursement purposes.

EXAMPLE

Molly Stevens sets up a $3,000 dependent care FSA and a $2,000 medical FSA at the beginning of the year. By the end of the year, she has used up all of the $3,000 of funds in the dependent care FSA, and still has $500 of funds available in the medical FSA. Ms. Stevens cannot apply additional dependent care expenses against the funds remaining in the medical FSA fund.

The following expenses cannot be reimbursed from a flexible spending account:
- Commuting benefits
- Educational assistance
- Employee discounts
- Lodging on the business premises
- Meals
- Moving expense reimbursements
- Scholarships or fellowships
- Tuition reduction
- Volunteer firefighter and emergency medical responder benefits
- Working condition benefits

For both types of funds, the FSA is usually administered by a third party, which holds the withheld funds and disburses them to those employees who have documented valid expenditures.

EXAMPLE

Mark Anderson has historically paid about $1,000 for the co-pay on a variety of prescriptions, which he reasonably expects to pay again in the next calendar year. At the beginning of the new year, he commits to have $1,000 withdrawn from his paycheck in increments over the entire year, to be deposited in a medical FSA.

During the year, as he pays for the co-pay associated with each prescription, he keeps the receipt and forwards it to his company's third-party FSA administrator, which reimburses him for the expense from the funds that the company has deducted from his pay.

If Mr. Anderson had only sought reimbursement for $900 of medical expenses, he would lose the $100 remaining in his FSA fund at the end of the year. If he had sought reimbursement for $1,200 of medical expenses, he would have been reimbursed for only $1,000, since that was the amount that he committed to have withheld during the year.

The net effect of an FSA is to reduce the amount of taxable income for an employee, which means that he or she pays fewer taxes. However, this benefit has an offsetting risk, in that employees must use all of the FSA funds withheld within a calendar year, or lose any remaining funds that were withheld from their pay but never used. Further, there is a risk that the amount withheld for an FSA may be lower than the amount of actual expenses incurred, since the withholding amount for an FSA is set up and then frozen at the start of each calendar year. If so, the employee loses the tax exemption on the excess amount of expense for which there are no offsetting FSA funds. The restriction on subsequent changes to an FSA does not apply if there is a change in an employee's marital status, number of dependents, or employment status that alters the underlying expenditures associated with an FSA.

EXAMPLE

Shelley Summers has enrolled in an FSA for her medical expenses, for which she authorizes annual deductions from her pay of $2,000. Midway through the year, she adopts a baby girl who was injured and orphaned in an earthquake. Ms. Summers expects that the girl will require extensive medical care, and accordingly wants to increase the amount of her FSA deduction.

This change in the number of dependents is a valid reason for altering the amount of her FSA deduction, since it alters the underlying expenditures associated with the FSA.

Tip: It is purely an employee decision regarding the proper deduction amount to use for an FSA. Either the human resources or payroll departments should certainly advise employees regarding the consequences of funding an excessive FSA amount. Otherwise, an employee might find at year-end that he has lost funds, and then vent his unhappiness on either department.

It is permissible to accelerate expenditures that are allowable under an FSA, in order to use up all remaining funds.

EXAMPLE

It is approaching the end of the year, and Ivan Berkowski finds that there is still $250 remaining in his medical FSA account. Accordingly, he fills several prescriptions in advance and buys a pair of prescription eyeglasses just before year-end, and submits the receipts for reimbursement from his FSA account. These are allowable expenses, so he is able to clear out the remaining FSA balance.

The effect of an FSA can be quite substantial to the net pay of an employee, since that person will not pay any of the following taxes on the amount of funds shifted into the FSA:

- Income taxes
- Social security taxes
- Medicare taxes

The exact percentage of a person's full-year net pay that will be increased by using an FSA is specific to the individual, since there is a cap on the amount of wages that are subject to social security taxes, and the amount of income taxes owed will depend upon a person's wage bracket and number of exemptions taken. Nonetheless, the savings are certainly worthwhile, which will make an FSA attractive to any employee – and this means that the FSA deduction is an extremely common one for the payroll department to manage.

EXAMPLE

Allison Foraker earns $60,000 per year. The total amount of all taxes withheld from her pay is 29%. She currently spends $1,500 per year on dependent care. The company that employs her starts an FSA plan. She calculates the following benefit from enrolling in the dependent care FSA in the amount of $1,500 per year:

	Before FSA	After FSA
Gross pay/year	$60,000	$60,000
FSA deduction	---	(1,500)
Adjusted gross pay	$60,000	$58,500
29% tax rate	$17,400	$16,965
Income differential	---	$435

Thus, Ms. Foraker keeps $435 of additional net income by enrolling in the dependent care FSA plan.

The effect of an FSA on the sponsoring company is generally beneficial, though there are some costs. The two cost issues are:

- *Funding risk.* A medical FSA allows employees to make claims against their FSA funds in excess of what they have thus far contributed during the year; if they leave the company before their contributions to the FSA match their claims against it, the company cannot obtain reimbursement from them for the difference. This scenario does not arise for a dependent care FSA, where employees can only withdraw funds to the extent that they have already contributed funds.
- *Administration fee.* If the company is using a third party administrator, it will pay a small fee to the administrator for each employee enrolled in either type of FSA plan.

EXAMPLE

Jonathan Strong signs up for a medical FSA in the amount of $2,400 per year, so his employer begins to deduct $200 from his gross pay each month in order to achieve the $2,400 goal by the end of the year. In February, Mr. Strong has major surgery and applies to the fund administrator for $2,400 of legitimate medical claims during that month. The administrator approves the claims and pays him $2,400. By the end of February, Mr. Strong has contributed $400 to the FSA fund and has taken $2,400 from it. In early March, Mr. Strong ceases employment, leaving the company with an unreimbursed liability of $2,000.

The main point of an FSA is to reduce the amount of taxes that employees pay. Since the sponsoring company matches some taxes, it reduces its compensation costs by encouraging employees to maximize their participation in FSAs. This is the primary benefit of an FSA from the corporate perspective.

EXAMPLE

Mulligan Imports sets up both dependent care and medical FSAs and encourages its employees to participate in the plans. The company has 300 employees, all of whom are paid amounts below the social security wage cap. Half of the employees participate, and fund their accounts for an average amount of $1,500 per year. This is a total of $225,000 that is protected from taxation (calculated as 150 employees × $1,500 each).

Mulligan would normally pay a matching amount of payroll taxes for the social security and Medicare taxes, which is 7.65% of employee pay. Since the FSAs are protecting $225,000 from taxation, this means that Mulligan is saving $17,213 in payroll taxes.

Tip: If a third party is being used to administer the employer's FSA plans, select one that offers a debit card to employees that they can use to make approved purchases. A debit card is very convenient for employees, since it essentially eliminates all of the paperwork that they would otherwise have to complete in order to obtain reimbursement.

If the employer has an FSA that favors highly compensated employees in regard to either their ability to participate in the plan or their contributions into the plan, or benefits received from it, report as part of their taxable compensation the value of taxable benefits they could have selected. The same rule applies to plans that favor key employees (which occurs when more than 25% of the total nontaxable benefits provided under the plan go to key employees). For the purposes of this rule, the definitions of highly compensated employees and key employees are:

Highly Compensated Employee Definition	Key Employee Definition
An officer; or	An officer having annual pay of more than $170,000; or
A shareholder owning more than 5% of the voting power or value of all classes of employer stock; or	An employee who is either a 5% owner of the business or a 1% owner whose annual pay is more than $150,000.
An employee who is considered highly compensated, based on the facts and circumstances; or	
The spouse or dependent of any of the above.	

Note: Any FSA plan maintained under a collective bargaining agreement is automatically considered to not favor highly compensated employees or key employees.

Health Savings Account

A health savings account is an account that is owned by a qualified individual who is either an employee or former employee. Any contributions made by a company into an HSA become the property of the individual. The balance in the account is used to pay for the medical expenses of the individual and that person's family.

The contributions by an employer into a health savings account (HSA) are not reported as taxable income to the employee, but only under the following restrictions (for 2016):

- The individual must be covered by a high deductible health plan; such a plan must have a single-person deductible of at least $1,300 or at least $2,600 for family coverage. Out-of-pocket annual expenses must be limited to $6,550 for single coverage and $13,100 for family coverage.
- The individual cannot be claimed as a dependent on another person's tax return.
- The individual cannot be enrolled in Medicare Part A or Part B.

The maximum exempt amount that a company can contribute to the HSA accounts of its employees is limited to $3,350 for single coverage and $6,750 for family coverage. These amounts increase by $1,000 if the individual is age 55 or older. If a married couple are both age 55 or older, the $1,000 increase applies to each of them, as long as they have separate HSA accounts.

If the contributions that a company makes to the HSA accounts of its employees are not comparable, the company must pay a 35% excise tax that is based on the amount the company contributed to all employee HSA accounts during the year.

Leaves of Absence

If a company has at least 50 employees, the Family and Medical Leave Act (FMLA) allows its employees to take up to 12 unpaid weeks of leave for a variety of reasons related to family and medical issues. Key reasons supporting a leave of absence are:

- Birth of a child
- Caring for a family member who has a serious illness
- Caring for an injured service member in the family
- Having a serious illness that renders the employee unable to perform his or her job

The FMLA restricts this leave of absence to those employees who:

- Have worked for the company a total of at least 12 months, including a minimum of 1,250 hours in the last 12 months.
- Work at a company facility where at least 50 of its employees work within a 75-mile radius.

> **Note:** Some states have enacted laws that make the FMLA applicable to businesses having as few as 15 employees, and have expanded the definition of a family. One should verify the applicability of these state laws to the business in question.

If employees fall under the protection of the FMLA and take leaves of absence for the reasons allowed under the Act, the employer must continue to provide them with the medical insurance for which they had already signed up before going on leave. It can continue to require them to pay the same employee deduction that had been in effect prior to their leave of absence. If an employee does not pay for his portion of the medical insurance within 30 days, the company is entitled to cancel the insurance for the remaining period of his leave of absence. A few additional conditions of the FMLA are:

- If the medical coverage or the terms of the employee-paid portion of the insurance are altered during a person's leave of absence, these changes will apply to the person on leave.
- If a person's medical insurance is cancelled due to non-payment, it must be restored once he returns to work.
- Only medical insurance is continued through a period of leave. Other benefits are not addressed by the FMLA.
- An employee must be given the same or equivalent job upon his or her return from leave.

- No seniority accrues to an employee who is on leave.
- If an employee is salaried and paid in the top ten percent of employees, and restoring this person to his or her previous position would cause "substantial and grievous economic injury," then this person's job is defined as a *key position*, and the company may deny reinstatement to the individual.

EXAMPLE

Jennifer Morris works for Suture Corporation. She takes a leave of absence to care for a terminally-ill child, which is covered under the FMLA. She had been covered under Suture's medical insurance plan prior to her leave of absence, under which she paid the company $300 per month as her portion of the expense.

While Ms. Morris is out on leave, the cost of Suture's medical insurance plan increases dramatically, causing the company to reduce benefits and increase the employee-paid portion of the cost to $500. Ms. Morris concludes that she cannot pay this increased amount, and stops paying Suture her share of the expense. Once her payment is 30 days overdue, Suture cancels her participation in the insurance plan.

Tip: Since the cost of providing medical coverage to an employee who is on leave can be quite high, consider adopting a formal review procedure and signed form that requires an employee to enumerate the reasons for going on leave, and the company's evaluation of whether the leave falls under the FMLA. Also, provide the employee with specific instructions regarding when his or her share of medical insurance payments are to be paid to the company, and the consequences of not making a timely payment.

Life Insurance

When a company selects a benefit package from a third party, it is common for the package to include a modest amount of group-term life insurance for each employee. The amount of such life insurance included in a basic benefits package is typically the amount of a person's annualized pay, and the cost of this insurance is so small that it is usually paid in full by the company. A common additional benefit is to make supplemental life insurance available to employees, which they pay for in full if they accept it.

A problem with group-term life insurance that is paid for by the company is that the IRS requires an employer to report as taxable income to the employee the amount of the benefit that exceeds $50,000 of life insurance. The company should not report such excess insurance coverage as income to the employees if the company is the beneficiary of the policy. The calculation of this benefit for employee tax reporting purposes is:

1. Round the amount of insurance coverage granted to the nearest $100.
2. Subtract $50,000 from the total amount of insurance coverage.

3. Multiply the number of thousands of dollars of insurance coverage remaining by the cost shown in the following table (accurate as of 2016). To determine the correct employee age, use the employee's age on the last day of the employee's tax year. The result is the cost of the insurance on a monthly basis.
4. Calculate the insurance cost for every month of coverage in the tax year.
5. Include the total of these amounts in the employee's W-2 form.

Employee Age	Insurance Cost
Under 25	$0.05
25 through 29	0.06
30 through 34	0.08
35 through 39	0.09
40 through 44	0.10
45 through 49	0.15
50 through 54	0.23
55 through 59	0.43
60 through 64	0.66
65 through 69	1.27
70 and older	2.06

EXAMPLE

The life insurance benefit provided by the Red Herring Fish Company to its employees is to provide them with one times their annualized pay as life insurance. Mr. Vernon Harness is 52 years old and is paid $150,000 per year, and so has life insurance coverage in the same amount. On July 1, Red Herring increases his annualized pay to $170,000, and alters his life insurance accordingly. The calculation of his taxable life insurance benefit is:

Time Period	Calculation	Total Benefit
Jan. to June	(($150,000 - $50,000) ÷ 1,000) × 0.23 multiplier × 6 months	= $138.00
July to Dec.	(($170,000 - $50,000) ÷ 1,000) × 0.23 multiplier × 6 months	= $165.60
	Total	= $303.60

In order for the amount of group-term life insurance under $50,000 to be exempt from reporting as taxable income for employees, the insurance coverage must meet all of the following requirements:

- It provides a general death benefit.
- It is provided to at least ten full-time employees at some point during the year. There are limited exceptions to this rule.

- The amount of insurance provided to each employee is based on such factors as age, years of service, pay, or position. These factors cannot be used to exclude an employee from coverage.
- The company directly or indirectly carries the insurance policy.

> **Tip:** The calculation and reporting of the life insurance benefit exceeding $50,000 is moderately time consuming, so consider eliminating the work load by capping all company-paid life insurance at $50,000, and making supplemental life insurance available to employees.

If the company is only providing life insurance to a few key employees, rather than to all employees, the company must report the entire insurance benefit as taxable income to employees. For this purpose, the reportable cost of the insurance is the greater of the actual premiums paid or the cost derived using the preceding IRS insurance cost table. For this rule, a key employee is considered to be one who is either an officer earning more than $170,000, a 5% owner of the business, or a 1% owner whose annual pay exceeds $150,000.

For the purposes of tax exemption, group-term life insurance does *not* include any of the following:

- Any insurance that does not provide a general death benefit. Examples are travel insurance or any policy that only provides accidental death benefits.
- Life insurance on the life of a spouse or dependent, unless the policy has a face value of no more than $2,000; if the face amount exceeds $2,000, include the coverage cost in income.
- Insurance that provides a multi-year benefit.

Lodging on Business Premises

If a company provides lodging to an employee, the value of this lodging is exempt from reporting as taxable income if all of the following conditions apply:

- The lodging is on the premises of the business
- The lodging is furnished for the convenience of the business
- The employee must accept the lodging as a condition of employment

This exemption does not apply if a company allows its employees to instead receive additional pay.

EXAMPLE

Enrico Montoya accepts employment as the desk clerk at the Sojourn Motel. As a condition of his employment, he lives in an apartment on the premises of the hotel, which is directly linked to the front desk where he works. The value of this lodging is exempt from reporting as income to Mr. Montoya.

Meals

It is acceptable to exclude the cost of de minimis meals from reported employee pay if the cost of these meals is so low that it would be unreasonable or administratively impractical to track them. The exclusion is also available for meals that a company provides to its employees at a company-operated eating facility, but only if the annual revenue from the facility equals or exceeds the direct costs of the facility.

The exemption does not apply to meal money that is calculated and paid based on hours worked.

EXAMPLE

The president of Milford Sound likes to have an occasional beer keg party after work hours on Friday. He also brings in donuts for the staff just prior to all major holidays. These are de minimis meal payments, and so are exempt from reporting as employee income.

Milford Sound has a policy of paying $20 in meal money to any employee who works on a weekend or more than 10 hours in a day. These payments are not exempt from reporting as employee income.

If a company provides meals at a company-operated eating facility to highly compensated employees that are not available to either all employees or to a group of employees that does not favor highly compensated employees, the value of these meals cannot be exempted from the income of the recipients. In this situation, a highly compensated employee is defined as either a 5% owner of the business at any time during this or the preceding year, or one who received more than $120,000 of compensation during the preceding year. The later criterion does not apply if the employee was not ranked in the top 20% of employees for compensation in the preceding year.

EXAMPLE

Gusher Corporation manages oil exploration teams around the world. Its president, Mr. Spout, dines regularly in the company's executive dining room, where only employees having the rank of vice president or above are allowed to dine. Gusher should report the value of Mr. Spout's meals in the dining room as taxable income.

If a company provides meals on the company premises for the convenience of the business, the value of these meals is exempt from reporting as taxable employee pay. This rule does not apply if the company allows its employees to elect to receive pay instead of meals.

EXAMPLE

Cajun Delights Restaurant provides meals to its service employees during their scheduled work shifts at the restaurant. These meals are provided for the convenience of the business, since the meals allow employees to continue working through the lunch and dinner periods. The value of these meals can be excluded from employee wages.

If Cajun Delights were to provide free meals to its employees during their days off, the company would have to report the value of such meals in taxable employee income.

If a business furnishes meals to its employees during work hours in order to have them on hand for emergencies, these meals are being provided for the convenience of the business, and should not be reported as employee pay.

EXAMPLE

Teton Helicopter Rescue operates two rescue helicopters in the area of the Grand Teton National Park. Its pilots must be available for immediate departure to rescue injured hikers and climbers during their shifts, so the company provides them with on-site meals during their shifts. These meals are provided at the convenience of the employer, and so are not reportable as employee wages.

If employees are restricted to a short meal period because of the nature of the business and employees cannot reasonably be expected to eat elsewhere during this time period, meals provided by the business are considered exempt from wage reporting. This exemption does not apply if the reason for the short meal period is to allow employees to leave work earlier in the day.

Similarly, if a business provides meals to its employees because they cannot otherwise obtain "proper" meals within a reasonable period of time, the value of these meals is also considered exempt from wage reporting. This rule implies that meals can be exempt from wage reporting even in the absence of a short meal period.

EXAMPLE

Emma Smith works at a payday loan business that has its peak period during the lunch hour. Accordingly, the company can only give Ms. Smith a 15-minute lunch break. Since she is unable to obtain lunch elsewhere within that time period, the company provides her with a meal on the premises. The value of this meal is not reportable as income.

If an employer would have provided a meal to an employee during working hours for business reasons, but the employee could not eat due to work duties, a meal provided immediately after working hours is considered exempt from wage reporting.

Medical Insurance

The primary benefit offered by most companies is medical insurance. The company typically arranges for a single health insurance plan with one provider, and then offers it to employees, with the provision that they accept a deduction from their pay to defray the total cost of the insurance. The amount of the deduction is entirely up to the employer. Typical deduction amounts are:

- Pay 80 percent of the employee's medical insurance
- Pay 80 percent of the employee's medical insurance and 50 percent of any incremental cost attributable to family members
- Pay for a minimum medical plan and allow employees to cover the entire incremental cost of a more comprehensive plan

There are a variety of health insurance providers available. The major types of providers are:

- *Health maintenance organization (HMO).* An HMO plan requires employees to only use doctors who have signed up to work with that specific plan.
- *Point of service plan (POS).* A POS plan requires employees to select a primary care physician who is the primary point of contact, but also allows consultations outside the plan's designated network of doctors.
- *Preferred provider organization (PPO).* A PPO plan allows employees to consult with doctors who fall outside of a core group of designated doctors, but at a higher co-pay and deductible cost.

Given the very high cost of medical insurance, some larger companies use *self-insurance,* rather than using an outside health care provider. Under this approach, employees submit their medical claims either to the company or a designated plan administrator, and are reimbursed by the company. Above a predetermined expenditure level for the entire plan, a *stop loss* insurance policy pays for all remaining claims for the year. The stop loss policy keeps a company from incurring catastrophic losses from major medical claims, while eliminating the profit that would otherwise have been paid to an outside health care provider.

The trouble with a self-insurance arrangement is that it can be considered discriminatory in favor of highly compensated employees, in which case all excess medical reimbursements made to this group are considered taxable income to those employees (though not for the purposes of calculating payroll taxes). The portion of medical reimbursements considered taxable is those payments made that exceed the average reimbursements paid to the other employees in the plan. Under these circumstances, a highly compensated employee is defined as:

- One of the five highest-paid officers; or
- An employee who owns more than 10% in value of the employer's stock; or
- An employee who is one of the highest-paid 25% of all employees.

EXAMPLE

Luminescence Corporation pays for a $2,000 cat scan and detailed doctor evaluation for the entire management team. This benefit is not provided to any other employees. Luminescence should include the entire cost of this procedure in the reportable income of each member of the management team, since it was not offered to the other employees.

Tip: If a self-insurance arrangement is to be considered non-discriminatory, the plan should benefit at least 70 percent of all employees. Thus, it may be necessary to use an extensive marketing campaign and a relatively high benefit level to ensure an adequate amount of participation.

From a payroll perspective, medical insurance deductions are usually taken from employee pay in a fixed amount in every regularly-scheduled payroll, but are not deducted from pay during special payrolls (such as for a payroll that is scheduled just for year-end bonuses).

Tip: When employees leave the employer part-way through a month, always charge them the full-month deduction for the medical insurance for the final month. The reason is that the insurance provider always charges for a full month of coverage for a departing employee, even if the employee is leaving just a day or two into the month, and the employee will benefit from that coverage through the end of the month. It is common to not charge this extra deduction, since deductions are usually automated in the payroll system, and a lesser amount is usually charged (since the deduction is spread over multiple payrolls in a month). Thus, include a medical insurance deduction in the checklist used to calculate a person's final pay check.

When a company pays for a portion (or all) of the medical insurance for an employee, this payment is not considered income to the employee (other than the exception just noted), so the employer should not report such payments as income in the year-end Form W-2 that it sends to the IRS. Further, if a company chooses to reimburse its employees for any deductibles or co-payments that they incur as part of their medical insurance, this is also not reportable income for the employees.

Medical Insurance - COBRA

When an employee ceases being employed by a company, he or she has the right to obtain medical insurance coverage through the former employer for 18 months following his or her termination date. The coverage period expands to a total of 36 months under certain limited circumstances. This benefit is required under the Consolidated Omnibus Budget Reconciliation Act, which is better known as COBRA.

COBRA coverage means that a former employee can buy insurance coverage through the company's medical insurance; however, it is at full price – the former employer is not required to pay for any portion of this insurance. Thus, the main point of COBRA is to give former employees *access to* insurance, not necessarily *low-cost* insurance. The COBRA requirement is applicable only to companies having at least 20 full time equivalent employees. Below that amount, an employer is not required to extend COBRA coverage to its former employees. A full-time equivalent is the total number of hours worked in a period divided by the normal number of working hours in that period. Thus, if a group of employees work 320 hours during a week, and the standard work week is 40 hours, the full-time equivalent for that period is eight, no matter how many people actually worked.

To comply with COBRA, a company must notify an employee of his or her rights regarding medical insurance coverage when there is a qualifying event. Anyone so notified has 60 days in which to accept insurance coverage under COBRA. If someone accepts coverage, the company can require them to pay up to 102 percent of the cost of the medical insurance (which allows the company room to recoup some of its COBRA administrative costs). There are four circumstances under which the employer can terminate COBRA coverage, which are:

- A person does not pay the company the full amount of the insurance within 30 days of the due date.
- The company stops providing medical insurance to its employees. This means there is no underlying health care coverage that the employer can offer its former employees.
- A person obtains coverage under another health insurance plan.
- A person obtains Medicare coverage.

EXAMPLE

Abraham Ibrahim is laid off by Snyder Corporation at the end of November. He receives a formal notification of his insurance rights under COBRA from Snyder at the layoff meeting. After 40 days, he fills out the COBRA documentation to accept insurance coverage. Mr. Ibrahim has filed in a timely manner, since he does so within the 60 day enrollment period. After six months, Mr. Ibrahim pays 35 days after the required due date for a monthly premium payment. Snyder now has a justifiable reason to terminate the coverage of Mr. Ibrahim.

The key problem with COBRA coverage from an employer's perspective is coordinating the receipt of payments from former employees with the ongoing provision of insurance by the health care provider. COBRA payments typically arrive in the accounting department and are processed in the normal manner as cash receipts. However, if there is a breakdown in the notification process for informing the human resources staff, there is a significant chance that either coverage will be dropped even though payment was made, or that coverage will continue even in the absence of a payment.

> **Tip:** To avoid any possibility of continuing the insurance coverage of a former employee who has not paid for the coverage, have a clerk maintain a list of all people receiving coverage under COBRA, and notify all people paying the company under COBRA to send their payments directly to this clerk. The clerk then logs in all cash receipts against the COBRA list and forwards the payments to the accounting staff for formal recordation as cash receipts. This approach eliminates any chance that the accounting staff will receive payments and not notify the human resources department of the receipts.

If a company chooses to pay for any portion of the accident or medical insurance premiums for a former employee, these payments are tax exempt for the former employee.

Moving Expense Reimbursement

A business can exclude from an employee's reportable wages any of the following moving expenses paid to a third party or reimbursed to the employee by the business:

- Reasonable expenses required to move household goods and personal effects from the old home to the new home
- Travel costs incurred to move from the old home to the new home

These expenses are only exempt from wage reporting if both of the following circumstances are true:

- The new job of the employee is at least 50 miles farther from the employee's old home than the old job location was; and
- The employee works at least 39 weeks during the first year after arriving in the general area of the new job location.

A moving expense is not deductible if it is a meal.

No-Additional-Cost Services

A no-additional-cost service is a service that a business provides to an employee which does not cause the company to incur any substantial additional cost. Such services must be ones that the business offers to its customers in its ordinary course of business, and in which an employee performs substantial services. No-additional-cost services are usually ones in which a business has excess capacity. Examples of no-additional-cost services include:

- Airline seats
- Bus seats
- Train seats
- Hotel rooms
- Telephone services

The cost incurred by a business in providing such services is considered to be substantial if the business or its employees spend a substantial amount of time in providing the service, even if such time would otherwise be idle or were provided outside normal business hours.

EXAMPLE

Mr. Emory Jacobson works for the Niagara Car Wash as a detailer. Niagara allows its employees to run their vehicles through the car wash at the end of the business day. The car wash system has excess capacity at that time, so there is no substantial incremental cost to the company. Thus, the value of this service should not be reported as taxable income to Mr. Jacobson.

If two businesses provide no-additional-cost services to each other's employees, these services may be exempt from reporting as taxable income. An exemption applies if all of the following are true:

- The service provided to the employees is the same type of service in which the employees work and which the businesses provide to their customers; and
- There is a written reciprocal agreement between the companies to provide reciprocal services to each other's employees; and
- The parties to the agreement all perform substantial services in the same line of business; and
- None of the companies involved incur a substantial additional cost to provide the services.

EXAMPLE

Excalibur Fitness enters into a reciprocal agreement with King Arthur Fitness, under which both companies allow their employees to work out for free in the fitness facilities of either company. Neither company incurs a substantial incremental cost by doing so, and the services provided are the same as the services that both companies provide to their customers. These services are therefore exempt from reporting as taxable employee income.

The services enumerated in this section are subject to the broadest IRS interpretation of an employee, which means that family members can make use of no-additional-cost services. The following individuals are all considered an employee for this benefit:

- Current employee
- Former employee who retired or is on disability
- A widow or widower of a person who died while an employee, or who retired or is on disability

- A leased employee who provides services to the company on a substantially full-time basis for at least a year, and those services are under the primary control of the business
- A partner who engages in services for a partnership

The IRS points out that one should consider any use of air transportation by the parent of an employee as having been used by the employee. Thus, such travel is exempt from reporting as taxable income.

No-additional-cost services are *not* exempt for highly compensated employees if the same services are *not* made available on the same terms to either all employees, or to a group of employees that does not favor highly compensated employees. For this analysis, a highly compensated employee is a person who was either a 5% owner of the business at any time during the year, or one who received at least $120,000 in compensation during the preceding year (which does not apply if the employee is not in the top 20% of employees when ranked by pay).

Pension Plans

A company can provide its employees with a number of different pension plans, all with varying tax treatments and administrative needs. These pension plans fall into two categories, which are qualified retirement plans and nonqualified retirement plans. We address the more common pension plans within the subheadings in this section.

A qualified retirement plan is a plan that meets all of the requirements of the Employee Retirement Income Security Act (ERISA), and Section 401(a) of the Internal Revenue Code. Under a qualified plan, the employer can deduct its contributions to the plan, while participants can defer their contributions to and earnings from the plan until they eventually withdraw funds from it. Participants can defer recognition even further by rolling their funds over into an Individual Retirement Account (IRA).

A nonqualified retirement plan is a plan that does not meet the requirements of ERISA or the Internal Revenue Code. A company using a nonqualified plan can pay key employees more than other participants in the plan. If a company contributes funds into a nonqualified plan, it cannot record the payments as an expense until the funds are eventually paid out to the targeted employees, which may be years in the future. Also, a plan participant being paid through a nonqualified plan cannot roll the funds over into an IRA.

Defined Contribution Plan

A defined contribution plan is a qualified retirement plan where the employer is responsible for contributing a specific amount into the plan, and is not responsible for the amount of any benefits eventually paid from the plan to participants. This means that the risk associated with subsequent performance of the fund is borne by participants, not the employer (which makes the defined contribution plan a much better choice for the employer than a defined benefit plan, as defined below).

Participants in a defined contribution plan may have a number of different investment options, which have varying risk profiles and possible returns on investment. The more common defined contribution plans are:

- *401(k) plan.* This is an investment account into which employees contribute funds, sometimes with additional matching funds contributed by the employer. The funds contributed by the employer are usually under a vesting arrangement, where the participants earn the funds by staying employed with the company for a certain period of time. Participants pay income taxes on the funds in a 401(k) account when they withdraw funds from the account. The net effect of a 401(k) is to defer the recognition of taxable income until retirement, when participants will presumably also be in a lower tax bracket, and so will pay fewer income taxes. With some hardship-based exceptions, a participant cannot withdraw funds from a 401(k) account until at least age 59 ½ without facing large penalties. To mitigate this problem for cash-strapped participants, a 401(k) account may provide for loans to participants up to the amount of their contributed funds, and on which they must pay interest.

> **Tip:** Make sure that there is a *force out provision* in the company's 401(k) plan, under which the company can require participants to close out their 401(k) funds if the balances are too low. This is important when the company is paying its third party fund administrator fees on all accounts, when the balances are very low and their owners have left the company. Even if there is no force out provision, communicate with former employees regularly to remind them of the existence of their 401(k) accounts and of their options to roll the balances into other retirement accounts. Doing so reduces the company's 401(k) administration costs.

- *403(b) plan.* This is a plan similar in concept and tax treatment to the 401(k) plan, but designed for public education and non-profit entities.
- *Money purchase plan.* This plan requires the employer to pay into each employee's plan account a percentage of his or her compensation for that year. The payments can be quite substantial, since the contribution cap per year is the lesser of 25% of employee compensation or $54,000 (in 2017). These payments are deferred income for participants until they withdraw the funds.
- *Profit sharing plan.* This plan is essentially the same as a money purchase plan, except that the employer funds any contributions with a portion of its profits. The amount of payments made is discretionary, and the employer can even choose to make contributions to the plan in the absence of company profits. Contributions are typically made to each participant's account based on his or her annual compensation as a percentage of all compensation among plan participants. The contribution per year per participant is the lesser of 25% of employee compensation or $54,000 (in 2017).

- *Roth 401(k).* This is similar to a 401(k) account, except that the participant pays taxes on funds when they are contributed to the account, rather than when the funds are later withdrawn. By doing so, all interest earned subsequent to placing funds in the account is tax-free.

The 401(k) plan has become the pension plan of choice for many companies, since it limits their liability for the amount of benefits eventually distributed to participants. However, this also means that participants are at some risk of not having sufficient pension funds to retire. To mitigate this risk, consider the following three changes to a 401(k) plan:

- *Automatic enrollment.* Enroll employees in the 401(k) plan at the earliest opportunity, so that they can start setting aside funds as soon as possible. Under this approach, an employee has to opt out of the plan.
- *Automatic contribution hikes.* Automatically increase the amounts contributed by employees, using as a trigger either an annual increase or whenever a person is granted a pay raise.
- *Offer a large match.* The best way to convince employees to participate in a 401(k) is to offer them hefty matching funds from the employer.
- *Portfolio rebalancing.* Automatically shift employee funds into more conservative investment portfolios as employees approach retirement.

> **Tip:** To encourage employees to invest more of their funds in a 401(k), extend the company match over a larger percentage of pay. For example, offering a 100% match for the first 3% of pay will only encourage employees to invest 3% of their wages. However, offering a 50% match for the first 6% of pay will encourage them to invest twice as much of their wages, while costing the company the same amount of matching funds.

Defined Benefit Plan

A defined benefit plan itemizes the exact payment that a participant will eventually receive, usually in the form of a fixed periodic payment for the remainder of the participant's life. This payment is based on a formula that can have a variety of components, but which usually involves the amount of wages paid and years of service, typically with a heavier weighting of wages paid near the end of a participant's period of employment. If a participant elects to receive his or her payment from the plan in a single lump sum, it is allowable to roll over the amount into an IRA. Otherwise, payments are subject to income taxes upon receipt. Two of the more common defined benefit plans are:

- *Cash balance plan.* Under this plan, the employer creates an account for each participant, and credits the account with a pay credit and an interest credit each year. The pay credit is based on a proportion of each participant's compensation. The interest credit can be a fixed or variable interest rate that tracks a baseline interest rate, such as a Treasury bill rate. This plan defines the participant benefit in terms of a stated account balance. Employees do not have to make their own contributions into this type of plan. The cash balance plan is less common than the target benefit plan.

- *Target benefit plan.* Under this plan, the employer is required to make annual contributions to the plan that is based on the actuarial estimates of the amount of funding needed to provide a certain level of benefits in the future. There are a multitude of assumptions involved in the actuarial estimate which are bound to vary somewhat from the eventual actual results, so a target benefit plan is likely to be somewhat overfunded or underfunded at any point in time. These funding issues are resolved in later periods, when the actuarial assumptions are further modified, resulting in altered funding requirements.

Defined benefit plans are much less favorable to a company than defined contribution plans, since a defined benefit plan places responsibility for the performance of amounts invested in the plan on the company, which may require substantial additional contributions over time.

Personal Retirement Account

The reporting requirements for a qualified retirement plan are substantial, so a smaller employer may not want to invest the amount of staff time and money in maintaining one. An alternative is to encourage employees to create their own personal retirement accounts. There are many types of these accounts, of which the more popular are:

- *Individual retirement account (IRA).* This is also referred to as a *traditional IRA.* This is an account that a person creates, and into which he or she can contribute the lower of total annual compensation or (as of 2016) $5,500 per year, or $6,500 for those at least 50 years old. Depending upon the circumstances, these contributions may be tax deductible for those employees with lower compensation levels. The key benefit of a traditional IRA is that any income earned on the funds invested in it is shielded from taxation until withdrawn. A person can begin withdrawing funds from the account as of age 59 ½, and is required to begin doing so as of age 70 ½. If a person does not withdraw the minimum required amount as of age 70 ½, the penalty for not doing so is 50% of the amount that should have been withdrawn.
- *Rollover IRA.* When an employee leaves a company where he or she has funds in a qualified pension plan, the best options are to either leave the funds in the plan, roll them into the qualified plan of the new employer, or to roll them into a rollover IRA. This last option is an IRA account that is specifically designed to accept funds from qualified pension plans. Since many people have multiple employers during their careers, many with qualified pension plans, it makes sense to consolidate the funds in these accounts into a rollover IRA.
- *Roth IRA.* This is similar to a traditional IRA account, except that the participant pays taxes on funds when they are contributed to the account,

rather than when the funds are later withdrawn. By doing so, all interest earned subsequent to placing funds in the account is tax-free. A participant can withdraw funds from the account as of age 59 ½. Since there is no subsequent taxation of the earnings in a Roth IRA, there is no reason for the government to require participants to draw down these funds, so there is no minimum draw down, as was the case for a traditional IRA.

- *Savings Incentive Match Plan for Employees (SIMPLE)*. As the acronym implies, this is a simplified retirement plan under which both the employer and employee can make contributions to an account. It is funded through a pre-tax reduction of employee gross pay. The maximum annual contribution to a SIMPLE account (as of 2017) was $12,500 and $15,500 for those at least 50 years old. A SIMPLE plan can only be created by an employer having fewer than 100 employees, or which has employed an average of 100 or fewer employees in either of the two preceding years. If a business subsequently increases its employment, it can still operate a SIMPLE plan as long as it does not employ an average of 100 or more people in a subsequent year. This plan requires a minimum contribution level by the employer, which can be either a flat 2% of each employee's compensation for the plan year, or at least 3% of an employee's compensation for the plan year. If a participant wants to withdraw funds from a SIMPLE account before age 59 ½, the penalty is 25% of the distribution.

- *Simplified employee pension (SEP)* IRA. This plan is designed for the self-employed person, but can be extended to all types of business entities. A SEP IRA can only be created if there is no qualified retirement plan already in place. Contributions to a SEP IRA are protected from income taxes until such time as they are withdrawn from the account. Participants may begin withdrawing funds from the account as of age 59 ½. The total contribution to a SEP IRA cannot exceed the lesser of 25% of a participant's annual compensation or $54,000 (as of 2017). These contribution levels make the SEP IRA one of the best ways to protect a substantial amount of funds from taxation.

Retirement Planning Services

If a company provides retirement planning services to its employees, the value of these services can be excluded from their reportable income. This exemption only applies if the company maintains a qualified retirement plan (see the Pension Plans section). The services provided under retirement planning can cover general advice and information on retirement, but cannot include tax preparation services, accounting, legal, or brokerage services.

This exemption only applies to highly compensated employees if the retirement planning services are also made available on the same terms to all members of a group of employees who are normally provided with information about the company's qualified retirement plan.

Stock Options

A stock option gives its recipient the option to buy a company's stock at a specific price, and within a specific range of dates. From a tax perspective, stock options are classified as either incentive stock options or nonqualified stock options. The characteristics of the two types of options are:

- *Incentive stock options (ISO)*. This is not reportable as taxable income to the employee at the time of grant, nor when the employee later exercises the options to buy stock. Once the employee eventually sells the stock, it is taxed as ordinary income; however, if he holds the stock for at least two years, it is taxable as a long-term capital gain. This type of option usually requires the recipient to either exercise or forfeit the option within 90 days of no longer being employed by the issuing company. An ISO is not valid for tax purposes unless it follows these rules:
  - *Company ownership*. Options cannot be granted to a person who owns more than ten percent of all classes of the employer's stock, unless the maximum option term is restricted to five years and the exercise is at least 110% of the fair market value of the stock.
  - *Employee only*. A company can only issue incentive stock options to its employees, and those individuals must continue to be employed by the company until 90 days before the exercise date.
  - *Maximum exercised*. The maximum aggregate fair market value of stock bought through an ISO exercise cannot exceed $100,000 in a calendar year. Any amount exercised in excess of $100,000 is treated as a nonqualified stock option (see below).
  - *Maximum term*. The maximum term of a stock option is ten years.
  - *Transfers*. Options cannot be transferred by the recipient and they must be exercised during that person's lifetime.
- *Nonqualified stock options*. This is reportable as taxable income to the employee when he exercises it to buy stock, at the ordinary income tax rate (*not* the long-term capital gains rate). The amount of taxable income is the difference between the option price and the fair market value of the stock on the exercise date. If the employee chooses to hold the stock thereafter, any additional gain in the value of the stock is taxable at the long-term capital gains tax rate.

Since an incentive stock option does not result in a tax for an employee until he sells the shares, this type of option tends to encourage a longer stock holding period by employees. Conversely, a nonqualified stock option is taxable when exercised, so an employee is more likely to sell the related stock at once, in order to pay taxes.

The incentive stock option is structured to be much more favorable to the recipient from a taxation perspective than the nonqualified stock option. Nonetheless, some companies may choose to issue nonqualified stock options because any terms at all can be used. For example, a company might issue options where the option price is substantially higher or lower than the fair market value of the stock on the date of issuance. Another possibility would be to extend the period subsequent to employment during which a recipient is still allowed to exercise his options.

If an employee acquires stock through an incentive stock option and is willing to hold the stock for at least two years, he can realize a significant tax savings by paying taxes at the long-term capital gains rate. However, waiting two years also presents the risk that the fair market value of the stock will decline, thereby offsetting any savings from paying at the lower tax rate. The IRS has created the Section 83(b) election to mitigate this risk. Under Section 83(b), a stock option recipient can recognize ordinary taxable income on the difference between the purchase price of the stock and its fair market value within 30 days of the option exercise date. When the employee sells the stock at a later date, any subsequent incremental gains are taxed at the long-term capital gains rate. An employee should be aware of the following points when evaluating whether to take the Section 83(b) election:

- Take the 83(b) election if there is only a small amount of reportable income at the time of the election, and there is a possibility of significant subsequent gains in the price of the stock.
- Do not take the 83(b) election if there is a large amount of reportable income at the time of the election, and there is little chance of significant subsequent gains in the price of the stock.

A major danger to the recipient of a stock option under an incentive stock option plan is the alternative minimum tax (AMT). The AMT is a separate calculation of the income tax that an individual owes, which is intended to keep certain high-income individuals from avoiding paying income taxes. If the AMT is higher than a person's normal income tax liability, they pay the AMT instead. The AMT requires an employee to calculate a tax liability for the difference between the exercise price of a stock option and the fair market value of the stock on the exercise date. If the AMT then applies to the employee, the employee may be forced to sell the shares at once in order to pay his tax bill. If an employee chooses to hold the stock instead, and the value of the stock later declines, the employee is still liable for the AMT tax that was based on the higher stock price. Thus, the net effect of the AMT is that a judicious employee usually sells his stock immediately, rather than risk a decline in the price of his stock holdings that could yield fewer funds with which to pay the AMT.

EXAMPLE

Nate Givens has stock options for 200,000 shares of Suture Corporation. He uses the options to buy Suture shares at an exercise price of $5, and which have a fair market value of $8, giving him a profit of $600,000. Mr. Givens exercises the options the day before Suture goes public. Under the terms of the stock agreement with Suture, he is restricted from selling the shares for six months. At the end of the six-month period, the fair market value of Suture stock has declined to $2 per share. Mr. Givens still owes the IRS the tax on $600,000, even though he can now only sell his stock at a loss.

If there is no active market for a company's stock, it can be quite difficult to determine the price of the stock that an employee acquires under a stock purchase plan. In such cases, the IRS will accept the price at which shares were sold under the company's last round of funding.

Stock Purchase Plans

A publicly held company may offer its employees a stock purchase plan under which they can obtain company stock at a discount from the fair market value. The payroll department typically creates a recurring payroll deduction for these payments, which the company then takes in exchange for stock that it issues periodically to employees.

EXAMPLE

Arnold Davis is an employee of Suture Corporation, which is publicly held. Suture has an employee stock purchase plan that offers employees a 15% discount from the market price. Mr. Davis enrolls in this plan and arranges to have $25 deducted from each paycheck for the stock purchase plan. He is paid twice a month. Suture issues stock under the plan twice a year, based on the average fair market value of the company's stock during the week preceding the stock issuance date. On June 30, Mr. Davis has accumulated $300 in the plan, and the average Suture stock price is $15. The company applies a 15% discount to arrive at a stock price of $12.75, from which it calculates that it can issue 23 shares to Mr. Davis (calculated as $300 ÷ $12.75). This issuance costs Mr. Davis $293.25, which leaves $6.75 in his account to which further payroll deductions will be added as of the next scheduled stock purchase.

Transportation Benefits

If a company provides a de minimis transportation benefit to its employees, exclude the value of the transportation from reportable employee pay. This is essentially any local transportation benefit that is so minor that it would be unreasonable or administratively impracticable to track. It certainly applies to occasional transportation fare for an employee who is working overtime, and which is not based on the number of hours worked.

EXAMPLE

Rachel Patterson is working late for her employer. She works so late that bus service is no longer available, so her manager pays for a cab to take her home. This benefit is exempt from reporting as taxable income.

Other types of transportation benefits are also exempt from being reported as taxable employee income, and are known as *qualified transportation benefits*. They include:

Benefit	Exclusion Cap	Discussion
Commuter highway transport	$255/month (combined with transit pass)	Between an employee's home and place of work, and involves a vehicle that seats at least six adults plus the driver.
Qualified parking	$255/month	Provided by a business to its employees on or near the business premises. Does not include parking at or near employee homes.
Qualified bicycle commuting reimbursement	$20 × number of qualified bicycle commuting months* during the year	Includes reimbursement of employees for the purchase of a bicycle, as well as bicycle improvements, repair, and storage.

* A *qualified bicycle commuting month* is one in which an employee uses a bicycle for a substantial proportion of commuting travel, and does not receive transportation in a commuter highway vehicle, or a transit pass, or qualified parking benefits.

These qualified transportation benefits are exempt whether the company provides them directly or reimburses employees for them.

Qualified transportation benefits do not apply to a self-employed individual.

Tuition Reduction

If an educational organization reduces the tuition that it charges its own employees, it can exclude the value of the reduced tuition from reported employee pay. A tuition reduction is qualified for this exemption if it is for the undergraduate education of any of the following:

- Current employee
- Former employee who is retired or on disability
- Widow or widower of an individual who died while an employee, retired, or on disability
- A dependent or spouse of any of the preceding individuals

Tuition reduction is generally limited to undergraduate education, unless it is for the education of a graduate student who performs teaching or research activities for the organization.

Vacation Benefit Reporting

A benefit that is highly valued by employees, and therefore subject to a great deal of examination, is the amount of earned vacation time remaining. In a company where this information is manually maintained, employees are likely to contact the payroll staff at any time to request the latest update on their remaining available hours. These requests can interfere with the orderly management of work within the payroll department, so here are some suggestions for improving the efficiency of reporting the vacation benefit:

- *Restrict review times.* Rather than allowing employees to impose themselves on the payroll staff at any time to request vacation information, have them fill out a request form, and then deal with the requests in a batch. This is more efficient for the payroll staff, and should not cause too much of a delay for the requesting employees.
- *Include in remittance advice.* Include the remaining vacation time in the remittance advice that accompanies each paycheck or notice of direct deposit. This pushes the information to employees, who no longer have a reason to visit the payroll department to inquire about this information. This approach works best when employees are paid frequently, since the information is more up-to-date.
- *Post in time tracking system.* If a web-based time tracking system is being used, consider adding to it a custom-designed vacation tracking application that employees can access. This application automatically updates employee vacation time available, based on their latest time sheets. Better yet, include an application that allows them to model how much vacation time they will have available at some date in the future. Such a system allows employees to view their vacation information based on the most recent information, rather than waiting for it to appear on their remittance advice at longer intervals. This approach only works when employees have computer access to a full-function time tracking system.

Tip: It can be extremely difficult to generate an accurate vacation benefit, especially when the vacation calculation is complex. For example, a "use it or lose it" clause, vacation buy outs, and changes in the accrual based on years in service can make the benefit difficult to understand. Thus, even if the calculations are correct, expect employees to complain about the results. The best solution is to adopt the simplest possible calculation, so there will be minimal cause for confusion.

Workers' Compensation Insurance

The government requires businesses to obtain workers' compensation insurance, which provides employees with benefits if they become ill or injured while on the job. The system also gives the business assurance that employees will not sue them.

A company may obtain workers' compensation insurance either through a fund that is sponsored by the local state government, or by a privately-owned insurance provider. Obtaining this insurance and managing employee claims is the responsibility of the human resources department. The sole issue for the payroll department involves the annual categorization of employees into different risk categories, along with their pay. The payroll staff slots each employee into a different category, such as sales, clerical, or manufacturing, along with their compensation, and reports this information to the insurance carrier. The carrier then calculates the cost of the insurance based on the categories to which employees are assigned, and this becomes the annual insurance premium for the company. The information is usually audited once a year by the insurance carrier, which may result in a retroactive adjustment to the premium paid.

The insurance cost related to each employee category is based on the probability of employee injury. Thus, assigning an employee to a clerical classification is best, since these employees are rarely injured, while a manufacturing classification implies a much higher injury rate. Due to the cost differential, the payroll staff should be careful to legitimately assign personnel to the lowest-cost classifications.

EXAMPLE

Lowry Locomotion manufactures toy cars and trucks. Lowry's payroll manager has just received the annual workers' compensation classification report from the company's insurance carrier. He knows that the clerical classification is by far the lowest-cost category, while the manufacturing classification involves an insurance premium that is five times higher than the clerical classification.

He peruses the payroll records and realizes that the jobs of three people in the production planning department are entirely clerical. He shifts these three people and their compensation into the clerical classification from the manufacturing classification, and documents his reasons for doing so.

EXAMPLE

For the upcoming year, Lowry Locomotion's workers' compensation insurer assigns a premium of $1.00 per $100 of wages for Lowry's clerical staff, and $5.00 per $100 of wages for its manufacturing staff. The estimated premium calculation is:

Job Classification	Premium Rate	Projected Total Wages	Projected Premium
Clerical	$1.00 per $100	$200,000	$2,000
Production	$5.00 per $100	1,200,000	60,000
			$62,000

At the end of the year, the insurer sends an auditor, who examines Lowry's payroll records and makes the following adjustments to the projected wage totals column in the preceding table, resulting in a different final premium:

Job Classification	Premium Rate	Actual Total Wages	Actual Premium
Clerical	$1.00 per $100	$193,000	$1,930
Production	$5.00 per $100	1,417,000	70,850
			$72,780

Based on this review, Lowry pays the insurer an additional $10,780, which represents the difference between the projected and actual wages.

Working Condition Benefits

Working condition benefits are those benefits that a company provides to its employees so that they can perform their jobs. Examples of working condition benefits are:

- A company car for business use
- A cash payment made to an employee to provide for an employee's specific business activities, and for which the employee verifies use of the funds and returns any unused cash
- Education provided to an employee in order to do his assigned job

Working condition benefits are exempt from reporting as employee taxable income. The value of a physical examination program is specifically excluded from classification as a working condition benefit.

The classification of an employee for working condition benefits is:

- A current employee
- A partner who provides services to a partnership
- A director
- An independent contractor who performs services for the company

Working condition benefits fall into several categories, as described in the following sub-sections.

Vehicles

If a company provides a vehicle to an employee for his use, the amount that is exempt from reporting as employee taxable income is the amount that would otherwise have been a deductible business expense if the employee had paid for it. Thus, if an employee were to also use such a vehicle partly for personal use, the value of the working condition benefit is strictly the amount that it is used for business purposes.

If a company's sales personnel use demonstrator vehicles, all of the use of these vehicles qualifies as a working condition benefit, as long as their use is primarily to help the sales staff in their jobs, and there are substantial restrictions on personal use of these vehicles.

If a vehicle is designated as a qualified nonpersonal-use vehicle, all of an employee's use of it is considered a working condition benefit. Such a vehicle is one that an employee is unlikely to use more than a minimal amount for personal purposes, due to its design. Examples of qualified nonpersonal-use vehicles are:

Ambulances	Hearses
Bucket trucks	Moving vans
Cement mixers	Passenger buses with a minimum 20-person capacity
Combines	Police, fire, and public safety vehicles that are clearly marked as such
Cranes and derricks	Refrigerated trucks
Delivery trucks with driver-only seating	Repair trucks
Dump trucks	School buses
Flatbed trucks	Tractors and other farm vehicles
Forklifts	Unmarked law enforcement vehicles that are officially authorized for use
Garbage trucks	Vehicles with a gross vehicle weight exceeding 14,000 pounds and designed to carry cargo

In addition, a pickup truck is considered a qualified nonpersonal-use vehicle if it has been specially modified in such a manner that it is not likely to be used for personal purposes. This requires at least the use of permanent decals or special painting to identify the business, as well as at least one of the following:

- A hydraulic lift gate, permanent tanks, permanent side boards or panels, or other heavy equipment that is attached to it; or
- The vehicle was specially designed or modified to transport a specific type of load, such as in the construction, farming, mining, or forestry trades.

Similarly, a van is considered a qualified nonpersonal-use vehicle if it has been modified in such a manner that it is not likely to be used for personal purposes. This requires at least the use of permanent decals or special painting to identify the business, as well as at least one of the following:

- Permanent shelving that fills the bulk of the cargo area; or
- An open cargo area, and the van carries merchandise or equipment as part of the business.

Education

If a company provides training to an employee, the training may be exempt from reporting as taxable employee income. To be exempt, one of the following conditions must apply:

- The education is required either by the employer or by law for an employee to retain his position or salary, and where the education must serve a bona fide business purpose; or

- The education improves or maintains the skills that an employee needs on the job.

Company-provided training is *not* exempt if it helps to qualify an employee for a new trade, or if it is needed to meet the *minimum* requirements of the employee's trade.

Outplacement Services

If a company provides outplacement services to an employee, the value of this service is exempt from reporting as taxable employee income if it meets all of the following conditions:

- The services are provided on the basis of need;
- There is a substantial benefit to the business from providing these services, rather than the benefit to be obtained from continuing to pay the employee; and
- The employee is seeking work in the same business of the employer.

A substantial business benefit can be construed as creating a positive image of the business, maintaining the morale of employees, and avoiding lawsuits for wrongful termination.

Outplacement services only qualify as a working condition benefit if employees cannot choose to receive cash or other taxable benefits instead of these services.

The tax exemption for specific working condition benefits is not available in the following two situations:

- The value of the use of consumer goods in a product testing program that are used by a director.
- The value of parking, transit passes in excess of $240 per month, or the use of consumer goods in a product testing program that are used by an independent contractor who is providing services to the business.

How to Value Benefits

The preceding discussion of benefits has not focused on the cost of benefits provided to employees, but rather on their *value*. The IRS has provided specific instructions about how to determine the value of benefits provided to employees that must be reported as taxable income to employees. The general rule for most benefits is that the value of a benefit is considered to be its fair market value. The fair market value of a benefit is the amount that an employee would be required to pay to obtain the benefit in an arm's length transaction. The cost that the company incurs to provide a benefit is *not* its fair market value.

The following sub-sections address special IRS rules for the valuation of certain types of benefits. These rules override the use of fair market value for reporting taxable employee income.

Cents per Mile

Under certain circumstances, the value of a vehicle provided to an employee for personal use is based on the *cents-per-mile rule*. Under this approach, multiply the standard mileage rate per mile by the number of miles driven by the employee for personal use.

> **Note:** The standard mileage rate for 2016 is 54 cents per mile.

It is allowable to use the cents-per-mile rule under either of the following circumstances:

- The vehicle meets the *mileage test*, where it is driven at least 10,000 miles (or proportionally less for part-year ownership), and it is used primarily by employees.
- The vehicle is expected to be used on company business throughout the calendar year. This is considered to be when at least 50% of vehicle mileage is related to the business, or a commuting group of at least three people uses the vehicle, or the vehicle is regularly used on company business.

> **Note:** Do not use the cents-per-mile rule if the value of an automobile first made available to an employee in 2016 exceeds $28,000, or $31,000 for a van or truck. This information for 2017 was not available as of the publication date.

EXAMPLE

David Jones is a buyer for the Cajun Delights restaurant chain. Part of Mr. Jones' job is to travel to various wharves to obtain fresh fish. Cajun provides Mr. Jones with a car for his job, which he is also allowed to drive for personal use. During the most recent calendar year, Mr. Jones drove the car 12,000 miles, of which 10,000 was on company business. This usage level passes the mileage test. Accordingly, Cajun reports $1,080 as a taxable wage benefit for Mr. Jones. The benefit is calculated as 2,000 miles of personal use, multiplied by the $0.54/mile mileage rate.

If the cents-per-mile rule is used, begin using it on the first day that a vehicle is made available to an employee for personal use. It is also allowable to switch to the cents-per-mile rule from the commuting rule (see next sub-section). In later years, the employer must use the cents-per-mile rule, or it can use the commuting rule if it qualifies. If a vehicle does not qualify for the cents-per-mile rule, use any other rule for which the situation qualifies. If vehicle that an employee was using is replaced, and the vehicle qualifies for the cents-per-mile rule, and the employer is doing so to reduce federal taxes, it must continue to use the cents-per-mile rule.

Commuting

If a vehicle qualifies for the *commuting rule*, determine the value of a vehicle provided to an employee for commuting purposes by multiplying each commute (one way) by $1.50. This $1.50 amount applies to each person who is commuting in the vehicle. Include this amount in the reported taxable income of each employee to which it applies. The commuting rule applies if *all* of the following conditions are met:

- The company requires the employee to commute in the vehicle provided (which applies automatically if the vehicle is used to carry at least three employees in an employer-sponsored commuting pool); and
- There is a written policy under which the employee is not allowed any personal use of the vehicle, other than for commuting and de minimis activities; and
- The employee does not in fact use the vehicle other than as noted in the preceding policy; and
- The employee using it is not a control employee or a highly compensated employee. A highly compensated employee is one who was either a 5% owner at any time during the past or preceding year, or who received over $120,000 compensation in the preceding year (which does not apply if the employee was not in the top 20% of employees when ranked by pay).

A control employee is usually considered to be either a board or shareholder-appointed officer whose pay is at least $105,000, or a director, or an employee whose pay is at least $215,000, or an employee who owns a 1% or more equity, capital, or profit interest in the business. For a government employer, a control employee is considered to be either an elected official or one whose compensation exceeds Federal Government Executive Level V.

Lease Value

The principal method for determining the value of an automobile provided to an employee is to use its annual lease value, which is called the *lease value rule*. If a vehicle is only provided for part of a year, prorate the annual lease value over the period provided.

Follow these steps to calculate the annual lease value of a vehicle under the lease value rule:

1. Determine the fair market value of the vehicle as of the first day on which the company makes it available to an employee for personal use. This is the amount a person would pay to buy the vehicle from a third party in an arm's length transaction in the geographic area where the vehicle is acquired. Include all purchase expenses (such as sales tax and title fees) in this assessment. It may be possible to use the safe-harbor value to derive the fair market value (see below).

2. Go to the IRS' Annual Lease Value Table (easily accessible with an Internet search), and find the annual lease value on the table that corresponds to the dollar range within which the fair market value of the vehicle falls.
3. Multiply the proportion of personal miles driven by the annual lease value.

EXAMPLE

Medusa Medical provides an automobile to Alex Lindsey. The fair market value of the vehicle on the day Medusa made it available to Mr. Lindsey was $35,000. According to the 2016 IRS Annual Lease Value Table, the car has an annual lease value of $9,250.

Mr. Lindsey keeps a log documenting his miles traveled, which reveals that he used the car 40% of the time for personal use during the year. Accordingly, Medusa reports $3,700 as taxable income to Mr. Lindsey for this benefit. The calculation is:

$9,250 Annual lease value × 40% Personal usage = $3,700 reportable benefit

---

The safe-harbor value (SHV) can be used to derive fair market value. The SHV is an available option when the company buys a vehicle in an arm's length transaction. In this situation, the fair market value is the purchase price, which includes the sales tax, title costs, and other purchase expenses. If the company leases a vehicle, the SHV is the manufacturer's invoice price plus 4%, or the manufacturer's suggested retail price minus 8%, or its retail value as estimated by a nationally recognized pricing source.

If the employee using a company-owned vehicle is using it on company business, reduce the lease value by the amount excluded from that person's wages as a working condition benefit (see the prior section).

Tip: In cases where employees are using company-provided vehicles on company business, require them to document the business-related use of those vehicles, including the miles driven, the time and place of travel, and the business purpose of the travel. The standard company policy should be that all miles not substantiated in this manner will be reported in an employee's taxable income.

The lease value rule must be used in the following manner:

- Use the lease value rule on the first day a vehicle is made available to an employee for personal use. However, if the employer has been using the commuting rule, it can change to the lease value rule if the commuting rule no longer applies. Or, if it has been using the cents-per-mile rule, it can change to the lease value rule if the cents-per-mile rule no longer applies.
- Use the lease value rule for all later years when the circumstances are the same, though one can use the commuting rule if it applies.
- Use the lease value rule if a replacement vehicle is provided and the primary reason for doing so is to reduce federal taxes.

If an employee is using a company vehicle for a period of 30 days or more, but less than an entire year, prorate the annual lease value by dividing it by 365 days to arrive at a daily rate, and then multiply the daily rate by the number of days of availability.

EXAMPLE

Anderson Palmer has personal use of a vehicle provided by his employer, Medusa Medical, for 90 days. The vehicle has an annual lease value of $8,500. To prorate the annual lease value over the 90-day period of personal usage, Medusa first divides the $8,500 annual lease by 365 days to arrive at a daily lease rate of $23.29. Medusa then multiplies the daily rate by the 90-day personal usage period to arrive at a total reportable benefit to Mr. Palmer of $2,096.10.

If an employee is using a company vehicle for a continuous period of less than 30 days, calculate the benefit to the employee using the *daily lease value*. To calculate the daily lease value, divide the annual lease value by 365 days to arrive at the daily rate, and then multiply the result by four times the number of days of availability. This quadrupled daily rate is the daily lease value. It is also allowable to value this lease benefit as though it had been available for a full 30-day period (which will effectively be a lower taxable benefit to the employee if the usage period exceeds seven days).

EXAMPLE

Carson Johnson has personal use of a vehicle provided by his employer, Medusa Medical, for 10 days. The vehicle has an annual lease value of $8,000. The associated taxable benefit is valued at $876.71 under the daily lease value calculation, which is derived as follows:

$$(\$8,000 \text{ annual lease value} \div 365 \text{ days}) \times 4 \times 10 \text{ days} = \$876.71$$

Under the alternative approach of valuing the benefit as though the usage period were 30 days, the valuation is derived as:

$$(\$8,000 \text{ annual lease value} \div 365 \text{ days}) \times 30 \text{ days} = \$657.53$$

Thus, the lower benefit amount of $657.53 is the one Medusa should use to report a taxable benefit for Mr. Johnson.

In short, the lease value rule is the baseline method for determining the fair market value of a vehicle. If an employer is using either the cents-per-mile rule or the commuting rule, and either one no longer applies, the fallback position is to use the lease value rule.

Unsafe Conditions Commuting

If a company provides commuting transportation to its employees solely because of unsafe conditions, the business should report a $1.50 one-way taxable benefit for each employee. Unsafe conditions exist when a reasonable person would consider it unsafe to walk or use public transportation at the time of day when that person commutes to work. This may be based on a history of crime in the region surrounding an employee's workplace or home. This rule applies if all of the following conditions are present:

- Employees would normally walk to work or use public transportation; and
- There is a written policy, stating that the company does not provide the transportation for personal purposes, but rather for commuting due to unsafe conditions; and
- Employees do not use such vehicles for personal purposes, other than to commute because of unsafe conditions.

An employee who is subject to the unsafe conditions commuting rule must be paid on an hourly basis, and not receive more than $120,000 during the year.

Rules for Withholding, Depositing, and Reporting Benefits

If a benefit should be reported as taxable income to an employee, calculate the value of the benefit no later than January 31 of the following year. It is reasonable to estimate benefit values prior to that date, in order to engage in pay withholdings.

Benefits can be treated as being paid to employees on essentially any basis, such as by pay period, quarterly, or annually – but no less frequently than annually. It is not necessary to use the same basis for all employees, and one can change the reporting period.

> **Tip:** The proper interval over which to report benefits should match the highest level of automation of the payroll system. Thus, if a benefit is earned in the same amount all year, set it up once as a recurring amount in the payroll system, and ignore it for the rest of the year. Alternatively, if the amount of a benefit changes over time, it will likely need to be entered into the payroll system manually; if so, entering it once at the end of each year is the most cost-effective solution.

> **Warning:** If the election is made to only report taxable benefits once a year, and an employee has left the company prior to the end of the year, the company is still liable to the IRS for any unpaid and uncollected taxes on noncash benefits. Thus, there is a risk in only reporting benefits at long intervals.

If the business is transferring property to an employee, report the benefit in the next regularly-scheduled payroll following the date of the transfer.

When deciding upon the proper amount of withholding to apply against a taxable benefit, use either of the following approaches:

- Add the value of the benefit to employee pay and calculate the income tax withholding on the total amount; or
- Withhold 25% of the value of the benefit (this flat rate option is 35% when an employee's supplemental wages exceed $1,000,000 per year).

In addition, withhold the applicable amounts of social security and Medicare taxes for the dates when the employer chooses to treat taxable benefits as having been paid.

It is allowable to treat the value of taxable noncash benefits as being paid in the next tax year, but only for those benefits that a company provides to employees during the last two months of the current year. Thus, the amount of taxable noncash benefits reported in the next year would encompass the final two months of the current year, plus the benefits provided during the first ten months of the next year. If the employer chooses to follow this rule, use it consistently for all employees receiving the specific benefit that is accounted for in this manner. It is possible to only use this rule for certain benefits.

EXAMPLE

Medusa Medical provides a variety of taxable noncash benefits to its employees, several of which require some time to calculate values that can be reported as taxable income. Given the time delay in calculating benefits, Medusa elects to shift the reporting of all noncash benefits forward for the last month of the year into the next year. Medusa sets up a formal policy for this treatment, so that the reporting of noncash benefits in any year is always comprised of December of the preceding year and January through November of the reporting year.

A company can elect not to withhold income taxes on the value of an employee's personal use of a vehicle that has been provided by the business. This election can be applied only to specific individuals, or to all employees receiving such a benefit. However, the employer must still withhold all applicable social security and Medicare taxes on this benefit. If the employer chooses to not withhold income taxes related to a vehicle, notify all affected employees in writing, and by the later of January 31 of each year or 30 days after the company provides a vehicle to an employee.

Report all taxable benefits on the Form W-2. The boxes in which this information is reported are:

Box Number	Box Description	Inclusions
1	Wages, tips, other compensation	Include all taxable benefits
3	Social security wages	Include all taxable benefits if applicable
5	Medicare wages and tips	Include all taxable benefits if applicable
14	Other	Option to show the total value of the benefits provided in the calendar year or other period

If there is a net reportable benefit, but the benefit is being provided to someone who is not classified as an employee, report it on either Form 1099-MISC (for an independent contractor) or Schedule K-1 (for a partner).

Benefit Authorization Form

A company may have a large number of benefits from which its employees can make selections, and those benefits may require certain amounts to be deducted from employee pay. The sheer volume of the benefits involved presents the risk that the company may not enroll an employee in a benefit plan that he requested. To keep this issue from arising, consider creating a master benefit enrollment form that lists all possible benefits, requires the employee to initial or sign next to each one they want, states the deduction amount, and the planned start and stop dates for each benefit. An example of the form is shown next.

Master Benefit Enrollment Form

I request the following benefits and related deductions from my pay (circle applicable items):

Benefit	Deduction	Start Date	End Date	Signature
Dental insurance				
FSA – Dependent care				
FSA – Medical				
Long-term disability				
Short-term disability				
Supplemental life				

Human resources approval: _____ Date: _____

Payroll deductions entered: _____ Date: _____

This master enrollment form is used by the human resources department to enroll employees in benefit plans, and by the payroll department to set up deductions in the payroll system. It should be used as part of a procedure that follows these steps:

1. The employee jointly fills out the form with a human resources employee, who explains the benefits, related deductions, and benefit start and stop dates (if any).
2. The human resources staff signs up the employee for all indicated benefits, signs the form to indicate that all benefits have been addressed, keeps a copy for itself, and sends a copy to the accounting department.
3. The accounting department enters the deductions into the payroll system that are noted on its copy of the form, signs the form to indicate successful data entry, and sends the form back to the human resources department.
4. The human resources staff matches the accounting document to its own document to verify that all benefits and related deductions have been addressed, and follows up on any incomplete items.

Taxability of Benefits

By default, any benefit provided to an employee is taxable, unless there is a specific exclusion for it. The following table notes the extent to which a benefit is classified as taxable income to an employee.

Employee Benefits

Benefit	Income Tax Withholding	Social Security, Medicare	Federal Unemployment
Achievement awards	$1,600 exemption for qualified plans, $400 otherwise	Same	Same
Adoption assistance	Exempt	Taxable	Taxable
Athletic facilities	Exempt	Same	Same
COBRA premium	Exempt	Same	Same
De minimis benefits	Exempt	Same	Same
Dependent care assistance	Exempt up to plan limits	Same	Same
Employee discounts	Exempt within IRS limits	Same	Same
Group term life insurance	Exempt	Exempt for cost of first $50,000 of coverage	Exempt
Health savings account	Exempt	Same	Same
Lodging on business premises	Exempt if condition of employment	Same	Same
Meals	Exempt	Same	Same
Medical insurance	Exempt, except for highly compensated employees in a self-insured plan	Exempt	Exempt
Moving expenses	Exempt if distance and time tests are met	Same	Same
No-additional-cost services	Exempt	Same	Same
Retirement planning services	Exempt	Same	Same
Stock options	See Stock Options section	Same	Same
Transportation	Exempt up to the limits noted in the Transportation Benefits section	Same	Same
Tuition reduction	Exempt for undergraduate, and graduate if do teaching or research	Same	Same
Working condition benefits	Exempt	Same	Same

If a company is required to report a benefit as income to an employee, report the amount by which the value of the benefit exceeds any amount that is excluded by law, or which the recipient paid for the benefit.

Summary

All of the topics described in this chapter are primary responsibilities of the human resources department. However, employees do not necessarily know that, and so are quite likely to instead come to the payroll department with their questions. Thus, the payroll staff needs a working knowledge of how these benefits operate, even though their main responsibilities are processing the employee deductions associated with each one, and entering taxable benefit information into the payroll system.

The primary focus of this chapter has been on whether or not a benefit is exempt from reporting as taxable employee income. The key determining factor in making this determination is whether a benefit is provided to all employees, or at least to a group of employees that are not considered highly compensated. Thus, as a general rule, if a company restricts its benefits to highly compensated individuals (such as to the family owning a business) it is likely that the IRS considers the benefits to be taxable income.

Chapter 6
Payroll Deductions

Introduction

A pay deduction is a subtraction from an employee's gross or net pay. We do not include payroll taxes in this definition, since payroll taxes are dealt with separately in the Payroll Taxes chapter.

This chapter describes the various types of deductions that are commonly applied to an employee's pay. The types of deductions addressed in this chapter are broken down into three categories, which are:

- *Benefits package*. This includes the employee-paid portion of various types of insurance, and pension payments (for which there may be a company-paid match).
- *Payments to third parties*. This includes charitable contributions, child support payments, garnishments, and union dues.
- *Financing situations*. This includes the repayment of asset purchases, advances, and loans.

There is also a discussion about reducing the number of deductions, which improves the efficiency of the payroll staff.

Deductions for the Corporate Benefits Package

A company that wants to retain its employees over the long term will likely offer them a benefits package that may include any or all of the following:

- Medical insurance
- Dental insurance
- Vision insurance
- Life insurance
- Supplemental life insurance
- Short-term disability insurance
- Long-term disability insurance

This benefits package usually contains a core set of benefits that are centered on medical insurance, with an ancillary group of other benefits from which employees can make selections. It is exceedingly rare for a company to pay for the entire cost of a benefits package, given the high and increasing cost of medical insurance. Instead, employees are required to pay varying proportions of either individual elements of a benefit package, or the cost of the package as a whole. In some instances, a company may elect not to pay for a benefit at all, and instead simply makes it available to employees, who must pay for it themselves. This last situation is most common for less critical benefits, such as supplemental life insurance coverage.

There are a variety of benefit deduction plans that are commonly used. Examples of these deduction formulas are:

- The company pays all of the medical insurance for an employee, but does not pay anything towards the additional cost of the insurance for an employee's family.
- The company pays for 80 percent of the cost of medical insurance for an employee, and 50 percent of the incremental amount of additional insurance for an employee's family.
- The company pays a flat percentage of an employee's medical insurance, irrespective of the number of people covered.
- The company pays all or most of an employee's insurance, but only for a lower-cost benefits package. The employee must pay for all of the incremental increase in cost for a more comprehensive benefits package.

The type and amount of insurance coverage that a company chooses to pay for can lead to some interesting reactions from employees, which may lead to some unexpected coverages.

EXAMPLE

A husband and wife both work for the same company. The company offers a benefits package under which the amount to be paid by the couple is least if they both sign up for individual coverage, rather than for employee and spouse coverage.

A husband and wife both work full-time for different companies. The husband's company only provides benefits to the employees themselves, with the employees having to shoulder the incremental cost of extending the coverage to their families. The wife's company pays a flat percentage of the benefits package for individual, spouse, and family coverage. They review the cost of their coverage and conclude that the husband should waive all coverage, while the spouse elects to take full family coverage.

The second of the two scenarios in the example is a common one. Those companies only offering benefits coverage to their employees – and not their families – find that a number of their employees do not take any coverage at all, in favor of their spouse's coverage at a different firm. While this may seem like a clever way to avoid a major expense, it also means that a person not taking advantage of a company's benefits package is less loyal to the company, and is therefore less likely to remain there.

When an employee signs up for various types of benefits, the human resources department should calculate the appropriate deductions for the various benefits, and forward them to the payroll department for entry into the payroll system.

> **Tip:** It may be tempting to aggregate all of the various benefits deductions into a single deduction line item, but this gives employees no information about the impact on deductions of individual benefits. Thus, it is better to provide more clarity by itemizing each deduction separately. This information should appear on the remittance advice that accompanies each payment to employees. This level of detail is, however, less efficient, as noted later in the Reduction of Deductions section.

EXAMPLE

Mole Industries has a benefits package under which it pays 80% of the cost of employee medical insurance, 50% of the incremental medical insurance attributable to family coverage, and 100% of life insurance up to a cap of $50,000. Mole makes supplemental life insurance, dental insurance, short-term disability, and long-term disability coverage available to its employees, but the employees must pay the full amount of these additional coverages. Mr. Gareth Harrington elects to take the family medical coverage, and has subscribed to all of the other types of insurance offered by Mole. The calculation of his total benefits-related pay deduction is:

Benefit	Cost	Employer Paid Portion	Employee Paid Portion
Medical insurance, single	$450	80%	$90
Medical insurance, family portion	620	50%	310
Life insurance	20	100%	0
Supplemental life insurance	15	0%	15
Dental insurance	65	0%	65
Short-term disability	80	0%	80
Long-term disability	15	0%	15
Totals	$1,265	0%	$575

> **Tip:** Some employees calculate their pay with great care and will be surprised if an unexpected deduction change appears on their paycheck. And when they are surprised, they will come to the payroll department to demand an explanation. To avoid spending time explaining the situation to employees, issue a memo to all affected staff in advance, warning them of the impending change.

EXAMPLE

Mole Industries makes long-term disability insurance available to its employees, which they pay for in full if they elect to take it. The insurance provider has enacted a 5% rate increase as of the first day of the following month. Mole's payroll manager issues the following memo to warn employees of the impending change:

> Dear ____:
>
> You have chosen to pay for long-term disability insurance, which we are providing to you through the Abe Lincoln Mutual Insurance Company. This provider has enacted a 5% rate increase, which will be effective as of March 1. You are currently paying $___ per paycheck for this coverage, so your deduction for long-term disability insurance will increase from $___ to $___ as of the March 15 paycheck. Please contact the payroll department at extension 123 if you have any questions.

When an employee is supposed to pay for a portion of a benefits package, the payment is usually taken from employee pay in the form of a deduction. This approach is vastly easier than having employees periodically pay the company for their share of the payments for a benefits package, since collecting amounts owed can be extremely difficult.

There may be deductions available to employees that allow them to either invest in a 401k pension plan or to buy company stock at a discount. A 401k plan is an excellent idea for a company, since there is usually some amount of company matching funds that employees will only be entitled to if they remain with the company for a certain number of years (known as *vesting*). This is an extremely common benefit, so the payroll staff is likely to see this deduction. It is a somewhat more labor-intensive deduction to handle, since there is usually no limitation on the number of times that employees are allowed to change it during a year; still, only a minority of employees usually engage in continuing 401k deduction changes.

Buying company stock at a discount through an employee stock purchase plan saves employees money, and also creates a ready source of cash for the company, so both parties win. Buying stock is usually only available to the employees of a publicly-held company that has filed a Form S-8 with the Securities and Exchange Commission, so this is a relatively rare deduction. If available, employees usually opt to have a standard amount deducted from their pay, and the company uses the money to periodically sell them shares in the company at a discount from the market price.

Deductions for Payments to Third Parties

Many deductions that can be taken from employee pay are forwarded to third parties. Examples of such deductions are for charitable contributions, child support payments, student loan garnishments, tax levies, and union dues. These deductions are addressed under separate subheadings within this section.

In all of the following cases, the payroll staff must take the extra step of accumulating the amounts deducted from employee pay and forwarding an authorization to the accounts payable staff to pay that amount to the third party. This extra step makes deductions for payments to third parties the most labor-intensive of all types of deductions – particularly when there is a penalty involved if the company does not make a payment on time and in the correct amount.

Charitable Contributions

Many employers encourage their employees to make contributions to local or national charities, and may also match these contributions to some extent. Under such an arrangement, an employee signs a pledge card, which authorizes the company to deduct certain contribution amounts from their pay on an ongoing basis. The company then periodically forwards the sum total of all contributions deducted to the targeted charities, along with any matching amount that the company is paying.

The Internal Revenue Service (IRS) requires that a person making a charitable contribution of $250 or more can only claim it on his tax return if he has a receipt. It can be quite difficult for the receiving charity to issue a receipt, since the company forwarding the payments to them is probably doing so in a batch, possibly without differentiating which employees are making the donations. This means that the next best form of receipt is to create a separate line item for each charity on the remittance advice that accompanies each pay check, noting the year-to-date amount of contributions made. Employees can then use the remittance advice as proof of payment to support their charitable contribution claims on their tax returns.

EXAMPLE

David Smythe fills out a pledge card to have his employer deduct $20 from each of his paychecks and forward the contribution to American Red Cross. There are two pay periods per month, so his total annual contribution is $480. Since the sum total of these contributions over the full year exceeds $250, Mr. Smythe must obtain written substantiation of the contributions, either from the American Red Cross or by other means, such as the total contribution deduction noted on his year-end pay remittance advice.

Garnishments Overview

Some people resist fulfilling their legal obligations to other parties, or they do not have the financial resources to do so. If such a person is employed, it is quite possible that the employer will receive a garnishment order, under which it must withhold specified amounts from an employee's pay and forward it to a third party. A garnishment order usually relates to either child support, unpaid taxes, or unpaid student loans. If a garnishment order is received, complete these steps:

1. Return a response form, stating whether the organization can begin the garnishment and the amount to be paid.

2. Use the garnishment calculation worksheet that accompanies the order to determine the amount to be garnished. There is a cap on the amount of a person's wages that can be garnished. Federal law limits the sum of all garnishments to 25 percent of a person's disposable pay. Further, there is a base amount of income that is protected from garnishment that is based on the minimum wage earned per week.
3. Set up the garnishment transaction in the payroll system with a stop date that is based on either the termination date listed in the order, or on the date when the garnishment amount is paid in full.
4. Set up a procedure to notify the accounts payable staff when garnishments are to be paid, the amount to be paid, and to which entity they are to be paid.

> **Tip:** Schedule a periodic internal audit review of garnishment payments to third parties, to ensure that there is a robust process of making the correct payments in a timely manner.

If an employee is in a difficult financial situation, it is quite possible that the employer will receive multiple garnishment orders for him. If so, one would generally satisfy garnishments against the wages of an employee in the order in which they are received, up to the maximum amount subject to that type of garnishment order, with a total cap of 25 percent of the employee's disposable pay. Many garnishments have a relatively short duration, so as soon as one order is satisfied, the next order in line is assigned a higher priority, and so on.

EXAMPLE

Robert Cratchit is in significant financial straits. He receives $3,000 of net pay from his employer, Chapman & Hall, at the end of each month. Chapman & Hall receives multiple garnishment orders for him, which are:

- $330/month student loan (received February 1)
- $500/month child support (received March 1)
- $150/month unpaid county taxes (received May 15)

The maximum amount of his net pay that can be garnished is $750 (calculated as 25% × $3,000 net pay). Of the available $750, the $500 child support garnishment takes absolute priority, irrespective of the garnishment receipt date, which leaves $250 for other garnishments. The student loan garnishment was received earliest, so that has second priority in the amount of $250 (which is also less than the maximum amount designated for student loan repayments – see the Student Loan Garnishment topic below). There are no funds remaining for the unpaid county taxes garnishment, which will have to wait until a higher-ranking garnishment has been completed.

The amount of deduction administration associated with a garnishment can be substantial, while the potential non-payment penalties make garnishments a particular cause for concern. Nonetheless, an employer is not allowed to terminate the employment of a person because of a garnishment order.

> **Tip:** The payroll department of a larger company may have a number of active garnishment orders. If so, it makes sense to maintain a schedule of these orders, itemizing the remaining balance on each one, the amount deducted in each successive payroll, and the date when each garnishment amount is completed. Also, since the first garnishment order received has priority over subsequent orders, be sure to list the order receipt date.

Child Support Garnishment

A garnishment order for child support is extremely common. This order has a higher priority than all other types of garnishment orders, even if it is issued at a later date than other orders. If a garnishment order for family support does arrive later than other garnishments that the employer is already paying to third parties, notify those third parties at once that future payments to them are to be curtailed or delayed.

Student Loan Garnishment

The government guarantees billions of dollars of student loans each year, and some of these loans become overdue for payment. If the federal government guarantees such a loan, the Department of Education can issue an administrative order to the employer of a person who is in default on paying back his student loan. This administrative order requires the employer to garnish the employee's wages in an amount up to 15 percent of the employee's disposable pay. This administrative order supersedes any state law governing wage garnishment. Several points to consider regarding a student loan garnishment are:

- If the employer neglects to garnish an employee's wages or forward this amount to the Department of Education, the government can sue the employer for the amount that should have been forwarded.
- The Department of Education will send a quarterly Employment Confirmation Report to the employer, in which the employer must confirm any changes in the employment status of the employee.

Tax Garnishment

If an employee does not pay his income taxes on a timely basis, the IRS may contact the company with a garnishment order (actually called a *tax levy notification*), not only to garnish the amount of unpaid taxes, but also quite possibly to garnish a substantial additional amount for penalties and related interest charges.

Part of an employee's compensation is exempt from an IRS tax levy. On a weekly basis, the amount of the exemption is the total of the employee's standard deduction and the amount deductible for exemptions on an income tax return for the applicable year, divided by 52. The amount the employee must pay in child support is also exempt.

If the IRS contacts the company about a tax levy, the contact will come in the form of a Notice of Levy on Wages, Salary and Other Income (Form 668-W). The employee should fill out part of the form relating to the amount of exemptions. This is a key part of the calculation to determine the amount of employee compensation that is exempt from garnishment, as just described. If the employee does not provide this information within three days, calculate the exemption as though the employee was married and filing separately with one exemption (which can be changed later if the employee provides the information). Use this calculation instead of the employee's Form W-4 to calculate the exemption amount. When the IRS sends a Form 668-W, it will be accompanied by Publication 1494, which is a useful table for calculating the applicable exemption amount based on the employee's filing status, number of exemptions, and applicable pay period. The following specific items apply to the calculation of exempt employee income:

- Generally, an employee can maintain any existing deductions when calculating the amount of pay subject to the garnishment.
- It is acceptable to allow an employee an increase in a deduction when the employee has no control over the change (such as an increase in the health insurance premium).
- It is acceptable to allow an employee a deduction that is required in order to be employed by the company (such as the payment of union dues as a condition of employment).
- Generally, any new voluntary deductions that an employee creates after a tax levy notification has been received will not reduce the amount of net pay subject to the tax levy.
- The IRS may disallow voluntary deductions from an employee's pay in calculating the amount of pay subject to the garnishment if these deductions are so large that they "defeat" the garnishment.
- Generally, apply any garnishments to the oldest assessment first. The employee has no say in the application of garnished amounts.

EXAMPLE

David Haven has not paid his federal income taxes for several years, so the IRS sends a tax levy notice to his employer, Mulligan Imports. Mulligan is required under the notification to garnish Mr. Haven's wages and forward the garnished amount to the IRS.

Mr. Haven receives $10,000 in monthly pay. His current deductions from that pay are as follows:

Monthly pay	$10,000
Federal and state income taxes	825
Social security and Medicare withholding	770
Medical insurance deduction	250
Charitable contribution	100
Stock purchase plan	55
Net pay	$8,000

Mulligan consults Publication 1494, which accompanied the tax levy notice, to determine how much of Mr. Haven's net pay is subject to the tax levy. Mr. Haven claims a filing status as head of household, with three exemptions. According to Publication 1494 for the year 2015, this means that $1,791.67 is exempt from the tax levy. Thus, the amount of his net pay that is subject to the tax levy is $6,208.33 (calculated as $8,000 net pay minus the $1,791.67 exemption).

If the company subsequently increases the medical insurance deduction because of a change in the premium charged by the health care provider, this is an acceptable increase that will reduce the amount subject to the tax levy.

If Mr. Haven subsequently increases the withholding for his stock purchase plan, this will have no impact on the amount subject to the tax levy.

In those rare cases where the company employs both spouses and there is a joint tax liability, garnish the compensation of the spouse receiving the higher income. The IRS states in its discussion of employee tax garnishments that the employer is required to garnish the compensation of both spouses only in "flagrant cases of neglect or refusal to pay."

When a tax garnishment order is received, prioritize it in front of all other garnishment orders, except for a child support order that has already been received. If multiple garnishment orders are received for taxes from different government entities and there are not sufficient employee wages available to satisfy all of the orders, prioritize them based on the order in which they were received.

Tip: If the net pay of an employee changes, the company must alter the amount of the related garnishment accordingly. If this is not done, the company may be liable to the government for any wages that should have been garnished. To keep this from happening, maintain a short list of all employees who are currently subject to tax levies, and review it during every payroll to see if any garnishments should be updated.

Union Dues

If a company has entered into a collective bargaining agreement with a labor union, the terms of the agreement usually stipulate that the company withhold union dues from employee pay and forward it to the union. In rare circumstances, the union may collect dues directly from its members, particularly in those jurisdictions where deducting union dues from pay has been banned. Halt any deductions for dues as of the date when a collective bargaining agreement expires.

Deductions for Financing Repayments

A company that produces consumer goods may find that its employees want to buy its products, or any company may find that employees ask it to buy products on their behalf. The latter situation is particularly common when a company can obtain substantial discounts on its purchases from suppliers. These situations are acceptable, as long as employees pay for the items in cash. The situation becomes more complex when employees request that the cost of the purchases be deducted from their pay over several pay periods instead. Doing so raises three issues:

- *Company acts as a bank.* The company is expending funds on behalf of its employees, and is in turn paid by them over a lengthy interval. Thus, the company is essentially extending an interest-free loan to its employees.
- *Employee departures.* If an employee leaves the company before paying back the full amount that the company paid on his behalf, it may be quite difficult to obtain payment for the outstanding balance.
- *Deduction tracking.* An employee may have acquired multiple products through the company, and is paying for them through a series of multi-layered deductions that are difficult to track.

Thus, if employees are allowed to buy goods through the company, insist on being paid at once (if not in advance) for any items purchased.

Similar issues arise when a company issues advances or loans to its employees. There may be a valid reason for issuing advances to employees, especially when they need cash for a business trip and have not yet been issued a company credit card. However, if the reason for issuing an advance or a loan to employees is to tide them over until their next paycheck, work with a local lender to provide them with short-term financing. Once employees realize that their employer is willing to give them interest-free advances, the employer will become their lender of choice, and the payroll and accounts payable departments will be burdened with an unending stream of employee requests for cash.

The situation becomes worse from a deductions perspective if the employer agrees to extend loans to its employees. The payroll department must now maintain a payment schedule that incorporates an interest rate, and which is subject to change if an employee requests a deduction deferral or pays a portion of it in advance. Thus, there is a potential for the loan deduction to be one of the most highly labor-intensive of all deductions.

> **Tip:** If the company is acting as a bank, have affected employees sign an agreement under which the company is allowed to deduct the maximum amount legally permissible from their final paycheck to reduce any remaining balance owed to the company.

The Reduction of Deductions

Whenever there are deductions from an employee's pay, this involves setting up the deduction as well as a goal amount that terminates the deduction when the total amount of the deductions (the goal) is reached. These additions to the payroll processing function require the time of the payroll staff to set up, and may include errors that require further investigation and correction. Ideally, minimize the number of deductions, so that the payroll staff has more time available for other, more value-added, activities. Here are several methods to consider that can reduce the number of deductions:

- *Benefit deductions.* There may be many deductions associated with employee benefits, such as the employee-paid portion of medical insurance, dental insurance, life insurance, and supplemental life insurance. These deductions are usually set up once a year, when insurance rates change, and are then copied forward automatically in all future payrolls until the next change in rates. These deductions can amount to a massive number of revisions when insurance rates change. One way to reduce the number of these deductions is to eliminate the employee-paid part of a benefit, so that the company pays the entire amount of the insurance. Since this can be a difficult alternative for a company that may be having trouble earning a profit, a simpler and less expensive alternative is to merge all benefits into a single package, and require just one deduction from employees for the entire package. A third option is to eliminate some lesser-used benefits, and thereby the deductions associated with them.

- *Change fee.* A few employees may constantly tweak their benefit plans and other related deductions. Every time they make these changes, the payroll staff has to spend time recording the transaction in the payroll system. Consider charging a change fee if an employee makes more than a certain maximum number of changes per year, thereby hopefully reducing the number of deduction change requests. However, this approach requires the use of a change tracking system, in order to know when to charge a change fee.

- *Deduction setting.* The human resources department is usually responsible for setting the amount to be paid by employees. This can be a complicated calculation, involving historical precedent, estimates of how many employees will want a benefit if they must pay a certain price, and employee perception of the value of the entire package with deductions included. The result can be an extremely complex set of employee deductions which the payroll department must now administer. A better way to create deductions is to include the payroll manager in the deliberations when deductions are being formulated, so that there is some additional focus on having a streamlined set of deductions that are easy to administer.

- *Employee advances.* Those employees with minimal cash reserves may get into the habit of requesting a pay advance from the company, which is then deducted from their next paycheck. If the company allows these advances, it can reasonably expect some employees to make continuing use of them, with an ongoing series of advances and offsetting deductions. This can be quite a problem for the payroll staff, since these entries cannot be automated. Further, the company loses any unpaid advances if an employee suddenly leaves the company. It is best to avoid this problem entirely by not allowing *any* employee advances. Instead, refer employees to a selection of local lenders who provide short-term loans.

- *Employee purchases.* If a company allows its employees to buy products from the company, or from other companies on their behalf, it is common practice to allow employees to pay for these purchases with a series of deductions from their paychecks. Some employees will take advantage of this situation to effectively use the company as their private bank, making a series of such purchases and requesting an unending stream of deductions from their paychecks to pay for the purchases. Also, employees may request that their deductions be altered (usually to extend the reimbursement period), which calls for more deduction calculations by the payroll staff. Since there is no operational need for these purchases, consider not allowing employees to buy anything through the company without paying for the purchases up front, in cash.

Tip: If a request is received from an employee to stop a deduction, insist that the employee make the request in writing, sign it, and state in the request the date as of which the deduction is to be stopped. By doing so, there is proof of authorization if the employee ever claims that he did not want to stop the deduction. This is a particular issue for insurance-related deductions, since stopping a deduction also stops the insurance, with possibly devastating results.

Garnishment Processing

When a government entity garnishes the wages of an employee, the company is required to withhold the designated amount from the employee's pay and forward the withheld amount to the government. A garnishment order sometimes allows the company to charge a small transaction fee either once a month or whenever a garnishment deduction occurs. If so, be sure to charge the employee the maximum transaction fee allowed. This fee will probably not cover the labor cost of setting up the garnishment transaction in the payroll system, and may not offset any garnishment fees charged by a payroll outsourcing company – but it can mitigate the cost to the company.

Garnishment processing is quite labor-intensive, since the payroll department must calculate the correct garnishment amount, monitor the remaining amount of garnishment to be withheld, and also coordinate payments with the accounts payable department. Any failure to complete these steps properly can result in fines and penalties. Thus, a good alternative for handling garnishments is to hand them off to a third party that is set up to handle these transactions.

If payroll is outsourced, take advantage of the garnishment processing service of the payroll supplier. For a fee, the supplier will track each garnishment on behalf of the employer, and make payments to the various governments that are requiring garnishments. If the employer is handling a large number of garnishments, this is a very cost-effective solution – but it is only available if payroll processing is already being outsourced.

Deduction Management by Employees

If an employer has a large number of employees, consider creating a software application that allows them direct access to their benefit and deduction alternatives. By doing so, the payroll staff no longer has to make any deduction changes on behalf of employees – they do it themselves.

Conceptually, an employee deduction management system presents employees with a set of benefit options, and shows them the amount of the related deduction if they want a certain benefit. Ideally, the system should present a running total of all deductions selected, and project what this does to a person's net pay. The system should also factor in whether a deduction (such as for a 401k plan) reduces the reported gross amount of a person's pay, which in turn reduces the amount of income taxes that would be withheld from their pay. It may be necessary to include limiters in the system, so that employees can only alter benefits a certain number of times per year (which may be imposed by the benefit providers).

Such a system is an awesome labor-saving device for the payroll department, since the department is completely removed from processing employee deductions. Further, if an employee makes a mistake, he is responsible for fixing it himself. In addition, the system gives employees advance knowledge of how their net pay will be altered, which should eliminate any surprises when they are paid.

There are two problems with a deduction management system. First, it is extremely expensive to create. This system requires not just a user-friendly interface, but also an interface into the payroll system (for deduction updates) and the human resources system (for benefit plan updates). The cost eliminates this system from consideration by all but the largest companies. The second issue is that an employee must be computer literate in order to use it, so it may be necessary to construct a user guide, or have a customer service staff that is available for consultation.

Summary

There can be a vast array of possible deductions from an employee paycheck, which can create a great deal of data entry and monitoring work for the payroll department. Most of these deductions originate elsewhere in a company – usually the human resources department – where there is little perception of the work that additional deductions cause for the payroll staff. It is the job of the payroll manager to educate the rest of the company regarding the amount of work involved, which may lead to a reduced number of deductions.

A large number of deductions may also originate in the executive suite, where senior management wants to offer a medley of benefits to employees in order to improve morale and retention levels. However, some benefits are used infrequently, and so do little for employees while increasing the administrative burden for both the human resources and payroll departments. Once again, this means that the cause of deductions is located outside of the payroll department, which calls for judicious lobbying from the payroll manager to mitigate the volume of payroll deductions.

Chapter 7
Payroll Taxes

Introduction

A company is required to withhold income taxes from the wages of its employees, as well as deduct social security and Medicare taxes. This chapter discusses tax rates, the mechanics of how to calculate the correct amount of withholdings, and whether the common paymaster rule can be used to reduce a company's tax matching liability.

Income Tax Withholding

If an individual is classified as an employee, the employer is responsible for withholding income taxes from that person's gross wages. There are some exceptions to this obligation by the employer, as noted in the Definition of an Employee chapter.

There are four inputs used by the employer to determine the correct amount of income tax to withhold from an employee's pay, which are gross pay, the number of exemptions claimed by an individual on his Form W-4, single or married status, and the tax indicated on the relevant IRS tax table. An example of a completed Form W-4 is shown on the following two pages.

The Form W-4 is completed by each employee, preferably every year, and it contains the number of withholding allowances that they want to claim. Each incremental withholding allowance claimed reduces the amount of federal income tax that the employer must withhold from their pay.

Tip: Encourage employees to use the Withholding Calculator located at www.irs.gov/individuals to assist in determining the appropriate number of withholding allowances that they should claim on a Form W-4.

Every employee should complete a Form W-4 when hired, but they are not required by law to do so. If a Form W-4 is not received from an employee, withhold income taxes as though the person were single, with zero withholding allowances (which results in the maximum possible income tax withholding).

Payroll Taxes

Form W-4, Employee's Withholding Allowance Certificate (page 1)

Form W-4 (2016)

Purpose. Complete Form W-4 so that your employer can withhold the correct federal income tax from your pay. Consider completing a new Form W-4 each year and when your personal or financial situation changes.

Exemption from withholding. If you are exempt, complete only lines 1, 2, 3, 4, and 7 and sign the form to validate it. Your exemption for 2016 expires February 15, 2017. See Pub. 505, Tax Withholding and Estimated Tax.

Note: If another person can claim you as a dependent on his or her tax return, you cannot claim exemption from withholding if your income exceeds $1,050 and includes more than $350 of unearned income (for example, interest and dividends).

Exceptions. An employee may be able to claim exemption from withholding even if the employee is a dependent, if the employee:
- is age 65 or older,
- is blind, or
- Will claim adjustments to income; tax credits; or itemized deductions, on his or her tax return.

The exceptions do not apply to supplemental wages greater than $1,000,000.

Basic instructions. If you are not exempt, complete the **Personal Allowances Worksheet** below. The worksheets on page 2 further adjust your withholding allowances based on itemized deductions, certain credits, adjustments to income, or two-earners/multiple jobs situations.

Complete all worksheets that apply. However, you may claim fewer (or zero) allowances. For regular wages, withholding must be based on allowances you claimed and may not be a flat amount or percentage of wages.

Head of household. Generally, you can claim head of household filing status on your tax return only if you are unmarried and pay more than 50% of the costs of keeping up a home for yourself and your dependent(s) or other qualifying individuals. See Pub. 501, Exemptions, Standard Deduction, and Filing Information, for information.

Tax credits. You can take projected tax credits into account in figuring your allowable number of withholding allowances. Credits for child or dependent care expenses and the child tax credit may be claimed using the Personal Allowances Worksheet below. See Pub. 505 for information on converting your other credits into withholding allowances.

Nonwage income. If you have a large amount of nonwage income, such as interest or dividends, consider making estimated tax payments using Form 1040-ES, Estimated Tax for Individuals. Otherwise, you may owe additional tax. If you have pension or annuity income, see Pub. 505 to find out if you should adjust your withholding on Form W-4 or W-4P.

Two earners or multiple jobs. If you have a working spouse or more than one job, figure the total number of allowances you are entitled to claim on all jobs using worksheets from only one Form W-4. Your withholding usually will be most accurate when all allowances are claimed on the Form W-4 for the highest paying job and zero allowances are claimed on the others. See Pub. 505 for details.

Nonresident alien. If you are a nonresident alien, see Notice 1392, Supplemental Form W-4 Instructions for Nonresident Aliens, before completing this form.

Check your withholding. After your Form W-4 takes effect, use Pub. 505 to see how the amount you are having withheld compares to your projected total tax for 2016. See Pub. 505, especially if your earnings exceed $130,000 (Single) or $180,000 (Married).

Future developments. Information about any future developments affecting Form W-4 (such as legislation enacted after we release it) will be posted at www.irs.gov/w4.

Personal Allowances Worksheet (Keep for your records.)

A Enter "1" for **yourself** if no one else can claim you as a dependent . . . . **A** ____

B Enter "1" if:
- You are single and have only one job; or
- You are married, have only one job, and your spouse does not work; or
- Your wages from a second job or your spouse's wages (or the total of both) are $1,500 or less.

B ____

C Enter "1" for your **spouse**. But, you may choose to enter "-0-" if you are married and have either a working spouse or more than one job. (Entering "-0-" may help you avoid having too little tax withheld.) . . . . **C** ____

D Enter number of **dependents** (other than your spouse or yourself) you will claim on your tax return . . . . . **D** ____

E Enter "1" if you will file as **head of household** on your tax return (see conditions under **Head of household** above) . . . **E** ____

F Enter "1" if you have at least $2,000 of **child or dependent care expenses** for which you plan to claim a credit . . . **F** ____
(**Note:** Do **not** include child support payments. See Pub. 503, Child and Dependent Care Expenses, for details.)

G **Child Tax Credit** (including additional child tax credit). See Pub. 972, Child Tax Credit, for more information.
- If your total income will be less than $70,000 ($100,000 if married), enter "2" for each eligible child; then **less** "1" if you have two to four eligible children or **less** "2" if you have five or more eligible children.
- If your total income will be between $70,000 and $84,000 ($100,000 and $119,000 if married), enter "1" for each eligible child . . . **G** ____

H Add lines A through G and enter total here. (**Note:** This may be different from the number of exemptions you claim on your tax return.) ▶ **H** ____

For accuracy, complete all worksheets that apply.
- If you plan to **itemize or claim adjustments to income** and want to reduce your withholding, see the **Deductions and Adjustments Worksheet** on page 2.
- If you are **single and have more than one job** or are **married and you and your spouse both work** and the combined earnings from all jobs exceed $50,000 ($20,000 if married), see the **Two-Earners/Multiple Jobs Worksheet** on page 2 to avoid having too little tax withheld.
- If neither of the above situations applies, **stop here** and enter the number from line H on line 5 of Form W-4 below.

-------- Separate here and give Form W-4 to your employer. Keep the top part for your records. --------

Form W-4 — Employee's Withholding Allowance Certificate

Department of the Treasury Internal Revenue Service

▶ Whether you are entitled to claim a certain number of allowances or exemption from withholding is subject to review by the IRS. Your employer may be required to send a copy of this form to the IRS.

OMB No. 1545-0074

2016

1 Your first name and middle initial	Last name	2 Your social security number
John D.	Smith	012-34-5678

Home address (number and street or rural route): 213 Main Street

City or town, state, and ZIP code: Overton, CO 80001

3 ☐ Single ☑ Married ☐ Married, but withhold at higher Single rate.
Note: If married, but legally separated, or spouse is a nonresident alien, check the "Single" box.

4 If your last name differs from that shown on your social security card, check here. You must call 1-800-772-1213 for a replacement card. ▶ ☐

5	Total number of allowances you are claiming (from line H above or from the applicable worksheet on page 2)	5	2
6	Additional amount, if any, you want withheld from each paycheck	6	$ 50

7 I claim exemption from withholding for 2016, and I certify that I meet **both** of the following conditions for exemption.
- Last year I had a right to a refund of **all** federal income tax withheld because I had **no** tax liability, and
- This year I expect a refund of **all** federal income tax withheld because I expect to have **no** tax liability.
If you meet both conditions, write "Exempt" here . . . . ▶ **7** ____

Under penalties of perjury, I declare that I have examined this certificate and, to the best of my knowledge and belief, it is true, correct, and complete.

Employee's signature (This form is not valid unless you sign it.) ▶ _____ Date ▶ _____

8 Employer's name and address (Employer: Complete lines 8 and 10 only if sending to the IRS.)	9 Office code (optional)	10 Employer identification number (EIN)
Big Widget Company		84-1234567

For Privacy Act and Paperwork Reduction Act Notice, see page 2. Cat. No. 10220Q Form **W-4** (2016)

Form W-4, Employee's Withholding Allowance Certificate (page 2)

Form W-4 (2016)

Page **2**

Deductions and Adjustments Worksheet

Note: Use this worksheet *only* if you plan to itemize deductions or claim certain credits or adjustments to income.

1	Enter an estimate of your 2016 itemized deductions. These include qualifying home mortgage interest, charitable contributions, state and local taxes, medical expenses in excess of 10% (7.5% if either you or your spouse was born before January 2, 1952) of your income, and miscellaneous deductions. For 2016, you may have to reduce your itemized deductions if your income is over $311,300 and you are married filing jointly or are a qualifying widow(er); $285,350 if you are head of household; $259,400 if you are single and not head of household or a qualifying widow(er); or $155,650 if you are married filing separately. See Pub. 505 for details		1	$
2	Enter: $12,600 if married filing jointly or qualifying widow(er) $9,300 if head of household $6,300 if single or married filing separately		2	$
3	**Subtract** line 2 from line 1. If zero or less, enter "-0-"		3	$
4	Enter an estimate of your 2016 adjustments to income and any additional standard deduction (see Pub. 505)		4	$
5	**Add** lines 3 and 4 and enter the total. (Include any amount for credits from the *Converting Credits to Withholding Allowances for 2016 Form W-4* worksheet in Pub. 505.)		5	$
6	Enter an estimate of your 2016 nonwage income (such as dividends or interest)		6	$
7	**Subtract** line 6 from line 5. If zero or less, enter "-0-"		7	$
8	**Divide** the amount on line 7 by $4,050 and enter the result here. Drop any fraction		8	
9	Enter the number from the **Personal Allowances Worksheet**, line H, page 1		9	
10	**Add** lines 8 and 9 and enter the total here. If you plan to use the **Two-Earners/Multiple Jobs Worksheet**, also enter this total on line 1 below. Otherwise, **stop here** and enter this total on Form W-4, line 5, page 1		10	

Two-Earners/Multiple Jobs Worksheet (See *Two earners or multiple jobs* on page 1.)

Note: Use this worksheet *only* if the instructions under line H on page 1 direct you here.

1	Enter the number from line H, page 1 (or from line 10 above if you used the **Deductions and Adjustments Worksheet**)	1	
2	Find the number in **Table 1** below that applies to the **LOWEST** paying job and enter it here. **However,** if you are married filing jointly and wages from the highest paying job are $65,000 or less, do not enter more than "3"	2	
3	If line 1 is **more than or equal to** line 2, subtract line 2 from line 1. Enter the result here (if zero, enter "-0-") and on Form W-4, line 5, page 1. **Do not** use the rest of this worksheet	3	
Note:	If line 1 is **less than** line 2, enter "-0-" on Form W-4, line 5, page 1. Complete lines 4 through 9 below to figure the additional withholding amount necessary to avoid a year-end tax bill.		
4	Enter the number from line 2 of this worksheet	4	
5	Enter the number from line 1 of this worksheet	5	
6	**Subtract** line 5 from line 4	6	
7	Find the amount in **Table 2** below that applies to the **HIGHEST** paying job and enter it here	7	$
8	**Multiply** line 7 by line 6 and enter the result here. This is the additional annual withholding needed	8	$
9	Divide line 8 by the number of pay periods remaining in 2016. For example, divide by 25 if you are paid every two weeks and you complete this form on a date in January when there are 25 pay periods remaining in 2016. Enter the result here and on Form W-4, line 6, page 1. This is the additional amount to be withheld from each paycheck	9	$

Table 1

Married Filing Jointly		All Others	
If wages from LOWEST paying job are—	Enter on line 2 above	If wages from LOWEST paying job are—	Enter on line 2 above
$0 - $6,000	0	$0 - $9,000	0
6,001 - 14,000	1	9,001 - 17,000	1
14,001 - 25,000	2	17,001 - 26,000	2
25,001 - 27,000	3	26,001 - 34,000	3
27,001 - 35,000	4	34,001 - 44,000	4
35,001 - 44,000	5	44,001 - 75,000	5
44,001 - 55,000	6	75,001 - 85,000	6
55,001 - 65,000	7	85,001 - 110,000	7
65,001 - 75,000	8	110,001 - 125,000	8
75,001 - 80,000	9	125,001 - 140,000	9
80,001 - 100,000	10	140,001 and over	10
100,001 - 115,000	11		
115,001 - 130,000	12		
130,001 - 140,000	13		
140,001 - 150,000	14		
150,001 and over	15		

Table 2

Married Filing Jointly		All Others	
If wages from HIGHEST paying job are—	Enter on line 7 above	If wages from HIGHEST paying job are—	Enter on line 7 above
$0 - $75,000	$610	$0 - $38,000	$610
75,001 - 135,000	1,010	38,001 - 85,000	1,010
135,001 - 205,000	1,130	85,001 - 185,000	1,130
205,001 - 360,000	1,340	185,001 - 400,000	1,340
360,001 - 405,000	1,420	400,001 and over	1,600
405,001 and over	1,600		

When an employee submits a signed Form W-4, that document remains in effect until such time as the employee submits a replacement form. Upon receipt of the new form, adjust the withholdings from the effective date of the form forward.

> **Tip:** Retain copies of all Forms W-4 in the employee file of each employee, so it is possible to justify when exemptions were changed in the payroll system, and the amount of those changes. This is a particular concern in cases where employees are under the assumption that they submitted allowances other than those being used as the basis for withholdings.

When employees complete the Form W-4, they have the option of basing their withholding amount on a fixed dollar amount, a percentage of gross wages, or a percentage of gross wages *and* an additional fixed dollar amount. The amounts specified in the form are the responsibility of the employee, not the company.

Be aware of two special cases involving the Form W-4 that may arise, which are as follows:

- *Reduced allowances.* An employee may claim fewer allowances than the amount they are entitled to claim, which is prudent for them if they have other income against which they need additional withholdings.
- *Exempt from withholding.* An employee can claim exemption from all federal income tax withholding if he or she had no income tax liability in the preceding year and expects none this year, as well. A Form W-4 claiming a complete exemption is only valid for the calendar year in which it is filed. If the employee does not submit a replacement form the next year, assume that the person is single and has zero withholding allowances in that year.

> **Tip:** The IRS may request that a Form W-4 be made available for inspection. If the IRS then notifies the employer that an employee is not entitled to claim exemption from withholding or a stated number of withholding allowances, use the replacement amounts and marital status specified in the IRS notice, as of the date specified in the notice. The employee must be notified of this notice within ten days of receipt. If the employee then submits a new Form W-4 that is more favorable to him or her than the IRS notice, continue to use the amounts specified in the IRS notice.

If nonresident aliens are employed, they should submit a Form W-4 on which they:

- Do not claim exemption from income tax withholding
- Request withholding as though they are single (irrespective of their actual status)
- Claim one allowance
- Write "Nonresident Alien" or "NRA" on line 6 of the form

If a nonresident alien claims exemption from income tax withholding under a tax treaty exemption, have them submit a Form 8233, Exemption from Withholding on Compensation for Independent (and Certain Dependent) Personal Services of a Nonresident Alien Individual.

> **Tip:** It is allowable to create a substitute Form W-4, as long as it contains language that is identical to the official Form W-4. Employees must be provided with all of the tables, instructions, and worksheets that accompany the official form. A substitute form cannot be accepted that was developed by an employee.

Social Security Tax

The social security tax began with the passage of the Social Security Act in 1935, which established Old Age and Survivor's Insurance. The insurance was to be funded by compulsory deductions from the pay of wage earners. Initially, these deductions were set at 1% of gross wages, and were to be paid by both the employer and the employee, and would continue until retirement age, which was set at 65. By 1948, the amount of these deductions had increased to 3%. Employers have been and continue to be responsible for withholding the social security tax from employee pay.

The tax rate for social security is now governed by the Federal Insurance Contributions Act (FICA). Because of this association, social security taxes are now closely associated with the acronym "FICA".

This tax has increased in size over time, along with the maximum wage cap (also known as the *wage base limit*) to which it applies. The social security tax rate is only applied to a person's wages up to the amount of the wage base cap. Do not apply the tax to any wages earned above the wage cap. For example, on earnings of $150,000 in 2017, the amount of employer tax paid would be $7,886.40, which is calculated as follows:

$$6.2\% \text{ Tax rate} \times \$127,200 \text{ Wage cap} = \$7,886.40$$

The following table shows the recent history of the social security tax for the past few years. Note the drop in the employee portion of the tax in 2011 and 2012.

Tax Year	FICA Tax Rate	Wage Cap
2017	6.2%	$127,200
2016	6.2%	118,500
2015	6.2%	118,500
2014	6.2%	117,000
2013	6.2%	113,700
2012	4.2% Employee / 6.2% Employer	110,100
2011	4.2% Employee / 6.2% Employer	106,800
2010	6.2%	106,800
2009	6.2%	106,800
2008	6.2%	102,000

Note that social security is matched by the employee, so the total tax amount paid to the government by the employer is 12.4% (with the exceptions of 2011 and 2012, as noted in the preceding table). A self-employed person is responsible for paying the full amount of the 12.4%.

EXAMPLE

Benjamin Mayhew earned $200,000 in 2017. Based on the $127,200 wage cap in place that year, his employer must deduct $7,886.40 from his gross pay and match it with another $7,886.40 for a total payment of $15,772.80.

> **Tip:** Withholding allowances have no impact on the social security tax.

The age at which full social security retirement benefits are payable depends on the year of birth of the individual. The following table states the full retirement age for different years of birth.

Age at Which Full Social Security Benefits Are Available

Year of Birth	Full Retirement Age
1943-1954	66
1955	66 and 2 months
1956	66 and 4 months
1957	66 and 6 months
1958	66 and 8 months
1959	66 and 10 months
1960+	67

An individual can retire as early as age 62, but will be paid roughly 25% less than the amount that would have been paid if the person had chosen to wait until his or her full retirement age.

Conversely, a person can choose to continue working beyond the full retirement age. If so, the individual is adding extra years of work to his or her social security record, which may result in higher benefits upon retirement. Further, one can choose to delay retirement until age 70 in exchange for an automatic increase by a certain percentage (usually about 8% per year) from the full retirement age until age 70.

Widows and widowers can begin receiving social security benefits at age 60, or at age 50 if they are disabled.

Medicare Tax

Medicare is a health insurance program that is administered by the United States government, and which is primarily available to those 65 years old or older, as well as to those with certain disabilities. It is funded through the Medicare tax, though participants must also pay a portion of all health insurance costs incurred. The program has been in existence since 1965.

Since 1986, the Medicare tax rate that is paid by an employee has been 1.45% (plus matching of the same amount by the employer), and 2.9% for self-employed workers. There is no cap on the Medicare tax for employed and self-employed people; thus, everyone must pay it, irrespective of the amount of money that they earn.

As of 2014, an additional Medicare tax of 0.9% was imposed, which applies to all wages earned in excess of $250,000 for married filers, and in excess of $200,000 for single and head of household filers.

> **Tip:** Withholding allowances have no impact on the Medicare tax.

EXAMPLE

Atlas Machining Company employs Mr. Smith, who earns $5,000 of gross pay in the most recent pay period. Atlas withholds $72.50 ($5,000 × .0145) from the pay of Mr. Smith, matches the $72.50 from its own funds and forwards $145.00 to the government.

EXAMPLE

Mr. Jones is self-employed and earns a total of $150,000 during the year. His total Medicare contribution during the year is $4,350 ($150,000 × .029).

Calculating Withholdings

There are three ways in which a company can withhold income taxes from the pay of an employee. These methods are:

- *Outsourced payroll.* If the payroll processing function is outsourced, the supplier handles this task using its own database of tax rates. The process is completely invisible to the company.
- *In-house payroll software.* If the company processes payroll within its payroll department using payroll software, the supplier of the software provides updated tax tables every year that are derived from the latest IRS updates. The payroll staff loads in the updates and, once again, the process is invisible to the company.
- *Manual calculations.* If the payroll manager elects to manually calculate income tax withholdings, there are multiple methods available that are acceptable to the IRS for doing so. The following sub-sections provide further details regarding the available methods.

Wage Bracket Method

The IRS provides a set of wage bracket tables for income tax withholdings in its Publication 15, Employer's Tax Guide. This publication is available as a PDF download on the www.irs.gov website. The IRS also provides wage bracket tables that show the total amount of the income tax withholding, social security deduction, and Medicare deduction; these tables are published by the IRS in its Publication 15-A, Employer's Supplemental Tax Guide.

The wage bracket tables are designed to be an easy way to derive the correct amount of income tax withholding for people claiming a reasonable number of withholding allowances (up to ten) and at lower wage levels. Each table calculates the proper amount of withholding under a different set of scenarios. Thus, there are separate wage bracket tables that address the following situations:

Payroll Type	Tables within Payroll Type
Daily	Single, Married
Weekly	Single, Married
Biweekly	Single, Married
Monthly	Single, Married

An extract from a combined wage bracket table is shown in the following exhibit, which is taken from the 2016 version of Publication 15-A. The table lists the amount of income tax withholding, social security deduction, and Medicare taxes to be withheld for a married person who is on a biweekly payroll period. The actual table presents information for a much larger range of income, and for more withholding allowances.

To use the wage bracket method, go to the table that corresponds to the company's payroll period and for the employee's married status (single or married). Within that table, go to the column corresponding to the number of withholding allowances claimed by the employee, and drop down that column to reach the row corresponding to the wages earned by the employee in the pay period. The amount in that cell represents either the amount of income tax to withhold (if a Publication 15 table is being used) or the entire amount of income tax, social security, and Medicare to withhold (if a Publication 15-A table is used).

Payroll Taxes

IRS Combined Wage Bracket Table for a Married Employee (Biweekly Payroll)

Wages are		The number of withholding allowances claimed is					
At least	But less than	0	1	2	3	4	5
		The amount of income, social security, and Medicare taxes to be withheld is					
1,005	1,025	146.65	130.65	114.65	99.65	83.65	77.65
1,025	1,045	150.18	134.18	118.18	103.18	87.18	79.18
1,045	1,065	153.71	137.71	121.71	106.71	90.71	80.71
1,065	1,085	158.24	141.24	125.24	110.24	94.24	82.24
1,085	1,105	162.77	144.77	128.77	113.77	98.77	83.77
1,105	1,125	167.30	148.30	132.30	117.30	101.30	86.30
1,125	1,145	171.83	151.83	135.83	120.83	104.83	89.83
1,145	1,165	176.36	155.36	139.36	124.36	108.36	93.36
1,165	1,185	180.89	158.89	142.89	127.89	111.89	96.89
1,185	1,205	185.42	162.42	146.42	131.42	115.42	100.42
1,205	1,225	189.95	166.95	149.95	134.95	118.95	103.95

Tip: A common error made with the wage bracket tables is to misread the zero allowances column as being for a single allowance. Employees sometimes use zero allowances if they have a significant amount of income earned outside of the company, and they want to have sufficient income taxes withheld against that additional income. To make sure that a clerk does not inadvertently use withholding figures from this column instead of withholdings from the one-allowance column, highlight or prominently circle the header for the zero allowance column, to more easily take note of it.

EXAMPLE

Albert Montaigne works for Mountain Arts, which manufactures propane-powered heating systems for residential homes. Mr. Montaigne is an hourly production employee of the company, which pays its staff on a biweekly basis. Mr. Montaigne earned $1,180 during the most recent biweekly period. He has claimed four withholding allowances on his Form W-4. According to the preceding extract from the IRS combined wage bracket table, the company should deduct a total of $111.89 from his wages to cover income tax withholdings, as well as social security and Medicare taxes.

Tip: Be certain that wage bracket tables are being used for the correct year, since the IRS updates the tables every year. If tables from a prior year are used, the employer is probably withholding the wrong amounts.

Percentage Method

The percentage method is essentially the formula used to compile the information in the wage bracket tables. This formula will work for any number of withholdings claimed by an employee, as well as for any amount of wages. Since the wage bracket tables are only available for a limited range of wages and allowances, the percentage method is the method of choice when an employer is faced with a broad range of wages and allowances. Use the following steps to calculate the proper income tax withholding under the percentage method:

1. Multiply one withholding allowance for the applicable payroll period by the number of allowances that an employee claims, using the withholding allowance in the following table (which is valid for the calendar year 2016):

Payroll Period	One Withholding Allowance
Weekly	$77.90
Biweekly	155.80
Semimonthly	168.80
Monthly	337.50
Quarterly	1,012.50
Semiannually	2,025.00
Annually	4,050.00
Daily	15.60

2. Subtract that amount from the gross wages of the employee.
3. Determine the amount to withhold from the applicable percentage method table. These tables are shown in the next two pages under the title Percentage Method Tables for Income Tax Withholding.

EXAMPLE

Molly Meister is single and claims three allowances on her Form W-4. She is paid $1,100 per week. This means that the amount of her wages subject to withholding is calculated as:

= $1,100 wages – ($77.90 withholding allowance × 3 allowances)
= $1,100 wages – $233.70
= **$866.30**

The percentage method table for 2016 states that the withholding for a single person earning $866.30 in a weekly pay period is $99.65 plus 25% of the amount over $767. Thus, her total income tax withholding is:

= $99.65 + (25% × ($866.30 - $767))
= $99.65 + $24.83
= **$124.48** withholding

Annualized Wages Method

Use an employee's annual wages to calculate the withholding under Table 7 of the percentage method tables listed in IRS Publication 15. Divide the amount listed in the table for the person's annual wages by the number of payroll periods, which yields the amount of income taxes to withhold in each payroll period.

Percentage Method Tables for Income Tax Withholding

(For Wages Paid in 2016)

TABLE 1—WEEKLY Payroll Period

(a) SINGLE person (including head of household)—

If the amount of wages (after subtracting withholding allowances) is:
Not over $43 . . . . $0

Over—	But not over—	The amount of income tax to withhold is:	of excess over—
$43	—$222	$0.00 plus 10%	—$43
$222	—$767	$17.90 plus 15%	—$222
$767	—$1,796	$99.65 plus 25%	—$767
$1,796	—$3,700	$356.90 plus 28%	—$1,796
$3,700	—$7,992	$890.02 plus 33%	—$3,700
$7,992	—$8,025	$2,306.38 plus 35%	—$7,992
$8,025	. . . .	$2,317.93 plus 39.6%	—$8,025

(b) MARRIED person—

If the amount of wages (after subtracting withholding allowances) is:
Not over $164 . . . . $0

Over—	But not over—	The amount of income tax to withhold is:	of excess over—
$164	—$521	$0.00 plus 10%	—$164
$521	—$1,613	$35.70 plus 15%	—$521
$1,613	—$3,086	$199.50 plus 25%	—$1,613
$3,086	—$4,615	$567.75 plus 28%	—$3,086
$4,615	—$8,113	$995.87 plus 33%	—$4,615
$8,113	—$9,144	$2,150.21 plus 35%	—$8,113
$9,144	. . . .	$2,511.06 plus 39.6%	—$9,144

TABLE 2—BIWEEKLY Payroll Period

(a) SINGLE person (including head of household)—

If the amount of wages (after subtracting withholding allowances) is:
Not over $87 . . . . $0

Over—	But not over—	The amount of income tax to withhold is:	of excess over—
$87	—$443	$0.00 plus 10%	—$87
$443	—$1,535	$35.60 plus 15%	—$443
$1,535	—$3,592	$199.40 plus 25%	—$1,535
$3,592	—$7,400	$713.65 plus 28%	—$3,592
$7,400	—$15,985	$1,779.89 plus 33%	—$7,400
$15,985	—$16,050	$4,612.94 plus 35%	—$15,985
$16,050	. . . .	$4,635.69 plus 39.6%	—$16,050

(b) MARRIED person—

If the amount of wages (after subtracting withholding allowances) is:
Not over $329 . . . . $0

Over—	But not over—	The amount of income tax to withhold is:	of excess over—
$329	—$1,042	$0.00 plus 10%	—$329
$1,042	—$3,225	$71.30 plus 15%	—$1,042
$3,225	—$6,171	$398.75 plus 25%	—$3,225
$6,171	—$9,231	$1,135.25 plus 28%	—$6,171
$9,231	—$16,227	$1,992.05 plus 33%	—$9,231
$16,227	—$18,288	$4,300.73 plus 35%	—$16,227
$18,288	. . . .	$5,022.08 plus 39.6%	—$18,288

TABLE 3—SEMIMONTHLY Payroll Period

(a) SINGLE person (including head of household)—

If the amount of wages (after subtracting withholding allowances) is:
Not over $94 . . . . $0

Over—	But not over—	The amount of income tax to withhold is:	of excess over—
$94	—$480	$0.00 plus 10%	—$94
$480	—$1,663	$38.60 plus 15%	—$480
$1,663	—$3,892	$216.05 plus 25%	—$1,663
$3,892	—$8,017	$773.30 plus 28%	—$3,892
$8,017	—$17,317	$1,928.30 plus 33%	—$8,017
$17,317	—$17,388	$4,997.30 plus 35%	—$17,317
$17,388	. . . .	$5,022.15 plus 39.6%	—$17,388

(b) MARRIED person—

If the amount of wages (after subtracting withholding allowances) is:
Not over $356 . . . . $0

Over—	But not over—	The amount of income tax to withhold is:	of excess over—
$356	—$1,129	$0.00 plus 10%	—$356
$1,129	—$3,494	$77.30 plus 15%	—$1,129
$3,494	—$6,685	$432.05 plus 25%	—$3,494
$6,685	—$10,000	$1,229.80 plus 28%	—$6,685
$10,000	—$17,579	$2,158.00 plus 33%	—$10,000
$17,579	—$19,813	$4,659.07 plus 35%	—$17,579
$19,813	. . . .	$5,440.97 plus 39.6%	—$19,813

TABLE 4—MONTHLY Payroll Period

(a) SINGLE person (including head of household)—

If the amount of wages (after subtracting withholding allowances) is:
Not over $188 . . . . $0

Over—	But not over—	The amount of income tax to withhold is:	of excess over—
$188	—$960	$0.00 plus 10%	—$188
$960	—$3,325	$77.20 plus 15%	—$960
$3,325	—$7,783	$431.95 plus 25%	—$3,325
$7,783	—$16,033	$1,546.45 plus 28%	—$7,783
$16,033	—$34,633	$3,856.45 plus 33%	—$16,033
$34,633	—$34,775	$9,994.45 plus 35%	—$34,633
$34,775	. . . .	$10,044.15 plus 39.6%	—$34,775

(b) MARRIED person—

If the amount of wages (after subtracting withholding allowances) is:
Not over $713 . . . . $0

Over—	But not over—	The amount of income tax to withhold is:	of excess over—
$713	—$2,258	$0.00 plus 10%	—$713
$2,258	—$6,988	$154.50 plus 15%	—$2,258
$6,988	—$13,371	$864.00 plus 25%	—$6,988
$13,371	—$20,000	$2,459.75 plus 28%	—$13,371
$20,000	—$35,158	$4,315.87 plus 33%	—$20,000
$35,158	—$39,625	$9,318.01 plus 35%	—$35,158
$39,625	. . . .	$10,881.46 plus 39.6%	—$39,625

Percentage Method Tables for Income Tax Withholding (continued)

(For Wages Paid in 2016)

TABLE 5—QUARTERLY Payroll Period

(a) SINGLE person (including head of household)—				(b) MARRIED person—			
If the amount of wages (after subtracting withholding allowances) is: Not over $563 . . . . $0		The amount of income tax to withhold is:		If the amount of wages (after subtracting withholding allowances) is: Not over $2,138 . . . . $0		The amount of income tax to withhold is:	
Over—	But not over—		of excess over—	Over—	But not over—		of excess over—
$563	—$2,881	$0.00 plus 10%	—$563	$2,138	—$6,775	$0.00 plus 10%	—$2,138
$2,881	—$9,975	$231.80 plus 15%	—$2,881	$6,775	—$20,963	$463.70 plus 15%	—$6,775
$9,975	—$23,350	$1,295.90 plus 25%	—$9,975	$20,963	—$40,113	$2,591.90 plus 25%	—$20,963
$23,350	—$48,100	$4,639.65 plus 28%	—$23,350	$40,113	—$60,000	$7,379.40 plus 28%	—$40,113
$48,100	—$103,900	$11,569.65 plus 33%	—$48,100	$60,000	—$105,475	$12,947.76 plus 33%	—$60,000
$103,900	—$104,325	$29,983.65 plus 35%	—$103,900	$105,475	—$118,875	$27,954.51 plus 35%	—$105,475
$104,325		$30,132.40 plus 39.6%	—$104,325	$118,875		$32,644.51 plus 39.6%	—$118,875

TABLE 6—SEMIANNUAL Payroll Period

(a) SINGLE person (including head of household)—				(b) MARRIED person—			
If the amount of wages (after subtracting withholding allowances) is: Not over $1,125 . . . . $0		The amount of income tax to withhold is:		If the amount of wages (after subtracting withholding allowances) is: Not over $4,275 . . . . $0		The amount of income tax to withhold is:	
Over—	But not over—		of excess over—	Over—	But not over—		of excess over—
$1,125	—$5,763	$0.00 plus 10%	—$1,125	$4,275	—$13,550	$0.00 plus 10%	—$4,275
$5,763	—$19,950	$463.80 plus 15%	—$5,763	$13,550	—$41,925	$927.50 plus 15%	—$13,550
$19,950	—$46,700	$2,591.85 plus 25%	—$19,950	$41,925	—$80,225	$5,183.75 plus 25%	—$41,925
$46,700	—$96,200	$9,279.35 plus 28%	—$46,700	$80,225	—$120,000	$14,758.75 plus 28%	—$80,225
$96,200	—$207,800	$23,139.35 plus 33%	—$96,200	$120,000	—$210,950	$25,895.75 plus 33%	—$120,000
$207,800	—$208,650	$59,983.65 plus 35%	—$207,800	$210,950	—$237,750	$55,909.25 plus 35%	—$210,950
$208,650		$60,264.85 plus 39.6%	—$208,650	$237,750		$65,289.25 plus 39.6%	—$237,750

TABLE 7—ANNUAL Payroll Period

(a) SINGLE person (including head of household)—				(b) MARRIED person—			
If the amount of wages (after subtracting withholding allowances) is: Not over $2,250 . . . . $0		The amount of income tax to withhold is:		If the amount of wages (after subtracting withholding allowances) is: Not over $8,550 . . . . $0		The amount of income tax to withhold is:	
Over—	But not over—		of excess over—	Over—	But not over—		of excess over—
$2,250	—$11,525	$0.00 plus 10%	—$2,250	$8,550	—$27,100	$0.00 plus 10%	—$8,550
$11,525	—$39,900	$927.50 plus 15%	—$11,525	$27,100	—$83,850	$1,855.00 plus 15%	—$27,100
$39,900	—$93,400	$5,183.75 plus 25%	—$39,900	$83,850	—$160,450	$10,367.50 plus 25%	—$83,850
$93,400	—$192,400	$18,558.75 plus 28%	—$93,400	$160,450	—$240,000	$29,517.50 plus 28%	—$160,450
$192,400	—$415,600	$46,278.75 plus 33%	—$192,400	$240,000	—$421,900	$51,791.50 plus 33%	—$240,000
$415,600	—$417,300	$119,934.75 plus 35%	—$415,600	$421,900	—$475,500	$111,818.50 plus 35%	—$421,900
$417,300		$120,529.75 plus 39.6%	—$417,300	$475,500		$130,578.50 plus 39.6%	—$475,500

TABLE 8—DAILY or MISCELLANEOUS Payroll Period

(a) SINGLE person (including head of household)—				(b) MARRIED person—			
If the amount of wages (after subtracting withholding allowances) divided by the number of days in the payroll period is: Not over $8.70 . . . . $0		The amount of income tax to withhold per day is:		If the amount of wages (after subtracting withholding allowances) divided by the number of days in the payroll period is: Not over $32.90 . . . . $0		The amount of income tax to withhold per day is:	
Over—	But not over—		of excess over—	Over—	But not over—		of excess over—
$8.70	—$44.30	$0.00 plus 10%	—$8.70	$32.90	—$104.20	$0.00 plus 10%	—$32.90
$44.30	—$153.50	$3.56 plus 15%	—$44.30	$104.20	—$322.50	$7.13 plus 15%	—$104.20
$153.50	—$359.20	$19.94 plus 25%	—$153.50	$322.50	—$617.10	$39.88 plus 25%	—$322.50
$359.20	—$740.00	$71.37 plus 28%	—$359.20	$617.10	—$923.10	$113.53 plus 28%	—$617.10
$740.00	—$1,598.50	$177.99 plus 33%	—$740.00	$923.10	—$1,622.70	$199.21 plus 33%	—$923.10
$1,598.50	—$1,605.00	$461.30 plus 35%	—$1,598.50	$1,622.70	—$1,828.80	$430.08 plus 35%	—$1,622.70
$1,605.00		$463.58 plus 39.6%	—$1,605.00	$1,828.80		$502.22 plus 39.6%	—$1,828.80

As of 2016, the annual income tax withholding for a single person and married person was as noted in the following table, which is extracted from Table 7 in IRS Publication 15:

TABLE 7—ANNUAL Payroll Period

(a) SINGLE person (including head of household)—					(b) MARRIED person—			
If the amount of wages (after subtracting withholding allowances) is:		The amount of income tax to withhold is:			If the amount of wages (after subtracting withholding allowances) is:		The amount of income tax to withhold is:	
Not over $2,250 . . . . $0					Not over $8,550 . . . . $0			
Over—	But not over—			of excess over—	Over—	But not over—		of excess over—
$2,250	—$11,525 . .	$0.00 plus 10%		—$2,250	$8,550	—$27,100 . .	$0.00 plus 10%	—$8,550
$11,525	—$39,900 . .	$927.50 plus 15%		—$11,525	$27,100	—$83,850 . .	$1,855.00 plus 15%	—$27,100
$39,900	—$93,400 . .	$5,183.75 plus 25%		—$39,900	$83,850	—$160,450 . .	$10,367.50 plus 25%	—$83,850
$93,400	—$192,400 . .	$18,558.75 plus 28%		—$93,400	$160,450	—$240,000 . .	$29,517.50 plus 28%	—$160,450
$192,400	—$415,600 . .	$46,278.75 plus 33%		—$192,400	$240,000	—$421,900 . .	$51,791.50 plus 33%	—$240,000
$415,600	—$417,300 . .	$119,934.75 plus 35%		—$415,600	$421,900	—$475,500 . .	$111,818.50 plus 35%	—$421,900
$417,300		$120,529.75 plus 39.6%		—$417,300	$475,500		$130,578.50 plus 39.6%	—$475,500

EXAMPLE

Ms. Elizabeth Bosworth is single and is paid a salary of $75,000 per year. If her employer were to use the 2016 annualized wages method to determine her income tax withholding, the calculation would be:

> = $5,183.75 + 25% of excess wages exceeding $39,900
> = $5,183.75 + (25% × ($75,000 salary - $39,990))
> = $5,183.75 + (25% × $35,010)
> = <u>$13,936.25</u> income tax withholding

Her employer pays on a semimonthly basis, which is 24 times per year. Thus, the amount of income tax withholding per paycheck should be $580.68 (calculated as $13,936.25 annual withholding ÷ 24 pay periods).

Average Estimated Wages Method

An employer can withhold income taxes for a payroll period based on the estimated amount of average wages for a calendar quarter.

Cumulative Wages Method

If an employee has asked, in writing, for the employer to withhold income taxes based on that person's cumulative wages, do so using the following method:

1. Add all wages paid to the employee thus far in the current calendar year to the wage amount in the current payroll period.
2. Divide this amount by the number of payroll periods completed so far in this calendar year, including the current payroll period.
3. Calculate the withholding based on this average wage amount per period.
4. Multiply the withholding by the number of periods calculated in step two.
5. Calculate the tax using the percentage method (see the preceding subsection).
6. Subtract the tax already deducted earlier in the calendar year from the total amount of tax calculated.
7. The excess remaining tax that has not yet been deducted is the amount to withhold in the current payroll period.

> **Tip:** There is no requirement that the employer must use this method, just because an employee requests that it be used. Thus, it is acceptable to turn down the request if the work required appears onerous.

Part-Year Employment Method

An employee who is only employed for part of a calendar year can ask his or her employer in writing to calculate income tax withholding based on the part-year employment method. The request must contain the following information:

- The last day of employment that year with any prior employer.
- A statement that the employee uses the calendar year accounting method.
- A statement that the employee reasonably anticipates being employed by all employers for no more than 245 days during the current calendar year.

Use the following steps to calculate a person's income tax withholding under this method:

1. Obtain the total amount of wages already paid to the employee in the current term of continuous employment.
2. Add the wages to be paid to the employee for the current payroll period to this amount.
3. Add the number of payroll periods used to accumulate information in the first two steps to the number of payroll periods between the person's last and current employment.
4. Divide the total in step two by the number of payroll periods derived in step three.
5. Locate the withholding amount in the withholding tax tables for the amount calculated in step four, using the employee's withholding allowances.
6. Multiply the total number of payroll periods derived in step three by the withholding amount in step five.
7. Subtract any tax already withheld during the current period of employment from the amount calculated in step six. Withhold any excess amount in the current payroll period.

A term of continuous employment begins on the first day that an employee begins work and earns pay, and ends on the earlier of the employee's last day of work. Alternatively, it ends on the last workday before a 30-day period, if the employee performs no services for the employer for more than 30 calendar days.

Other Methods

Other methods are allowable for withholding taxes, as long as the amount of tax withheld is "consistently about the same" as it would have been using the percentage method. The IRS recommends that the full range of wage and allowance situations be tested on any alternative methods to ensure that they are within the following tolerances:

If the tax required to be withheld under the annual percentage is:	Then the annual tax withheld under the employer's method may not differ by more than:
Less than $10.00	$9.99
$10 or more but under $100	$10 plus 10% of the excess over $10
$100 or more but under $1,000	$19 plus 3% of the excess over $100
$1,000 or more	$46 plus 1% of the excess over $1,000

Earnings Not Subject to Payroll Taxes

There are many types of earnings besides wages, and some of them are exempt from social security and Medicare tax deductions. When the employee is exempt from these taxes, it also means that the employer is also exempt from paying matching amounts to the government. Thus, the payroll staff should be fully aware of which types of earnings are exempt, if only to save the company from paying taxes that it does not owe. The following table shows the extent to which earnings are taxable. FUTA deductions are not shown in the table, but are generally the same as for social security and Medicare taxes.

Taxability of Earnings

Class of Employment or Earnings Type	Income Tax Withholding	Social Security and Medicare Deductions
Cafeteria plan withholdings	Exempt	Exempt
Deceased worker, wages paid to beneficiary or estate in year of death	Exempt	Taxable
Deceased worker, wages paid to beneficiary or estate after year of death	Exempt	Exempt
Disabled worker wages paid after year in which disabled	Withhold	Exempt, if did not provide services to employer during the payment period
Employee business expense reimbursement under an accountable plan and not exceeding government guidelines*	Exempt	Exempt
Employee business expense reimbursement under accountable plan for amounts exceeding government guidelines*	Withhold	Taxable
Employee business expense reimbursement under nonaccountable plan*	Withhold	Taxable
Child employed by parent	Withhold	Exempt until age 18, or until age 21 for domestic work
Fringe benefits	**	**

Class of Employment or Earnings Type	Income Tax Withholding	Social Security and Medicare Deductions
Insurance – Accident and health insurance	Exempt	Exempt
Insurance – Group term	Exempt	Exempt except cost includable in employee gross wages*
Insurance agent wages	Withhold only if common law employee	Taxable
Officers or shareholders of S corporation distributions	Withhold	Taxable
Pension plan: Employer contributions to qualified plan	Exempt	Exempt
Severance pay	Withhold	Taxable
Sick pay	Withhold	Exempt after end of six calendar months after month in which last worked for employer
Tips: If more than $20 in a month	Withhold	Taxable
Tips: If less than $20 in a month	Exempt	Exempt
Workers' compensation	Exempt	Exempt

* See the Employee Benefits chapter for more information
** Taxable in excess of fair market value of the benefit over any employee-paid portion and any amount legally excludable

Underwithheld Taxes

If an employer does not withhold income, social security, or Medicare taxes from employee pay, or does so at reduced levels, the employer still owes the government the full amount of these withholdings. The employer can make up the underwithheld difference from later pay to employees. Underwithheld income taxes must be recovered from an employee by the last day of the calendar year.

Overwithheld Taxes

If an employer withholds too much income, social security, or Medicare taxes from employee pay, employees must be refunded the excess amount. Overwithheld income taxes must be refunded to employees by the last day of the calendar year. The employer should keep a receipt that shows the date and amount paid back to employees. If no refund is made, report the overage in the next quarterly Form 941 filing.

Employee Taxes Paid by the Employer

What if the employer pays the employee portion of social security and Medicare taxes? This is essentially a form of additional compensation for the employee, and is treated as such for tax reporting. Therefore, include the amount of the additional taxes paid on behalf of the employees in their reportable wages. This additional compensation is, in turn, subject to social security and Medicare tax deductions.

The IRS has provided two calculations in its Publication 15-A for determining the amount of an employee's increased wages in this situation, which are:

- *Stated pay of $109,434.75 or less in 2016.* Divide the stated amount of wages by 1 minus the combined employee social security and Medicare tax rate for the year in which wages are being paid. The result is used for the calculation of FUTA tax and federal income tax withholding.
- *Stated pay of more than $109,434.75 in 2016.* If an employee has stated pay of more than $109,434.75, he or she has exceeded the social security wage cap (calculated as $118,500 × 0.9235), and no further social security tax applies. However, there is no wage cap for the Medicare tax. To calculate the amount of wages subject to Medicare, follow these steps:
  1. Subtract $109,434.75 from the stated pay of the employee.
  2. Divide the result by 0.9855 (calculated as 1 − 0.0145) and add $118,500.

Once calculated, enter the amount of the Medicare wages in box 5 of Form W-2.

Note: The additional 0.9% Medicare tax may also apply for higher wage earners. See the Medicare Tax section for more information.

Stated pay is the amount that an employer pays to an employee as wages prior to any additional payments by the employer for the employee's share of social security and Medicare taxes.

EXAMPLE

Ms. Emma Thompson earns $55,000 in 2016, on which her employer pays her share of social security and Medicare taxes. The calculation of her increased wages is:

$$= \$55,000 \text{ wages} \div (1 - 0.0765)$$
$$= \$55,000 \text{ wages} \div 0.9235$$
$$= \underline{\$59,556.04} \text{ reportable wages}$$

$59,556.04 should be used for the calculation of the FUTA tax and federal income tax withholding.

EXAMPLE

Mr. Michael Dorne earns $125,000 in 2016, on which his employer pays his share of social security and Medicare taxes. The calculation of his increased wages for Medicare purposes is:

> Step 1. $125,000 wages - $109,434.75 = $15,565.25
> Step 2. $15,565.25 ÷ 0.9855 = $15,794.27
> $15,794.27 + $118,500 = <u>$134,294.27</u>

The reportable amount of Medicare wages is $134,294.27.

Although these tax amounts are not actually withheld from employee pay, report them to the IRS as withheld, and then pay this amount as the employer's share of the social security and Medicare taxes.

> **Note:** This methodology for increasing the reportable wages of an employee does not apply to household and agricultural employees. If the employer pays the employee share of social security and Medicare taxes, the additional payment must still be included in employee wages – but the wage increase is not subject to additional social security or Medicare taxes.

The Earned Income Credit

The earned income credit (EIC) is intended to provide a tax credit to working individuals and families at the low to moderate income level. The EIC provides an incentive to work, and also partially offsets the burden of social security taxes. The information in this section regarding the EIC is provided for the 2015 tax year, since the IRS has not provided updated information since that year. The following are the qualifications that a person must meet in order to qualify for the EIC:

- Adjusted gross income must be less than:
  - $47,747 ($53,267 for married filing jointly) if there are three or more qualifying children
  - $44,454 ($49,974 for married filing jointly) if there are two qualifying children
  - $39,131 ($44,651 for married filing jointly) if there is one qualifying child
  - $14,820 ($20,330 for married filing jointly) if there is no qualifying child
- Have a valid social security number
- Cannot file as "married filing separately"
- Must be a U.S. citizen or resident alien for the entire year
- Cannot file Form 2555 or Form 2555-EZ (related to foreign earned income)
- Investment income must be $3,400 or less

- Must have "earned" income, of which examples are wages, net earnings from self-employment, strike benefits, and taxable disability benefits
- Children meet the relationship, age, residency, and joint return tests, which are:
    o *Relationship test.* A child must be a son, daughter, stepchild, foster child, brother, sister, half-brother, half-sister, stepbrother, stepsister, or a descendant of any of them.
    o *Age test.* A child must be under age 19 at the end of the year, or under age 24 if a student, or any age if permanently and totally disabled.
    o *Residency test.* A child must have lived with the individual in the United States for more than half of the year.
    o *Joint return test.* A child cannot file a joint return for the year.
- A qualifying child cannot be used by more than one person to claim the EIC
- The person filing cannot be a qualifying child of another person

If the filing person does not have any qualifying children, he or she must meet the following rules in order to claim the EIC:
- Must be at least age 25 but under age 65
- Cannot be the dependent of another person
- Cannot be a qualifying child of another person
- Must have lived in the United States for more than half of the year

The normal method by which an individual calculates the EIC is to fill in all lines on the Form 1040 tax return that apply to the EIC, and let the IRS calculate it. It is also possible to manually calculate the EIC based on tables included in the back of IRS Publication 596, *Earned Income Credit.*

How does the EIC impact payroll? After all, it is the responsibility of an individual to file for the EIC. The following tip clarifies the role of the employer in the EIC.

Tip: The IRS mandates that the employer must notify employees who have no federal income tax withheld that they may be able to claim a tax refund due to the EIC. The easiest way to meet this requirement is to issue the year-end Form W-2 to employees with the EIC notice printed on the back of Copy B. An alternative is to provide Notice 797, Possible Federal Tax Refund Due to the Earned Income Credit, or a company-issued statement that provides the same text.

Tax Deductions for the Self-Employed Person

A self-employed person is responsible for deducting both the employee and employer portions of the social security and Medicare taxes. A self-employed person is assumed to operate under either a sole proprietorship or partnership business structure.

Use the following steps to determine the correct deduction amount for a self-employed person:

1. Calculate the gross income of the business.
2. Subtract from the gross income all allowable business deductions (essentially all operating expenses). This yields the net income of the sole proprietorship or partnership.
3. Calculate the person's share of the net income. This should be 100% of the net income of a sole proprietorship, or a reduced distribution under the operating agreement that governs a partnership. This share is taxable, whether or not it is actually distributed to the person.
4. Multiply the person's share of net income by 15.3% to arrive at the payroll tax deduction. The 15.3% figure is comprised of 12.4% for the social security tax and 2.9% for the Medicare tax.

> **Note:** It is not necessary to report the results of self-employment income if it is less than $400.00 per year.

EXAMPLE

Robert Franklin is one of two members of a partnership, in which net income is split evenly between the partners. The business earns $400,000 of gross income in 2016, and incurs $150,000 of expenses. This leaves $250,000 to be split evenly between the two partners, so Mr. Franklin's share is $125,000. This amount is subject to the $118,500 social security wage cap, so his social security tax deduction is $14,694.00 (calculated as $118,500 × 12.4%) and his Medicare tax deduction is $3,625.00 (calculated as $125,000 × 2.9%).

The Common Paymaster Rule

When a parent company owns a number of subsidiary entities, there is a possibility that employees will transfer between the various subsidiaries during a calendar year. If so, and payroll is computed at each individual subsidiary, and the transferring employees are paid more than the social security wage cap, too much of the social security tax will be deducted from their pay, and the company as a whole will match all of that extra deduction. This is a problem for the employee, who is having too much tax deducted, and for the company, which is incurring an excessive payroll expense. Though an employee can recover the excess amount deducted, the employer cannot do so.

EXAMPLE

Milford Sound, the audio equipment company, has two subsidiaries, Puget Sound and Long Island Sound. Mr. Arnold Saxon works for the Puget Sound subsidiary from January 1 to June 30 of 2016 as the division manager and is paid compensation of $100,000 during that time. He then transfers to the Long Island Sound subsidiary and works there from July 1 to December 31 of 2016, earning another $100,000. The payroll department of the Puget Sound subsidiary deducts $6,200 from his pay and the payroll department of the Long Island Sound subsidiary does the same. Since the 2016 social security wage cap is $118,500, the maximum amount that should have been deducted from his pay is $7,347, rather than the $12,400 that was actually deducted. Mr. Saxon can apply for a return of the excess $5,053 deducted from his pay, but Milford Sound cannot recover the matching amount of $5,053 that it also paid.

If a business experiences this problem and is organized as a corporation, it can take advantage of the common paymaster rule to eliminate the excess amount of taxes paid. Under this rule, the parent company calculates payroll taxes for any employees being paid by more than one subsidiary as though they are being paid by a single entity for the entire calendar year. To do so, the parent company designates one entity within its group of controlled businesses to pay the employees. This designated entity is called the *common paymaster*.

The common paymaster is responsible not only for paying designated employees, but also for maintaining the payroll records for them. It is allowable for the common paymaster to pay an employee with a single paycheck, despite that person working for multiple entities, or it may pay them with separate checks that are drawn on the bank accounts or the entities for which an employee works. The common paymaster's administrative duties also include remitting payroll taxes to the government.

Note: The only risk involved in using the common paymaster rule is that all subsidiaries using a common paymaster are jointly and severally liable for their shares of payroll taxes to be remitted. Thus, if one subsidiary were to fall behind on its payroll tax remittances to the government, the government could force a different subsidiary to pay the overdue amount.

In order to qualify for the common paymaster rule, a business must meet *all* of the following conditions:
- The parties paying employees must be related, where:
  - One company owns at least half the stock of the other related companies; or
  - At least 30% of the employees of one company must be concurrently employed by the other company; or
  - At least half of the officers of one company must be officers of the other company.

- If a company is a non-stock corporation, at least half of the board of directors of one company must serve on the board of directors of the other company.
- All payments made to employees must be made through a single legal entity. This means that an employee cannot be individually paid by more than one payroll department within the same company.

> **Tip:** To make the last of the preceding requirements effective, it makes sense to consolidate all payroll departments within the entire business entity to the greatest extent possible.

The common paymaster rule is also effective for paying the employees of a newly-acquired company. See the next section.

Payroll Taxes for a Successor Employer

The problems just noted for a multi-subsidiary company also arise in an acquisition, since the employees of the acquiree may switch to being employees of the acquirer, and experience an excessive amount of social security deductions. The IRS has a successor employer rule for this scenario, under which the acquiring entity can include the wages previously paid by the acquiree in its calculation of the remaining social security tax for the employees of the acquiree. The rule applies if the acquirer has acquired substantially all of the assets of the acquiree.

EXAMPLE

Ms. Andrea Price is the marketing director of Spade Designs, which is bought by Mole Industries. Ms. Price received compensation of $50,000 from Spade during 2016 and prior to the acquisition by Mole Industries. Subsequent to the acquisition, the payroll function is centralized at Mole, which then pays Ms. Price an additional $100,000 through the end of the calendar year. The wages that Mole pays Ms. Price are subject to the social security tax on the first $68,500 that it pays her. This amount is calculated as the social security wage cap for 2016 of $118,500, minus the $50,000 of wages already paid to her by Spade.

Payroll Taxes for Part-Time Employees

There is no difference in the taxation applied to someone who is considered a part-time employee versus someone who is classified as a full-time employee. The situation is the same for someone who is only hired for a short period of time, or who has another job in addition to the one with the employer.

State Payroll Taxes

Nearly all states have a state-level income tax. Those that do not are:

Alaska	New Hampshire	Texas
Florida	South Dakota	Washington
Nevada	Tennessee	Wyoming

The remaining 41 states use a variety of income tax rates and withholding allowance methods that require a detailed knowledge of the requirements of each state. This issue is mitigated from the perspective of income tax calculation if payroll is outsourced to a supplier, since they handle the calculations. However, a state may require a separate withholding allowance form than the federal Form W-4, which the company must have its employees complete.

When a company registers to do business in a state, doing so places the company on the state's mailing list of updates regarding business information, so there should be a steady stream of notices coming from the state regarding changes in tax rates and forms. In particular, each state will likely have its own wage bracket tables or percentage calculation methods that are similar in layout to the federal wage bracket tables (see the Calculating Withholdings section). The same information is usually also available on the secretary of state web site for each state.

One area of difficulty is when a company is registered to do business in one state, but some employees commute to work from their residences in other states. In these cases, the company usually must withhold income on behalf of the state of residence, not the state of employment. A more simplified approach that is allowed by some states is to withhold income taxes on behalf of the state in which the company operates, and have employees claim an offsetting credit on their state tax returns.

Totalization Agreements

A totalization agreement is one in which the United States has an agreement with another country to eliminate dual taxation under their two social security systems. The agreement provides that employees pay social security taxes only to the country where they work. This means that any employees and employers who are subject to foreign social security taxes under a totalization agreement are exempt from both United States social security and Medicare taxes.

The United States has totalization agreements with the following countries:

Australia	France	Poland
Austria	Germany	Portugal
Belgium	Greece	Slovak Republic
Canada	Ireland	South Korea
Chile	Italy	Spain
Czech Republic	Japan	Sweden
Denmark	Luxembourg	Switzerland
Finland	Netherlands	United Kingdom
	Norway	

Summary

Realistically, most of the types of employee earnings and tax deduction calculation methods noted in this chapter will arise only at infrequent intervals, if at all. When in doubt regarding whether a wage situation calls for a withholding, contact the IRS directly at 800-829-4933. Another potential source of information is the employer's payroll processor (if payroll processing is being outsourced), or this book, or Publication 15, *Employer's Tax Guide*, which the IRS revises annually.

Chapter 8
Tax Remittances

Introduction

An employer has a legal obligation to forward to the government all income taxes that it has withheld from employee pay, as well as social security and Medicare taxes. These remittances must be forwarded to the government in accordance with a specific payment schedule and method that is described in the following sections. In this chapter, we review when tax deposits should be made, how to remit funds, related reporting requirements, and a variety of rules related to tax remittances.

If an employer were to miss a timely remittance, or pay an insufficient amount, the related penalty would be severe. For this reason alone, it is important to have a detailed understanding of tax remittances.

Types of Tax Deposit Schedules

There are two deposit schedules, known as the *monthly deposit schedule* and the *semiweekly deposit schedule*, that state when to deposit payroll taxes. Which of these deposit schedules will be followed must be determined before the beginning of each calendar year. The selection of a deposit schedule is based entirely on the tax liability reported during a *lookback period*.

The deposit schedule is based on the total taxes (i.e., federal income taxes withheld, social security taxes, and Medicare taxes) reported in line 8 of the Forms 941 in a four-quarter lookback period. The lookback period begins on July 1 and ends on June 30. The decision tree for selecting a deposit period is:

- If the employer reported $50,000 or less of taxes during the lookback period, use the monthly deposit schedule.
- If the employer reported more than $50,000 of taxes during the lookback period, use the semiweekly deposit schedule.

Note: Do not select a deposit schedule based on how often the employer pays employees or make deposits. It is solely based on the total tax liability reported during the lookback period.

EXAMPLE

Norrona Software had used the monthly deposit schedule in previous years, but its payroll expanded considerably in the past year, which may place it in the semiweekly deposit schedule. Norrona's payroll manager calculates the amount of taxes paid during its lookback period to see if the semiweekly deposit schedule now applies. The calculation is:

Lookback Period	Taxes Paid
July 1 – September 30, 2016	$8,250
October 1 – December 31, 2016	14,750
January 1 – March 31, 2016	17,500
April 1 – June 30, 2017	19,000
Total	$59,500

Since the total amount of taxes that Norrona paid during the lookback period exceeded $50,000, the company must use the semiweekly deposit schedule during the next calendar year.

The specific payment schedules for the monthly and semiweekly deposit schedules are addressed in the next two sections.

Tip: A new employer has no lookback period, and so is automatically considered a monthly schedule depositor for its first calendar year of business.

The schedule for depositing state withholding taxes varies by state. Consult with the applicable state government for this deposit schedule. If payroll processing is outsourced, the supplier will handle these deposits on the employer's behalf.

Monthly Deposit Schedule

If a business qualifies to use the monthly deposit schedule, deposit employment taxes on payments made during a month by the 15th day of the following month.

EXAMPLE

Quest Clothiers is a monthly schedule depositor that pays its staff on the 15th and last business day of each month. Under the monthly deposit schedule, Quest must deposit the combined tax liabilities for all of its payrolls in a month by the 15th day of the following month. The same deposit schedule would apply if Quest had instead paid its employees every day, every other week, twice a month, once a month, or on any other payroll schedule.

The total payroll taxes withheld for each of Quest's payrolls in September are noted in the following table, along with the amount of its tax liability that will be due for remittance to the government on October 15:

Tax Remittances

	Federal Income Tax Withheld	Social Security Tax Withheld	Medicare Tax Withheld
Sept. 15 payroll	$1,500.00	$620.00	$145.00
Sept. 30 payroll	1,250.00	558.00	130.50
Sept. total withheld	$2,750.00	$1,178.00	$275.50
Employer tax matching	--	1,178.00	275.50
Tax deposit due Oct. 15	$2,750.00	$2,356.00	$551.00

Quest's tax liability to be remitted on October 15 is $5,657.00, which is calculated as the total of all withholdings and employer matches for federal income taxes, social security taxes, and Medicare taxes ($2,750.00 + $2,356.00 + $551.00).

Semiweekly Deposit Schedule

If an employer qualifies to use the semiweekly deposit schedule, remit payroll taxes using the following table:

Payment Date	Corresponding Deposit Date
Wednesday, Thursday, or Friday	Following Wednesday
Saturday, Sunday, Monday, Tuesday	Following Friday

If an employer has more than one pay date during a semiweekly period and the pay dates fall in different calendar quarters, make separate deposits for the liabilities associated with each pay date.

EXAMPLE

Norrona Software has a pay date on Wednesday, June 29 (second quarter) and another pay date on Friday, July 1 (third quarter). Norrona must make a separate deposit for the taxes associated with each pay date, even though both dates fall within the same semiweekly period. Norrona should pay both deposits on the following Wednesday, July 6.

EXAMPLE

Nascent Corporation uses the semiweekly deposit schedule. The company only pays its employees once a month, on the last day of the month. Although Nascent is on a semiweekly deposit schedule, it can only make a deposit once a month, since it only pays its employees once a month.

Note that the semiweekly deposit method does not mean that an employer is required to make two tax deposits per week – it is simply the name of the method.

Thus, if a company has one payroll every other week, it would remit taxes only every other week.

The differentiating factor between the monthly and semiweekly deposit schedules is that an employer must remit taxes much more quickly under the semiweekly method. The monthly method uses a simpler and more delayed tax deposit schedule, which is ideal for smaller businesses.

Federal Unemployment Deposit Schedule

The federal unemployment tax is to be deposited on a quarterly basis. The deposit dates are:

Relevant Calendar Quarter	Last Possible Deposit Date
First quarter of the calendar year	April 30
Second quarter of the calendar year	July 31
Third quarter of the calendar year	October 31
Fourth quarter of the calendar year	January 31

$100,000 Next-Day Deposit Rule

The $100,000 next-day deposit rule overrides both the monthly and semiweekly deposit schedules. This rule states that, if an employer accumulates $100,000 or more in taxes on any day during a monthly or semiweekly deposit period, it must deposit the amount by the next business day. The rule does not apply if there is an incremental increase in a tax liability *after* the end of a deposit period.

EXAMPLE

Norrona Software pays a large bonus to its CEO on a Friday, which results in a $120,000 tax liability. The company should deposit the $120,000 by the next business day, which is the following Monday.

EXAMPLE

Norrona Software is a semiweekly schedule depositor, and accumulates a $90,000 tax liability through a Tuesday, which it must deposit on the following Friday. Norrona then accumulates another $15,000 tax liability on Wednesday. The company should pay the $90,000 deposit on Friday, and the $15,000 deposit on the following Wednesday, in accordance with the normal semiweekly deposit schedule.

EXAMPLE

Puller Corporation is a semiweekly schedule depositor. Through the period Saturday through Monday, it accumulates taxes of $108,000, and is required to deposit on the following business day, which is Tuesday. On Tuesday, Puller accumulates an additional $25,000 of taxes. Puller can deposit this residual $25,000 amount on the following Friday, which is the regularly-scheduled deposit date under the semiweekly deposit schedule.

Note: If an employer is on a monthly deposit schedule, and accumulates a $100,000 tax liability on any day, it automatically shifts to the semiweekly deposit schedule on the following day, and remains on that schedule through the remainder of that calendar year, as well as for the following calendar year.

Accuracy of Deposits Rule

The entire tax liability must be deposited no later than the deposit due date. However, if an amount is deposited that is slightly less than the total tax liability, there will be no penalty as long as both of the following conditions are met:
- The shortfall does not exceed the greater of $100 or 2% of the total amount of taxes that should have been deposited; and
- The shortfall is deposited by the makeup date.

The *makeup date* for a deposit shortfall for a monthly schedule depositor is the due date of the next Form 941 quarterly federal tax return. The makeup date for a semiweekly schedule depositor is the earlier of the first Wednesday or Friday (whichever comes first) that falls on or after the 15th day of the month following the month in which the shortfall occurred, or the due date of the next Form 941 quarterly federal tax return.

Deposits not on Business Days

If the applicable deposit schedule mandates that a tax deposit be made on a day that is not a business day, it is acceptable to make the deposit by the close of the immediately following business day. A business day is considered to be any day other than a Saturday, Sunday, or legal holiday.

EXAMPLE

Norrona Software is required to make a tax deposit on a Friday, but that day is a national holiday. It is acceptable to the IRS if Norrona makes the deposit on the following Monday instead.

An employer using the semiweekly deposit schedule is always allowed at least three business days in which to make a tax deposit. Thus, if any of the three business days following a semiweekly period is a legal holiday, there will be an additional number of corresponding business days in which to make the deposit.

EXAMPLE

Norrona Software has a pay date on a Friday, and so would normally deposit taxes on the following Wednesday under the semiweekly deposit schedule. However, the following Monday is a legal holiday, so Norrona can instead make the deposit on the following Thursday, thereby allowing three business days in which to make the deposit.

In the United States, the following are all considered to be legal holidays, with their 2017 dates listed:

Holiday	Date in 2016
New Year's Day	January 2
Birthday of Martin Luther King, Jr.	January 16
Washington's Birthday	February 20
Memorial Day	May 29
Independence Day	July 4
Labor Day	September 4
Columbus Day	October 9
Veterans' Day	November 10
Thanksgiving Day	November 23
Christmas Day	December 25

Remittance Method

An employer must pay all federal tax deposits by electronic funds transfer. Use the Electronic Federal Tax Payment System (EFTPS) to make these deposits. EFTPS is a free service that is maintained by the Department of Treasury. EFTPS can be used directly or via an intermediary, such as the employer's payroll supplier (if payroll is outsourced) to deposit funds on the employer's behalf. Go to www.eftps.gov to enroll in EFTPS. If the employer is new, it will likely have been pre-enrolled in EFTPS when it applied for an employer identification number (EIN); if so, the company will receive a personal identification number for the EFTPS system as part of the initial EIN package of information.

Tip: If an employer is running late on making a tax deposit, use a financial institution to make a same-day wire payment on its behalf. The financial institution will likely charge a fee for this service.

In order to make an EFTPS deposit on time, initiate the deposit no later than 8 p.m. Eastern time the day before the date when the deposit is due.

When remitting taxes to the government, the remittance should include the following types of taxes:

- Withheld income taxes
- Withheld and matching employer social security taxes
- Withheld and matching employer Medicare taxes

When making a deposit, EFTPS will provide a deposit trace number, which can be used as a receipt or to trace the payment.

> **Tip:** If the company deposited too much, one can choose on the Form 941 for that quarter to either have the overpayment refunded or applied as a credit to the next quarterly return.

The Form 941 Quarterly Federal Tax Return

Following each calendar quarter, any employer that pays wages subject to income tax withholding, or social security and Medicare taxes, must file a Form 941, the Employer's Quarterly Federal Tax Return. The Form 941 must be filed by the last day of the month following the calendar quarter to which it applies. Thus, the filing dates for the Form 941 are:

Quarter Ending	Form 941 Due Date
March 31	April 30
June 30	July 31
September 30	October 31
December 31	January 31

An employer does not have to file a Form 941 under any of the following circumstances:

- *Agricultural workers.* If wages are paid to agricultural employees, report this information on Form 943, Employer's Annual Federal Tax return for Agricultural Employees.
- *Household employer.* If wages are paid to household employees, report this information on Schedule H of Form 1040, Household Employment Taxes.
- *Puerto Rico.* Employers based in Puerto Rico should use Form 941-PR.
- *Seasonal employer.* If there are calendar quarters where there is no tax liability because no wages were paid, check the "Seasonal employer" box on every Form 941 filed.
- *Withholding exemption.* If employees are exempt from income tax withholding, use Form 941-SS instead. If there is a mix of employees who are and

are not subject to income tax withholding, report their combined information on Form 941.

The following exhibit contains a sample of the Form 941, as completed by a semiweekly filer that has no unusual exceptions from the normal tax reporting. In the form, the filer is identifying the employer and the reporting period in the header block, calculating the amount of taxes to be deposited and the amount already deposited in Part 1, and describing the company's deposit schedule in Part 2. These are the key parts of the Form.

The form shown in the exhibit is sufficient for all employers on a monthly filing schedule. An employer on the semiweekly filing schedule must also add Schedule B to the form, which itemizes the dates on which all payroll tax liabilities were incurred during the calendar quarter. Schedule B is shown below. In some situations, an employer may need to make a payment alongside the Form 941. If so, complete Form 941-V, Payment Voucher, to document the amount of the payment. In the exhibit, we have not entered a payment amount in Form 941-V, since all deposits related to the calendar quarter were already made and listed in Schedule B.

Form 941, Employer's Quarterly Federal Tax Return

Form 941 for 2016: Employer's QUARTERLY Federal Tax Return
(Rev. January 2016) Department of the Treasury — Internal Revenue Service

950114
OMB No. 1545-0029

Employer identification number (EIN): 8 4 – 0 1 2 3 4 5 6

Name (not your trade name): Norrona Software

Trade name (if any):

Address: 123 Main Street
Number Street Suite or room number

Anywhere CO 80111
City State ZIP code

Foreign country name Foreign province/county Foreign postal code

Report for this Quarter of 2016
(Check one.)

[X] 1: January, February, March
[ ] 2: April, May, June
[ ] 3: July, August, September
[ ] 4: October, November, December

Instructions and prior year forms are available at www.irs.gov/form941.

Read the separate instructions before you complete Form 941. Type or print within the boxes.

Part 1: Answer these questions for this quarter.

1 Number of employees who received wages, tips, or other compensation for the pay period including: *Mar. 12* (Quarter 1), *June 12* (Quarter 2), *Sept. 12* (Quarter 3), or *Dec. 12* (Quarter 4) **1** 28

2 Wages, tips, and other compensation **2** 284000 . 00

3 Federal income tax withheld from wages, tips, and other compensation **3** 28400 . 00

4 If no wages, tips, and other compensation are subject to social security or Medicare tax [ ] Check and go to line 6.

	Column 1		Column 2	
5a Taxable social security wages	284000 . 00	× .124 =	29536 . 00
5b Taxable social security tips	.	× .124 =	.
5c Taxable Medicare wages & tips	284000 . 00	× .029 =	8236 . 00
5d Taxable wages & tips subject to Additional Medicare Tax withholding	.	× .009 =	.

5e Add Column 2 from lines 5a, 5b, 5c, and 5d **5e** 37772 . 00

5f Section 3121(q) Notice and Demand—Tax due on unreported tips (see instructions) **5f** .

6 Total taxes before adjustments. Add lines 3, 5e, and 5f **6** 66172 . 00

7 Current quarter's adjustment for fractions of cents **7** .

8 Current quarter's adjustment for sick pay **8** .

9 Current quarter's adjustments for tips and group-term life insurance **9** .

10 Total taxes after adjustments. Combine lines 6 through 9 **10** 66172 . 00

11 Total deposits for this quarter, including overpayment applied from a prior quarter and overpayments applied from Form 941-X, 941-X (PR), 944-X, or 944-X (SP) filed in the current quarter **11** 66172 . 00

12 Balance due. If line 10 is more than line 11, enter the difference and see instructions **12** .

13 Overpayment. If line 11 is more than line 10, enter the difference . Check one: [ ] Apply to next return. [ ] Send a refund.

▶ You MUST complete both pages of Form 941 and SIGN it. Next ➡

145

Form 941, Employer's Quarterly Federal Tax Return - continued

Name (not your trade name)	Employer identification number (EIN)
Norrona Software	84-0123456

Part 2: Tell us about your deposit schedule and tax liability for this quarter.

If you are unsure about whether you are a monthly schedule depositor or a semiweekly schedule depositor, see section 11 of Pub. 15.

14 Check one:

☐ Line 10 on this return is less than $2,500 or line 10 on the return for the prior quarter was less than $2,500, and you did not incur a $100,000 next-day deposit obligation during the current quarter. If line 10 for the prior quarter was less than $2,500 but line 10 on this return is $100,000 or more, you must provide a record of your federal tax liability. If you are a monthly schedule depositor, complete the deposit schedule below; if you are a semiweekly schedule depositor, attach Schedule B (Form 941). Go to Part 3.

☐ **You were a monthly schedule depositor for the entire quarter.** Enter your tax liability for each month and total liability for the quarter, then go to Part 3.

Tax liability: Month 1 ☐ .

Month 2 ☐ .

Month 3 ☐ .

Total liability for quarter ☐ . Total must equal line 10.

☐ **You were a semiweekly schedule depositor for any part of this quarter.** Complete Schedule B (Form 941), Report of Tax Liability for Semiweekly Schedule Depositors, and attach it to Form 941.

Part 3: Tell us about your business. If a question does NOT apply to your business, leave it blank.

15 If your business has closed or you stopped paying wages . . . . ☐ Check here, and

enter the final date you paid wages ☐ / / .

16 If you are a seasonal employer and you do not have to file a return for every quarter of the year . . ☐ Check here.

Part 4: May we speak with your third-party designee?

Do you want to allow an employee, a paid tax preparer, or another person to discuss this return with the IRS? See the instructions for details.

☒ Yes. Designee's name and phone number | John Smith | 303-238-1234

Select a 5-digit Personal Identification Number (PIN) to use when talking to the IRS. ☐ ☐ ☐ ☐ ☐

☐ No.

Part 5: Sign here. You MUST complete both pages of Form 941 and SIGN it.

Under penalties of perjury, I declare that I have examined this return, including accompanying schedules and statements, and to the best of my knowledge and belief, it is true, correct, and complete. Declaration of preparer (other than taxpayer) is based on all information of which preparer has any knowledge.

X Sign your name here

Print your name here | Arlo Jones
Print your title here | Controller

Date / /

Best daytime phone | 303-238-1234

Paid Preparer Use Only	Check if you are self-employed . . . ☐
Preparer's name	PTIN
Preparer's signature	Date / /
Firm's name (or yours if self-employed)	EIN
Address	Phone
City	State	ZIP code

Form **941** (Rev. 1-2016)

Tax Remittances

Form 941, Employer's Quarterly Federal Tax Return – Schedule B

Schedule B (Form 941):

Report of Tax Liability for Semiweekly Schedule Depositors

960311

OMB No. 1545-0029

(Rev. January 2014)   Department of the Treasury — Internal Revenue Service

Employer identification number (EIN): 8 4 – 0 1 2 3 4 5 6

Name (not your trade name): Norrona Software

Calendar year: 2 0 1 6   (Also check quarter)

Report for this Quarter...
(Check one.)

[X] 1: January, February, March
[ ] 2: April, May, June
[ ] 3: July, August, September
[ ] 4: October, November, December

Use this schedule to show your TAX LIABILITY for the quarter; DO NOT use it to show your deposits. When you file this form with Form 941 or Form 941-SS, DO NOT change your tax liability by adjustments reported on any Forms 941-X or 944-X. You must fill out this form and attach it to Form 941 or Form 941-SS if you are a semiweekly schedule depositor or became one because your accumulated tax liability on any day was $100,000 or more. Write your daily tax liability on the numbered space that corresponds to the date wages were paid. See Section 11 in Pub. 15 (Circular E), Employer's Tax Guide, for details.

Month 1

Tax liability for Month 1: 19250 . 00

15: 9625 . 00
23: 9625 . 00

Month 2

Tax liability for Month 2: 20050 . 00

20: 10025 . 00
15: 10025 . 00

Month 3

Tax liability for Month 3: 26872 . 00

15: 13436 . 00
31: 13436 . 00

Fill in your total liability for the quarter (Month 1 + Month 2 + Month 3) ▶
Total must equal line 10 on Form 941 or Form 941-SS.

Total liability for the quarter: 66172 . 00

For Paperwork Reduction Act Notice, see separate instructions.   IRS.gov/form941   Cat. No. 11967Q   Schedule B (Form 941) (Rev. 1-2014)

Form 941-V, Payment Voucher

Form 941-V	**Payment Voucher**	OMB No. 1545-0029
Department of the Treasury Internal Revenue Service	▶ Don't staple this voucher or your payment to Form 941.	**2016**

1 Enter your employer identification number (EIN). 84-0123456	2 **Enter the amount of your payment.** ▶ Make your check or money order payable to "United States Treasury"	Dollars	Cents

3 Tax Period	4 Enter your business name (individual name if sole proprietor).
⦿ 1st Quarter ◯ 3rd Quarter ◯ 2nd Quarter ◯ 4th Quarter	Norrona Software Enter your address. 123 Main Street Enter your city, state, and ZIP code or your city, foreign country name, foreign province/county, and foreign postal code. Anywhere, CO 80111

> **Note:** In some cases, the IRS allows an employer to file the Form 944, Employer's Annual Federal Tax Return, instead of the quarterly Form 941. If a firm qualifies for the Form 944, file it by the last day of the month following the end of the year.

An employer is allowed to make a tax deposit with the Form 941 filing instead of a normal tax deposit without incurring a penalty under either of the following two conditions:

- The total Form 941 tax liability for the current or preceding quarter is less than $2,500 and the company did not incur a $100,000 next-day deposit obligation during the current quarter.
- The employer is a monthly schedule depositor and makes a payment in accordance with the accuracy of deposits rule (see the preceding Accuracy of Deposits Rule section).

If an employer goes out of business, file a final return for the last quarter in which wages were paid.

If an employer does not file a Form 941 in a timely manner (not including filing extensions), the IRS imposes a failure-to-file penalty of 5% of the unpaid tax due with that return, up to a maximum penalty of 25% of the tax due. In addition, for each whole month or part of a month that is paid late, there is an additional failure-to-pay penalty of ½% of the amount of the tax, up to a maximum of 25% of the tax due. If both penalties apply in a month, the failure-to-file penalty is reduced by the amount of the failure-to-pay penalty. The IRS may waive these penalties if one can present a reasonable cause for failing to file the Form 941 or pay the tax due.

Form 941 Discrepancies

If there are discrepancies between the information in an employer's quarterly Form 941 and the Forms W-2 issued to employees following the calendar year-end, the IRS may contact the employer to resolve the discrepancies. To avoid this reconciliation, consider using one or more of the following preventive measures:

- *Bonuses*. Report bonuses as wages and as social security and Medicare wages on Forms W-2 and 941.

- *EIN*. If an EIN was entered on any Form 941 during the year that was different from the EIN used on the Form W-3, enter this alternative EIN on Form W-3 in the box for "Other EIN used this year."
- *Medicare taxes*. Do not report the employee share of Medicare taxes on Form W-2 as Medicare wages, but rather in the box for Medicare tax withheld.
- *Noncash wages*. Do not report noncash wages that are not subject to social security or Medicare taxes as social security or Medicare wages.
- *Reconcile Form W-3 to Form 941*. Match the amounts on the Form W-3 to the four quarterly Forms 941.
- *Reconcile Form W-3 to Forms W-2*. Match the amounts on the Form W-3 to the total amounts from Forms W-2.
- *Social security taxes*. Do not report the employee share of social security taxes on Form W-2 as social security wages, but rather in the box for social security tax withheld.
- *Wage base limit*. Verify that the social security withholdings for employees did not exceed the wage base limit for that year.

The key issue with these preventive measures is to ensure that the totals on the Forms W-2 summarize up into the totals on the Form W-3, and that these totals match the amounts on the Forms 941. Doing so ensures that the complete package of payroll reports is internally consistent.

> **Tip:** If there is a valid reason why the amounts on the Forms W-2, W-3, and 941 do not match, construct a reconciliation of the differences, which is useful in case the government asks about the discrepancy.

For detailed explanations of the Forms W-2 and W-3, see the Payroll Reports chapter.

Prior Period Adjustments

When an error is detected on a Form 941 or Form 944 that had been filed on an earlier date, correct the error on a Form 941-X or Form 944-X, respectively. File a separate Form 941-X or Form 944-X for each original filing that is being corrected. Use the Form 941-X even for corrections to Forms 941 that were filed within the current calendar year.

In a situation where corrections are being made for both over reported and underreported amounts and the employer is also requesting a refund, file a separate report for the over reported amounts and another for the underreported amounts. Using this approach allows one to maximize the amount of refund claimed.

If an employee repays the employer for wages that he or she received in error, do not offset the repayments against current-year wages unless the repayments are for amounts that were received in error within the current calendar year. Follow these correction rules for reporting wage repayments:

- *Current year wage repayment.* If the employer receives the repayment of wages that were paid during a prior quarter of the current year, report the adjustment on Form 941-X. This recovers the income tax withholding and social security and Medicare taxes on the repaid wages.
- *Prior year wage repayment.* If the employer receives the repayment of wages that were paid during a prior year, report the adjustment on either Form 941-X or 944-X. This recovers the social security and Medicare taxes, but not the income tax withholding. The employer must also file Forms W-2c and W-3c with the Social Security Administration to correct social security and Medicare wages and taxes.

Federal Tax Deposit Penalties

An employer can be penalized if it makes a tax deposit too late, or in an amount that is less than the required amount. The penalties are:

Penalty Amount	Description
2%	Deposits are made 1 to 5 days late.
5%	Deposits are made 6 to 15 days late.
10%	Deposits are made more than 15 days late. Also applicable for amounts paid within 10 days of the first IRS notice date regarding a tax due.
10%	Deposits are paid directly to the IRS or paid with the employer's tax return.
15%	Amounts still unpaid more than 10 days after the date of the first IRS notice date regarding a tax due, or the date of receipt of a demand for immediate payment.

The IRS calculates penalties using calendar days, beginning on the due date of the tax liability.

Tip: An employer can receive a penalty waiver if a deposit problem was caused by a reasonable cause and not willful neglect. A business may also receive a waiver if it did not make a deposit in the first quarter when it was required to deposit unemployment tax, or in the first quarter when its frequency of deposits changed.

In addition to the penalties just noted, the IRS also charges interest on the unpaid tax balance from the date when it was due for remittance to the government. The IRS formulates the interest rate as follows:

- *Underpayment.* The interest rate is the federal short-term rate plus three percentage points.

- *Underpayment by large corporate filers.* The interest rate is the federal short-term rate plus five percentage points.

EXAMPLE

Spud Potato Farms does not remit payroll taxes of $10,000 for September (due October 15) until November 20. Thus, the deposit is made 35 days late. Spud has not received a tax due notice from the IRS. The IRS assesses the following failure to pay penalty against Spud:

Failure to pay tax ($10,000 × 10%)	=	$1,000.00
Interest on taxes due ($10,000 × 5% × 35/365)	=	47.95
Total penalty =		$1,047.95

The official IRS interest rate during the penalty period was 5%.

The IRS applies deposits to the most recent tax liability within a quarter, which tends to leave older liabilities still outstanding, if an employer had not paid the entire amount of a liability at an earlier date. If an organization receives a failure-to-deposit notice from the IRS, it can designate how to apply the deposits, thereby minimizing the amount of the penalty. An employer can only make this designation if it does so within 90 days of the date of the IRS notice.

EXAMPLE

Norrona Software is supposed to make a $20,000 tax deposit on August 15 and another deposit of $22,500 on September 15. Norrona inadvertently does not pay the $20,000 that was due on August 15. On September 15, Norrona deposits $30,000. Using the deposits rule, the IRS applies $22,500 of this deposit to the amount due on September 15, and the remaining $7,500 to the August deposit. This leaves $12,500 of the June liability undeposited.

Tip: To avoid a penalty, do not adjust the tax liability on Form 941 to account for prior period errors. Instead, file an adjusted return for these errors on Form 941-X.

Trust Fund Recovery Penalty

If an employer does not deposit the federal income, social security, and Medicare taxes that it owes to the United States Treasury, the government can apply the trust fund recovery penalty. This penalty is the full amount of the tax owed. It can apply to individuals if the government cannot collect the applicable taxes from the business. The trust fund recovery penalty is an enormous issue, since employees can be held personally liable for unpaid taxes owed by the business.

The IRS can impose the trust fund recovery penalty on anyone to whom both of the following circumstances apply:

- The person is responsible for collecting, accounting for, and paying the taxes. The IRS defines this person as an officer or employee of a business, an accountant, or a volunteer director or trustee. It can also include anyone who signs checks for the business, or who has the authority to cause the spending of business funds.
- The person acted willfully (i.e., voluntarily, consciously, and intentionally) in not paying the taxes. Such a person knows the required actions are not taking place, and either intentionally disregarded the law or was indifferent to its requirements.

The IRS can take collection action against a person's personal assets under this penalty, including such actions as a federal tax lien or the seizure of assets.

Note: The trust fund recovery penalty has that name because an employer holds employee's money in trust until it pays the funds to the government with a tax deposit.

EXAMPLE

Mr. Arlan Spud is running short of cash to run his business, Spud Potato Farms, of which he is the president, and uses unremitted payroll taxes to pay his other creditors. This action falls within the IRS definition of acting willfully to not deposit taxes, and leaves Mr. Spud personally liable for the trust fund recovery penalty.

State Tax Remittances

Each state government has its own system for reporting and depositing state-level payroll taxes. The types of taxes can vary from those collected at the federal level, and may include the following:

- State income tax
- Unemployment insurance tax
- Disability insurance tax
- Special district taxes (such as for a transportation district)

The forms used to report this information vary by state. The primary reports that may be required are:

- *Reconciliation statement.* Compares the amount of state taxes remitted to the amount withheld from employee pay.
- *Tax withholdings.* Reports wages paid to employees, and the state taxes withheld from their pay.

Most state governments provide preprinted tax remittance and reporting forms to those employers registered to do business within their boundaries. If an employer outsources its payroll, the supplier is responsible for completing and submitting these forms.

The required remittance dates also vary by state, as do the modes of payment – either check or electronic payments may be required. In some cases, an employer can choose between modes of payment, though it is customary to require electronic payment for all future payments, once an employer has switched to that type of payment.

Each state government publishes an explanatory guide to its tax structure, in which it describes the state's reporting and remittance system. These guides are usually also available online as PDF documents or web pages.

Local Tax Remittances

Some city and county governments impose their own payroll taxes. These taxes are usually in the form of licenses or headcount fees, but may occasionally also be income tax withholdings. In these situations, the employer must fill out a form and remit the designated amounts to the applicable city or county government. The remittance schedule and form of payment is designated by the recipient government. If an employer outsources its payroll, the supplier is responsible for reporting and remitting these taxes.

Summary

Tax remittances and the penalties resulting from an incorrect (or missing) filing are among the chief annoyances of the payroll manager. These can be mitigated by imposing a strict procedural regimen for every tax deposit. One can also tie staff bonuses to the reduction of remittance errors, and include remittance problems in the performance reviews of the payroll staff. If these measures do not improve the situation, consider outsourcing payroll processing; doing so shifts the tax remittance problem to the payroll supplier, which is presumably structured to efficiently process remittances with a high degree of accuracy.

Chapter 9
Unemployment Taxes

Introduction

The federal and state governments of the United States provide unemployment compensation to workers who have lost their jobs. This compensation is paid for primarily by employers, who pay both federal and state unemployment taxes. This chapter describes when an employer should pay unemployment taxes, how to calculate and remit the tax, and how to report it to the government. It also addresses the possibility of reducing costs with voluntary unemployment tax payments, as well as how to transfer an unemployment experience rating.

Responsibility for Unemployment Tax Payments

An employer is responsible for the payment of federal unemployment taxes (FUTA) if any of the following tests apply:

- *General test.* It paid wages of at least $1,500 in any calendar quarter in 2015 or 2016, or it had one or more employees for some portion of a day in at least 20 weeks in 2015 or in at least 20 weeks in 2016. This test does not apply to farmworkers or household workers.
- *Farmworkers test.* It paid cash wages of at least $20,000 to farmworkers during any calendar quarter in 2015 or 2016, or employed at least 10 farmworkers for some portion of a day in at least 20 weeks in 2015 or in at least 20 weeks in 2016.
- *Household employees test.* It paid total cash wages of at least $1,000 to household employees in any calendar quarter in 2015 or 2016. A household employee is an employee who performs household work in a private home, local college club, or local fraternity or sorority chapter.

The employer is responsible for FUTA taxes only for those employees falling into the preceding categories for which the employer is liable.

EXAMPLE

Aardvark Industries, maker of bulletproof upholstery, is only open for business when there are firm, prepaid orders for its very expensive upholstery products. Upon receipt of these orders, Aardvark farms out the work to a network of local stay-at-home parents who stitch together the materials and forward the completed goods back to the company for final assembly. Aardvark was founded in the immediately preceding year, when the owner worked for no wages for three months while he designed the product. In the fourth quarter, there was only one order, which required the payment of $1,200 in wages. Thus, Aardvark had no FUTA liability in that year.

In the next year, Aardvark received an increasing stream of orders, resulting in it surpassing both the wage and time thresholds of the general FUTA test. Aardvark is liable for FUTA taxes in the next year.

FUTA Tax Calculation

After June 2011, the FUTA tax rate is 6.0% (it was 6.2% prior to that date). Calculate the FUTA tax based on only the first $7,000 paid to each employee in the form of wages during the year (i.e., there is no FUTA tax on wages higher than $7,000 in each calendar year). Then subtract a credit from the FUTA tax for the amount of tax paid into the state unemployment tax fund. The maximum (and most common) amount of this credit is 5.4%, which means that the actual amount of FUTA tax is only 0.6% (after June 2011).

> **Tip:** When constructing the annual budget, be sure to calculate the FUTA tax to appear in the first calendar quarter of the year. Most employees have exceeded the maximum $7,000 cap on wages applicable to the FUTA tax by the end of that quarter. However, if there is an intention to hire new employees later in the year, budget FUTA tax for them that begins as of their first pay date.

EXAMPLE

Genomic Research has 100 employees, all of whom earn more than $100,000 per year. Thus, they all earn more than the $7,000 FUTA wage cap in the first quarter of the year. Within the first quarter, Genomic has $700,000 of wages eligible for the FUTA tax (calculated as 100 employees × $7,000). Its FUTA tax liability is the 6.0% federal rate minus the 5.4% state rate, multiplied by the $700,000 of eligible wages. Genomic's FUTA tax liability is therefore $4,200 (calculated as $700,000 eligible wages × 0.6%).

FUTA Tax Deposits

FUTA taxes must be remitted on a quarterly basis. If the total amount of tax payable is less than $500 in any quarter, an employer can opt to carry the liability forward to the next quarter. One may continue to roll the liability forward through additional quarters if the liability remains less than $500.

If the amount of FUTA tax liability is $500 or more, the company may pay it by electronic funds transfer. A third party can do this by prior arrangement, or the funds can be remitted through the Electronic Federal Tax Payment (EFTPS) system. Consult the EFTPS website at www.eftps.gov for information about this payment system. When an EFTPS remittance is made, the system issues an electronic funds transfer trace number, which can be used as evidence of payment.

An employer may also pay with a credit card or debit card. See the irs.gov/e-pay site for more information.

FUTA Tax Payment Timing

The FUTA tax must be remitted by the end of the last day of the month immediately following the end of a calendar quarter. If that date falls on a weekend or holiday, remit the tax on the next business day. In order to qualify for a timely remittance, pay into the EFTPS system by 8 p.m. Eastern time on the designated due date. The due dates for each quarter are noted in the following table:

FUTA Remittance Due Dates

Quarter	Ending Date	Due Date
Jan. – Feb. – Mar.	March 31	April 30
Apr. – May – Jun.	June 30	July 31
Jul. – Aug. – Sep.	September 30	October 31
Oct. – Nov. – Dec.	December 31	January 31

If funds are not remitted in accordance with the IRS remittance schedule, an employer may be subject to a 10% penalty for failure to deposit on time.

FUTA Tax Reporting

An employer should report the FUTA liability and remittances for the preceding year on Form 940, Employer's Annual Federal Unemployment Tax Return. The filing date for the Form 940 is January 31 of the next year. If all FUTA taxes are deposited when due, an employer may file the Form 940 as late as February 10 of the next year.

A sample of the Form 940 is shown on the following two pages.

State Unemployment Taxes

Each state has its own unemployment insurance program, which evaluates unemployment claims and administers the payment of benefits to individuals. Each of the states has its own rules regarding who is eligible for unemployment benefits, the amounts to be paid, and the duration of those payments, within guidelines set by the federal government.

State governments impose a state-level unemployment tax on employers that can be quite high – even more than the 5.4% credit allowed under FUTA, as noted earlier. A state typically assigns a relatively high default tax rate to a new business, and then subsequently adjusts that rate based on the history of unemployment claims made by employees of the business (known as the *experience rating*). If a business rarely lays off its staff, it will eventually be assigned a lower tax rate, with the reverse being true for a business with an uneven employment record.

States mail unemployment rate notices for the upcoming year to businesses near the end of the current calendar year. Include the tax rate noted on the form in the employer's payroll calculations for all of the following year.

156

Tip: If payroll is outsourced to a third party, forward the tax rate notice to that supplier. If the payroll staff forgets to do so, the supplier will likely contact the entity to request this information.

Form **940 for 2015:** Employer's Annual Federal Unemployment (FUTA) Tax Return
Department of the Treasury — Internal Revenue Service

850113
OMB No. 1545-0028

Employer identification number (EIN): 84-0123456

Name (not your trade name): Norrona Software

Trade name (if any):

Address: 123 Main Street

City: Anywhere   State: CO   ZIP code: 80111

Type of Return (Check all that apply.)
- a. Amended
- b. Successor employer
- c. No payments to employees in 2015
- d. Final: Business closed or stopped paying wages

Instructions and prior-year forms are available at www.irs.gov/form940.

Read the separate instructions before you complete this form. Please type or print within the boxes.

Part 1: Tell us about your return. If any line does NOT apply, leave it blank. See instructions before completing Part 1.

1a If you had to pay state unemployment tax in one state only, enter the state abbreviation . **1a** `C` `O`
1b If you had to pay state unemployment tax in more than one state, you are a multi-state employer . . . . . **1b** ☐ Check here. Complete Schedule A (Form 940).
2 If you paid wages in a state that is subject to CREDIT REDUCTION . . . . . **2** ☐ Check here. Complete Schedule A (Form 940).

Part 2: Determine your FUTA tax before adjustments. If any line does NOT apply, leave it blank.

3 Total payments to all employees **3** 1000000.00
4 Payments exempt from FUTA tax **4** 25000.00

Check all that apply: 4a ☐ Fringe benefits 4c ☐ Retirement/Pension 4e ☐ Other
4b ☐ Group-term life insurance 4d ☐ Dependent care
5 Total of payments made to each employee in excess of $7,000 . . . . . **5** 825000.00
6 Subtotal (line 4 + line 5 = line 6) **6** 850000.00
7 Total taxable FUTA wages (line 3 – line 6 = line 7) (see instructions) **7** 150000.00
8 FUTA tax before adjustments (line 7 x .006 = line 8) **8** 900.00

Part 3: Determine your adjustments. If any line does NOT apply, leave it blank.

9 If ALL of the taxable FUTA wages you paid were excluded from state unemployment tax, multiply line 7 by .054 (line 7 x .054 = line 9). Go to line 12 . . . . . **9** .
10 If SOME of the taxable FUTA wages you paid were excluded from state unemployment tax, OR you paid ANY state unemployment tax late (after the due date for filing Form 940), complete the worksheet in the instructions. Enter the amount from line 7 of the worksheet . . **10** .
11 If credit reduction applies, enter the total from Schedule A (Form 940) . . . . . **11** .

Part 4: Determine your FUTA tax and balance due or overpayment. If any line does NOT apply, leave it blank.

12 Total FUTA tax after adjustments (lines 8 + 9 + 10 + 11 = line 12) **12** 900.00
13 FUTA tax deposited for the year, including any overpayment applied from a prior year . **13** 900.00
14 Balance due (If line 12 is more than line 13, enter the excess on line 14.)
- If line 14 is more than $500, you must deposit your tax.
- If line 14 is $500 or less, you may pay with this return. (see instructions) . . . . . **14** .
15 Overpayment (If line 13 is more than line 12, enter the excess on line 15 and check a box below.) . . . . . **15** .
▶ You MUST complete both pages of this form and SIGN it. Check one: ☐ Apply to next return. ☐ Send a refund.

Next ▶

Name (not your trade name)	Employer identification number (EIN)
Norrona Software	84-123456

Part 5: Report your FUTA tax liability by quarter only if line 12 is more than $500. If not, go to Part 6.

16 Report the amount of your FUTA tax liability for each quarter; do NOT enter the amount you deposited. If you had no liability for a quarter, leave the line blank.

16a 1st quarter (January 1 – March 31)	16a	600 . 00
16b 2nd quarter (April 1 – June 30)	16b	200 . 00
16c 3rd quarter (July 1 – September 30)	16c	100 . 00
16d 4th quarter (October 1 – December 31)	16d	.

17 Total tax liability for the year (lines 16a + 16b + 16c + 16d = line 17) **17** 900 . 00 **Total must equal line 12.**

Part 6: May we speak with your third-party designee?

Do you want to allow an employee, a paid tax preparer, or another person to discuss this return with the IRS? See the instructions for details.

☐ Yes. Designee's name and phone number

Select a 5-digit Personal Identification Number (PIN) to use when talking to IRS

☐ No.

Part 7: Sign here. You MUST complete both pages of this form and SIGN it.

Under penalties of perjury, I declare that I have examined this return, including accompanying schedules and statements, and to the best of my knowledge and belief, it is true, correct, and complete, and that no part of any payment made to a state unemployment fund claimed as a credit was, or is to be, deducted from the payments made to employees. Declaration of preparer (other than taxpayer) is based on all information of which preparer has any knowledge.

X Sign your name here

Print your name here Joel Smith

Print your title here CEO

Date / /

Best daytime phone 303-123-4567

Paid Preparer Use Only Check if you are self-employed . ☐

Preparer's name		PTIN	
Preparer's signature		Date	/ /
Firm's name (or yours if self-employed)		EIN	
Address		Phone	
City	State	ZIP code	

Page **2** Form **940** (2015)

The wage base for state-level unemployment taxes can differ dramatically from the current $7,000 annual limit used for the calculation of the federal unemployment tax. The following table shows the amount of wages subject to state unemployment tax, as well as the range of the tax and the amount charged to a new employer, as of January 2015.

Summary of State Unemployment Taxes as of June 2016[1]

State	Wages Subject to Tax	Minimum Tax Rate	Maximum Tax Rate	New Employer Rate
Alabama	$8,000	0.65%	6.80%	2.70%
Alaska	39,700	1.00%	5.40%	1.69%
Arizona	7,000	0.03%	8.91%	2.00%
Arkansas	12,000	0.50%	14.40%	3.30%
California	7,000	1.50%	6.20%	3.40%
Colorado	12,200	0.77%	10.14%	2.12%
Connecticut	15,000	1.90%	6.80%	4.30%
Delaware	18,500	0.30%	8.20%	1.90%
District of Columbia	9,000	1.60%	7.00%	2.70%
Florida	7,000	0.10%	5.40%	2.70%
Georgia	9,500	0.04%	8.10%	2.70%
Hawaii	42,200	0.00%	5.60%	2.40%
Idaho	37,200	0.43%	5.40%	1.50%
Illinois	12,960	0.55%	7.75%	3.55%
Indiana	9,500	0.50%	7.40%	*
Iowa	28,300	0.00%	8.00%	1.00%
Kansas	14,000	0.20%	7.60%	2.70%
Kentucky	10,200	1.00%	10.00%	2.70%
Louisiana	7,700	0.10%	6.20%	1.22%
Maine	12,000	0.57%	5.40%	2.04%
Maryland	8,500	0.30%	7.50%	2.60%
Massachusetts	15,000	0.73%	11.13%	1.87%
Michigan	9,000	0.06%	10.30%	2.70%
Minnesota	31,000	0.10%	9.00%	1.59%
Mississippi	14,000	0.24%	5.64%	1.24%
Missouri	13,000	0.00%	9.75%	3.51%
Montana	30,500	0.13%	6.30%	*
Nebraska	9,000	0.00%	5.40%	1.25%
Nevada	28,200	0.30%	5.40%	3.00%
New Hampshire	14,000	0.10%	7.50%	1.70%
New Jersey	32,600	0.50%	5.80%	2.80%
New Mexico	24,100	0.33%	5.40%	1.00%
New York	10,700	1.70%	9.50%	4.10%
North Carolina	22,300	0.06%	5.76%	1.00%
North Dakota	37,200	0.28%	10.72%	1.62%
Ohio	9,000	0.30%	8.70%	2.70%
Oklahoma	17,500	0.10%	5.50%	1.50%
Oregon	36,900	1.20%	5.40%	2.60%
Pennsylvania	9,500	2.80%	10.89%	3.68%
Puerto Rico	7,000	2.40%	5.40%	3.30%

---

[1] Sources: Department of Labor's Employment and Training Administration, and ADP Fast Wage and Tax Facts

Unemployment Taxes

State	Wages Subject to Tax	Minimum Tax Rate	Maximum Tax Rate	New Employer Rate
Rhode Island	22,000	1.69%	9.79%	2.27%
South Carolina	14,000	0.06%	5.46%	1.39%
South Dakota	15,000	0.00%	9.50%	1.75%
Tennessee	8,000	0.01%	10.00%	2.70%
Texas	9,000	0.45%	7.47%	2.70%
Utah	32,200	0.20%	7.20%	*
Vermont	16,800	1.30%	8.40%	1.00%
Virginia	8,000	0.17%	6.27%	2.57%
Virgin Islands	23,000	1.50%	6.00%	2.00%
Washington	44,000	0.13%	7.73%	*
West Virginia	12,000	1.50%	8.50%	2.70%
Wisconsin	14,000	0.05%	12.00%	*
Wyoming	25,500	0.27%	8.77%	*

* Industry average

The difference in wage base can have a dramatic effect on the amount of state unemployment that a business pays, as noted in the following example:

EXAMPLE

Albatross Flight Systems is considering moving its 100 employees to a facility in another state. The average annual pay of its employees is $55,000 and no one earns less than $30,000. The best sites selected by the CEO of Albatross are Nevada and Colorado. Assuming that Albatross is assigned a new employer rate when it moves, the calculation of the annual amount of state unemployment taxes that it would pay is:

State	Expense Calculation	Total Expense
Colorado	100 staff × $12,200 wage base × 2.12% rate =	$25,864
Nevada	100 staff × $28,200 wage base × 3.00% rate =	$84,600

Thus, the lower state unemployment tax for Colorado could pay for an additional staff person, when compared to the rate for Nevada.

Tip: If management is contemplating the expansion of a business into a new state, and the cost of state unemployment taxes is a significant factor in the decision, peruse the preceding summary table of state unemployment taxes to see which ones have a combination of the lowest amount of wages subject to tax and the lowest new employer rate.

Each state requires that employers use its form for reporting unemployment tax information. The typical report requires the itemization of gross wages paid by individual employee, to be reported on a quarterly basis. The state then uses this information to determine the amount of gross wages falling within the unemployment wage cap, which it multiplies by the unemployment tax rate applicable to the business in order to derive the total amount of unemployment tax that should have been paid by the business at the end of the quarter. It then matches this amount to the employer's reported amount of unemployment tax paid to see if there is a variance. This information is supplied automatically by the payroll supplier, if payroll is being outsourced, and is a standard report in many off-the-shelf payroll software packages.

Unemployment Benefit Claims

Employees who have left a business are responsible for filing unemployment claims with the state government. Once an individual files such a claim, the state unemployment agency forwards a summary of the claim to the person's former employer. The claim summary includes a request to review and correct any information on the claim, as well as to provide additional information about dates worked and wages paid.

An individual who has lost his job through no fault of his own (such as a lay off) will generally be granted unemployment benefits by the state government. Most states use the ABC test to determine whether an individual is a contractor (and therefore not able to collect unemployment benefits). The three elements of the ABC test are:

1. There is an **a**bsence of control by the entity; and
2. **B**usiness conducted by the individual is substantially different from that of the entity or is conducted away from entity premises; and
3. The individual **c**ustomarily works independently from the entity as a separate business.

If the employer becomes aware of a claim from a person who was let go for cause or who left voluntarily, it should protest the claim. By protesting unjustified claims, an employer can reduce the amount of unemployment benefits paid, and thereby keep its experience rating as high as possible. The higher experience rating keeps it from paying an excessive amount of state unemployment taxes in future periods.

Calculation of the State Unemployment Tax Rate

By far the most common method for calculating the state unemployment tax rate is the *reserve ratio method*. Under this method, the government wants to have each employer maintain a balance of paid-in unemployment taxes of roughly six to ten percent of their net taxable wages. This is called the *reserve ratio*. The calculation of the reserve ratio is:

$$\frac{\text{Unemployment contributions} - \text{Benefits paid out}}{\text{Average payroll}}$$

The state government applies this employer-specific reserve ratio to a tax rate table to determine the unemployment tax that it will charge to the employer in the next year. In brief, if the reserve ratio is too small (caused by a large number of unemployment payouts), the employer can expect a larger unemployment tax in the next year in order to replenish its paid-in unemployment taxes. Conversely, the higher the reserve ratio, the lower the tax rate applied to an employer.

EXAMPLE

The state of Serendipity uses the following rate table to determine the unemployment tax rate that it charges employers:

Reserve Ratio	Tax Rate
13%+	0.8%
10%+ to 13%	1.5%
7%+ to 10%	2.5%
0% to 7%	3.5%
Negative ratio	4.5%

Arcturus Tours had average payroll of $220,000 during the past year, as well as unemployment contributions of $23,000 and benefits paid out of $5,500. This results in a reserve ratio of 8%, which is calculated as:

$$\frac{\$23,000 \text{ Unemployment contributions} - \$5,500 \text{ Benefits paid out}}{\$220,000 \text{ Average payroll}}$$

Given the 8% reserve ratio, Serendipity charges Arcturus an unemployment tax of 2.5% for the next year.

Three other methods are also used to calculate the unemployment tax rate. The following table describes these methods and the states in which they are used. By default, all states not noted in this table use the reserve ratio method.

Alternative Unemployment Tax Calculation Methods

Method Name	Calculation	States Using Method
Benefit Ratio	Proportion of unemployment benefits paid to former employees during a measurement period, divided by the total payroll during the period. A high proportion results in a high tax rate.	Alabama, Connecticut, Florida, Illinois, Iowa, Maryland, Michigan, Minnesota, Mississippi, Oregon, Texas, Utah, Vermont, Virginia, Washington, Wyoming
Benefit Wage Ratio	Proportion of total taxable wages for laid-off employees to total payroll during the period. A high proportion results in a high tax rate.	Delaware, Oklahoma
Payroll Stabilization	Assesses higher tax rates to those employers with shrinking payrolls.	Alaska

Voluntary Unemployment Contributions

In some states, an employer can make voluntary contributions to the state unemployment insurance fund in order to increase its reserve ratio, and therefore be assigned a lower unemployment tax percentage. The basic concept is that a state maintains a tax rate table in which a certain tax rate is assigned if a company falls within a specific reserve ratio range. If a company has a reserve ratio that is near the upper edge of a range for which a certain tax rate is applied, it is possible to voluntarily pay in a small additional amount in order to move the company into a higher reserve ratio, where a lower unemployment tax rate applies. Ideally, a voluntary contribution is only made if the amount of the contribution is lower than the savings expected to be achieved with a lower tax rate in the following year.

EXAMPLE

Orion Devices receives a notification from the state of Serendipity that its reserve ratio is currently 12.98%, and that contributing an additional $200 will increase the ratio to 13.01%. Doing so will change Orion's state unemployment tax rate from its current 1.5% to 0.8% (based on the rate table noted in the preceding example). Since Orion has an applicable wage base of $400,000 per year, paying the $200 voluntary contribution means that the company will experience a 0.7% reduction in its state unemployment tax, which translates into a $2,800 reduction in taxes. Thus, the $200 contribution will result in a net expense reduction of $2,600.

The following states allow voluntary contributions:

States Allowing Voluntary Unemployment Fund Contributions

Arkansas	Massachusetts	North Dakota
Arizona	Michigan	Ohio
Colorado	Minnesota	Pennsylvania
Georgia	Missouri	Rhode Island
Indiana	Nebraska	South Dakota
Kansas	New Jersey	Texas
Kentucky	New York	Washington
Louisiana	North Carolina	West Virginia
Maine		Wisconsin

Some states notify employers of the amount of voluntary contribution required to improve the reserve ratio. However, in most cases, the payroll manager must calculate the amount of the contribution, based on information provided with the annual notice issued by the state government of the tax rate for the following year.

Tip: A voluntary contribution is nonrefundable, so do not pay unless it is fairly certain that doing so will result in a significant savings in the following year. Realistically, most companies will have reserve ratios that are too near the center of the ranges in the tax table to warrant the use of a voluntary contribution.

States only allow a short period of time during which an employer can make voluntary contributions; typically, contributions must be received within 30 days of when the state mails notices of next-year tax rates to employers.

Transferring an Unemployment Experience Rating

A business may sometimes find that it must change to a new form of legal organization, such as to a "C" corporation or a limited liability company. When it reorganizes under the new format, the state in which it operates assigns it a new unemployment experience rating that is a default value assigned to all newly-organized businesses. This default rate can be fairly high, and may very well exceed the experience rating that it had earned with the old legal entity.

It may take several years to return to a low experience rating through the ongoing avoidance of layoffs, and the business will pay an excessive amount of unemployment taxes in the interim. To avoid this expense, apply to have the new entity take over the experience rating of the old business that it is replacing. This is accepted practice when the new entity is essentially taking over all of the business of the old entity, and also intends to continue the business activities of the old entity.

This is the baseline situation, but use of another entity's unemployment experience rating actually applies to any of the following three situations:

- *One entity replaces another entity.* This is the situation just described.
- *One entity acquires another entity.* The acquirer can use the experience rating of the acquiree.
- *Two or more entities acquire portions of another entity.* The acquiring entities can split the original entity's experience rating, which is based on the proportion of taxable payroll that is shifted to each acquiring entity.

When an entity successfully transfers to itself the unemployment experience rating of another business, it obtains the following items from the acquiree:

- The unemployment funds reserve
- Charges against the acquiree's unemployment funds reserve
- Contributions into the unemployment funds reserve

In order to transfer an experience rating, apply for the transfer through either the offices of the secretary of state, the department of unemployment, or the department of revenue (which varies by state). Most state governments restrict the time period during which one can apply for a transfer of experience rating.

Tip: Include the transfer of experience rating on the company's standard acquisition checklist. It should be one of the activities to be completed immediately after the completion of an acquisition agreement.

Summary

The amount of federal unemployment tax paid by a business is relatively small. However, the state unemployment tax can be substantially higher, and so can be a greater cause for concern. Further, there can be a large difference in the state unemployment taxes charged by the various states. This difference is comprised of both the tax percentage and the wage base to which it applies, which can result in more than a 4x difference between the taxes paid in different states. Thus, if management is considering where to locate a facility, the state unemployment tax is a sufficiently sizeable issue to be included in the decision.

Chapter 10
Payments to Employees

Introduction

This chapter describes two methods for physically handing a payment to an employee, and two methods for electronically transferring funds to them instead. All four methods are still in use, despite the obvious efficiencies of electronic payment. In this chapter, we will describe each method and the circumstances under which it works best.

Related podcast episodes: Episodes 126 through 129 of the Accounting Best Practices Podcast discuss the streamlining of payroll. They are available at: **www.accountingtools.com/podcasts** or **iTunes**

Payments with Cash

Paying employees in cash is rarely used outside of situations where they are day laborers or farm workers, since it is excessively time-consuming to obtain the necessary amounts of cash and transport it to employees in pay envelopes. There is also some risk in keeping large amounts of cash on hand.

EXAMPLE

Arbor Lawn Care hires a group of high school students to issue brochures in local neighborhoods during a one-day marketing campaign for its lawn mowing service. Given the brevity of the work period, the easiest way to pay the students is with cash.

The procedure for paying employees with cash is:
1. Calculate gross and net pay in the normal manner (which is the same irrespective of the payment method).
2. Calculate the exact number of each type of bills and coins needed for the payroll. Use the Payroll Cash Requirement Form shown later to make this determination. To use the form, list the net pay due to each employee in the Net Pay column, and then calculate the largest denomination of bills and coins required to pay the employee. Then create totals across the bottom of the form to determine the total amounts of each kind of bill or coin needed. As an example, see the bill and coin distribution in the sample form for Jeff Arnold; he is listed first on the form. His net pay is $153.17. We calculate the number of bills and coins due him in the following descending order:

a. The maximum number of $20 bills that can be paid to him is seven, which leaves $13.17.
b. The maximum number of $10 bills that can be paid to him is one, which leaves $3.17.
c. The maximum number of $1 bills that can be paid to him is three, which leaves $0.17.
d. The maximum number of dimes that can be paid to him is one, which leaves $0.07.
e. The maximum number of nickels that can be paid to him is one, which leaves $0.02.
f. The maximum number of pennies that can be paid to him is two, which completes the calculation.
3. Withdraw the required sums of bills and coins from the bank.
4. Obtain enough envelopes from supplies for each person to be paid with cash.
5. Obtain a fill-in-the-blanks stamp and use it to stamp a form on the outside of each envelope. A sample of the stamp is shown below. It states the detailed calculation of the pay earned by each employee.
6. Fill in the stamped form on the outside of each envelope, and insert the cash due to each person.
7. Give the pay envelopes to employees, and have each employee sign a receipt, stating the amount received and the date of receipt. A sample of the receipt is shown below. The receipt provides evidence that the company paid the correct amount to the employee on the official pay date.

The sheer volume of steps required to pay employees with cash makes it clear that this is not the most efficient payment method.

Payroll Cash Requirement Form

Name	Net Pay	$20	$10	$5	$1	$0.25	$0.10	$0.05	$0.01
Arnold, Jeff	$153.17	7	1		3		1	1	2
Beasley, Beau	214.26	10	1		4	1			1
Chico, David	305.48	15		1		1	2		3
Donner, Al	226.11	11		1	1		1		1
Ender, Mary	93.82	4	1		3	3		1	2
Fagan, Nancy	148.90	7		1	3	3	1	1	
Grieg, Vlad	175.34	8	1	1		1		1	4
Hope, Lilly	302.66	15			2	2	1	1	1
Totals	$1,619.74	77	4	4	16	11	6	5	14

Cover Stamp for Pay Envelope

Employee name	Kathy Orton
Pay date range	June 24 - 30
Regular hours worked	40
Regular pay rate	$9.00
Regular pay total	$360.00
Overtime hours worked	4
Overtime pay rate	$13.50
Overtime pay total	$54.00
Total pay	$414.00
Pay deductions	
Federal income tax	$74.52
State income tax	20.70
Social security tax	25.67
Medicare tax	6.00
Total deductions	$126.89
Net pay	$287.11

Pay Envelope Receipt Form

For Pay Period Ended: June 30, 20x1

Name	Cash Paid	Date Paid	Recipient Signature
Matthews, Oliver	$193.12	July 3, 20x1	*Oliver Matthews*
Nonesuch, Jaime	207.43	July 3, 20x1	*Jaime Nonesuch*
Orton, Kathy	248.99	July 3, 20x1	*Kathy Orton*
Paulson, Paula	160.57	July 3, 20x1	*Paula Paulson*
Quigley, Anna	195.75	July 3, 20x1	*Anna Quigley*

There are special control problems associated with paying employees in cash, which are addressed in the Payroll Controls chapter.

Payments by Check

The standard method for paying employees for many years was the check, though it has been largely supplanted by direct deposit (see the next section). A check is usually accompanied by a *remittance advice* (also known as a *check stub*), on which is listed an employee's gross pay, tax deductions and other withholdings, and net pay. A simplified sample remittance advice for a one-week pay period is:

Employee Name: Arturo Johansson							[company name]
Ending Pay Date	Hours Worked	Rate	Gross Pay	Federal Inc. Tax	Social Security	Medicare	Net Pay
5/15/xx	Regular 40 OT 10	$20.00 $30.00	$1,100.00	$197.25	$68.20	$15.95	$818.60

Paying by check is inefficient, because it involves many steps to complete. Consider this process flow:

1. Transfer the required amount of funds into the payroll checking account
2. Record the transfer of funds in the accounting system
3. Print checks
4. Sign checks or use a signature stamp to replace the check signer
5. Stuff checks into envelopes
6. Mail checks to outlying company locations for distribution
7. Hand checks to employees and retain checks when employees are not present
8. Follow up on remaining undistributed checks
9. Follow up on those checks not cashed
10. Cancel and replace any lost checks

In addition, all unused check stock should be locked up, since there is a risk that it could be stolen and used to fraudulently create paychecks.

If payroll is outsourced to a supplier, the supplier prints the paychecks, stuffs them into envelopes, and returns them to the employer for distribution.

Despite this array of problems, many companies continue to issue paychecks because they do not have ready access to a direct deposit or pay card solution. Issuing payments with checks is an extremely low-tech solution, and so is easy enough for anyone to use – especially those companies still calculating payrolls manually.

> **Tip:** The labor associated with distributing paychecks by hand can be eliminated if the checks are instead mailed directly to employee residences. The company must incur the additional cost of postage, but avoids having to follow up on undistributed paychecks. Checks can be mailed a day or two early in order to have them in employee hands on the designated pay date.

The controls associated with check payments are described in the Payroll Controls chapter.

Tip: It is best to pay employees with checks drawn on a separate bank account, rather than the main corporate checking account. This makes it easier to reconcile the corporate checking account, since the activity level is lower. A separate account is not needed if payroll is outsourced, since the supplier merely withdraws a lump sum from the corporate bank account to pay for each payroll, which is a minor item to reconcile.

Tip: If a separate payroll checking account is maintained, consider retaining a small excess balance in the account to provide funding for the small number of manual checks that may be issued between normal payrolls.

Payments by Direct Deposit

Direct deposit involves the electronic transfer of funds from the company to the bank accounts of its employees, using the Automated Clearing House (ACH) system. ACH is an electronic network for the processing of both debit and credit transactions within the United States and Canada. ACH payments include direct deposit payroll, social security payments, tax refunds, and the direct payment of business-to-business and consumer bills. Within the ACH system, the *originator* is the entity that originates transactions, and the *receiver* is the entity that has authorized an originator to initiate a debit or credit entry to a transaction account. The transactions pass through sending and receiving banks that are authorized to use the ACH system.

The payment process is to calculate pay in the same manner as for check payments, but to then send the payment information to a direct deposit processing service, which initiates electronic payments to the bank accounts of those employees being paid in this manner. The processing service deducts the funds from a company bank account in advance of the direct deposits, so cash flow tends to be somewhat more accelerated than is the case if a company were to issue checks and then wait several days for the amounts on the checks to be withdrawn from its bank account.

Direct deposit is more efficient than payments by check, because it does not require a signature on each payment, there are no checks to be delivered, and employees do not have to waste time depositing them at a bank. Further, employees who are off-site can still rely upon having cash paid into their accounts in a timely manner. Finally, all of the controls used to monitor checks are eliminated.

Direct deposit can also be more efficient from the perspective of the remittance advice. A number of payroll suppliers offer an option to simply notify employees by e-mail when their pay has been sent to them, after which employees can access a secure website to view their remittance advice information. This approach is better than sending a paper version of a remittance advice, because employees can also access many years of historical pay information on-line, as well as their W-2 forms.

Despite its efficiency advantages, direct deposit is not perfect, for it requires employees to have bank accounts. If this is an issue, consider using a blended solution with pay cards (see the next section) for those employees who do not have a bank account. Also, banks charge a fee for direct deposit payments, though the net cost of this fee is less than the cost of check stock, mailing costs, and check processing fees if an employer were to instead pay employees by check.

> **Tip:** The cost of ACH transactions can be reduced by cutting back the number of pay periods per year. Thus, if a switch is made from a weekly payroll to a semi-monthly payroll, there are 26 fewer payrolls, so that the cost of direct deposit is reduced by half.

The implementation of direct deposit can cause some initial difficulties, because one must correctly set up each person's bank account information in the direct deposit module of the company's payroll software (or software provided by the outsourced payroll supplier). This initial setup is remarkably prone to error, and also usually requires a test transaction (the *pre-notification*) that delays implementation by one pay period. Consequently, even if a new employee signs up for direct deposit immediately, the payroll staff must still print a paycheck for that person's first payroll, after which direct deposit can be used.

> **Tip:** If employees want to be paid by direct deposit, require them to submit a voided check for the checking account into which they want the employer to send funds. The routing and account numbers can be more reliably taken directly from such a check, rather than risking a transposition error if an employee copies this information onto a form. Also, do not accept a deposit slip instead of a check – the information on the deposit slip may not match the routing and account number information on the check.

> **Tips:** Employees periodically switch bank accounts, close their old accounts, and do not inform the employer of the change, resulting in payments bouncing from the closed accounts. If there is a company newsletter, include an occasional notice, reminding employees to notify the payroll department if they want their direct deposit payments to go into a different account.

A final issue with direct deposit is being able to do so from an in-house payroll processing function. If the payroll software does not provide for direct deposit, it will be necessary to contract with a third party to make the payments on behalf of the company. Direct deposit is much easier to implement if an employer is outsourcing payroll, since direct deposit is part of the standard feature set for all payroll suppliers.

> **Note:** It might be tempting to force all employees to be paid by direct deposit. Before doing so, check the applicable state laws to see if this is possible. It may be necessary to allow them the option of an alternative form of payment.

Payments by Pay Card

If there are employees who do not have a bank account and who do not want one, they are either asking for payment in cash or are taking their paychecks to a check cashing service that charges a high fee. The situation can be improved for these workers by offering them a *pay card*, which is also known as a *payroll card* or *debit card*. The company transfers funds directly into the pay card, so there is no need for a check cashing service. Employees can make purchases directly with the card, or use it to obtain cash through an ATM. The company still issues a remittance advice to all pay card holders, so they can see the detail behind the amounts being paid to them.

Here are several additional advantages of having pay cards:

- *Check fees.* Pay cards eliminate the possibility of having to pay the occasional stop payment fee for a lost paycheck.
- *First payment.* Direct deposit is not usually possible for an employee's first payment, but can be achieved with a pay card.
- *Low fees.* ATM cash withdrawal fees are much lower than the fees charged by check cashing services.
- *Security.* The pay card is protected by a personal identification number.
- *Special payments.* There is no need to cut a check for special payments, such as for an award or pay adjustment. Instead, simply send the cash to the pay card.
- *Statement.* Employees receive a monthly statement, detailing payments into and withdrawals from their account.
- *Unclaimed property.* Once funds are transferred to a pay card, they are the property of the recipient, so the company no longer has to concern itself with remitting unclaimed pay to the state government under escheatment laws.

When compared to direct deposit, pay cards are the more attractive option for many employees. However, since direct deposit has been available far longer, pay cards have not gained as much traction in the marketplace.

> **Tip:** To encourage the use of pay cards, consider installing an ATM right on the company premises, so that employees with pay cards can have immediate access to cash. Doing so also reduces employee time away from the office, since they no longer have to travel to a bank or outside ATM to obtain cash. Given the lease and maintenance fees involved, this option is only viable if there are a number of pay card users on the premises.

Flexible Spending Account Debit Cards

Under a flexible spending account arrangement (see the Employee Benefits chapter), employees can elect to have a predetermined amount withheld from their gross pay before taxes are deducted, and then use those funds to pay for health care expenses.

The most labor-intensive approach to reimbursing employees for such expenses follows these steps:
1. The employee completes a reimbursement form and attached a receipt
2. The employer or processing service determines whether the request is valid
3. If so, a check is issued to the employee
4. The employee deposits the check to receive funds

These steps can span a long period of time. For example, employees tend to let receipts pile up until they can submit them all at one time on a single reimbursement form; there may be a delay before the employer or processing service can examine them, and another delay while the check is cut and mailed. Thus, it may be several months before an employee is reimbursed for a valid expenditure.

A vastly better approach is to outsource FSA administration to a third party that offers flexible spending account debit cards. Such a card is funded by the available FSA cash balance, and allows one to directly purchase the following types of expenditures related to health care:
- Prescription co-payments
- Doctor's office co-payments
- Some types of over-the-counter health care items
- Coinsurance, deductible, and other out-of-pocket expenses for medical, dental, and vision plans

Though employees may still have to submit receipts in some situations, the FSA debit card is still a massive improvement over the traditional system for two reasons:
- Employees can largely avoid expense reimbursement paperwork
- Employees can access available funds immediately

These improvements are primarily for the benefit of employees, rather than the company, since the company may not experience any direct cost savings. However, there may be an indirect benefit, in that ease of use may increase the level of employee FSA participation, which in turn reduces the amount of their gross pay subject to social security and Medicare taxes, which in turn reduces the company's obligatory matching of those taxes.

Unclaimed Wages

If an employee does not cash a check, the employer is required to remit these funds to the state government after a certain period of time. The company reports this information on an annual unclaimed property report to the government, after which the employee can still reclaim the funds from the government. Thus, it is not acceptable to simply reverse the payroll expense associated with a check that was never cashed, since that constitutes retaining funds that are, by law, supposed to be remitted to the government.

Summary

This chapter showed how to pay employees with cash, checks, direct deposit, and pay cards. Of these methods, the one whose usage is most likely to decline in the future is check payments, since it is a less efficient approach than direct deposit or pay cards. Cash payments will likely continue to be useful for situations where employees are paid very frequently. Ultimately, a combination of direct deposit and pay cards will likely be the payment method of choice, since the two methods jointly present the best blend of rapid and efficient payments to employees; direct deposit will be the more likely alternative for those people with bank accounts, and pay cards for those without bank accounts.

Chapter 11
Accounting for Payroll

Introduction

The payroll system may be entirely separate from a company's primary system of recording accounting transactions. This is especially true if it has outsourced the payroll function entirely. Thus, one should have a process for transferring the information accumulated in the payroll system to the accounting system. The chief tool for doing so is the journal entry, which is used to transfer a variety of types of expense-related information at a summary level into the accounting system. This chapter describes where payroll information is stored in an accounting system, and the journal entries used to record payroll information in that system.

> **Note:** The accounting system does not contain information about employee-specific wage and benefit information. The payroll system must be accessed to obtain this information.

The Accounting Journal Entry

An accounting journal entry is the method used to enter an accounting transaction into the accounting records. There must be a minimum of two line items in a journal entry, though there is no upper limit to the number of line items that can be included in it. A two-line journal entry is known as a *simple* journal entry, while one containing more line items is called a *compound* journal entry. A company may use a great many journal entries in just a single accounting period, so it is better to use a larger number of simple journal entries than a smaller number of compound journal entries in order to clarify why the entries are being made.

Whenever an accounting transaction is created, at least two accounts are always impacted, with a debit entry being recorded against one account and a credit entry against the other account. A debit is an accounting entry that either increases an asset or expense account, or decreases a liability or equity account. It is positioned to the left in an accounting entry. A credit is an accounting entry that either decreases an asset or expense account, or increases a liability or equity account. It is positioned to the right in an accounting entry.

The totals of the debits and credits for any transaction must always equal each other, so that an accounting transaction is said to be "in balance." If a transaction were not in balance, it would not be possible to create financial statements. Thus, the use of debits and credits in a two-column transaction recording format is the most essential of all controls over accounting accuracy.

A journal entry should include the following information:
- The accounts into which the debits and credits are to be recorded

- The date of the entry
- The accounting period in which the journal entry should be recorded
- The name of the person recording the entry
- Any managerial authorizations
- A unique number to identify the journal entry
- Whether the entry is a one-time entry, a recurring entry, or a reversing entry
- Documentation to prove why the journal entry is being recorded

EXAMPLE

Oberlin Acoustics accrues for a $10,000 bonus payable to its president with the following entry, which includes many of the features needed for a comprehensive journal entry:

J/E #0780		Debit	Credit
Acct. 4300	Bonus expense	10,000	
Acct. 3210	Accrued bonus liability		10,000
May 18 – To record accrued bonus for Mr. Smythe, Oberlin president			

The "J/E #" in the journal entry in the preceding example is the field in which is recorded the unique number assigned to the journal entry to identify it.

There are two special types of journal entries that can be of use when accounting for payroll. A *reversing journal entry* is one that is either reversed manually in the following accounting period, or which is automatically reversed by the accounting software in the following accounting period. A *recurring journal entry* is one that repeats in every successive accounting period until a termination date is reached. This can be done manually, or can be set up to run automatically in an accounting software system.

The Chart of Accounts

The chart of accounts is a listing of all accounts used in the general ledger, usually sorted in order by account number. The accounts are typically numeric, but can also be alphabetic or alphanumeric. The account numbering system is used by the accounting software to aggregate information into a company's financial statements. Accounts are usually listed in order of their appearance in the financial statements, starting with the balance sheet and continuing with the income statement. Thus, the chart of accounts begins with cash, proceeds through liabilities and shareholders' equity, and then continues with accounts for revenues and then expenses. Many organizations structure their chart of accounts so that expense information is separately compiled by department. For example, the sales department, engineering department, and accounting department may all have the same set of expense accounts.

The following chart of accounts shows only those accounts most likely to be used for payroll-related transactions (the account numbers used are examples only – any employer's account numbers will likely differ):

Payroll-Related Accounts in the Chart of Accounts

Number	Description	Usage
Assets		
1000	Cash	Source of payments to employees
1100	Payroll advances	Tracks advances that have not yet been paid back to the company
Liabilities		
2100	Federal unemployment taxes payable	Tracks federal unemployment taxes owed but not yet paid
2110	Federal withholding taxes payable	Tracks federal income taxes withheld from employee pay but not yet remitted to the government
2120	Garnishments payable	Tracks garnishments withheld from employee pay but not yet remitted to the garnishing authority
2130	Medicare taxes payable	Tracks Medicare taxes withheld and matched, but not yet remitted to the government
2140	Social security taxes payable	Tracks social security taxes withheld and matched, but not yet remitted to the government
2150	State unemployment taxes payable	Tracks state unemployment taxes owed but not yet paid
2160	Accrued benefits liability	Tracks benefits expenses incurred but not yet paid
2170	Accrued bonus liability	Tracks bonus expense incurred but not yet paid
2180	Accrued commissions	Tracks commission expense incurred but not yet paid
2190	Accrued payroll taxes	Tracks payroll taxes associated with accrued wages that have not yet been paid
2200	Accrued salaries and wages	Tracks salaries and wages that have been earned by employees but not yet paid

Number	Description	Usage
Expenses		
3100	Direct labor expense	Tracks the incurred labor expense associated with the cost of goods sold
4200	Bonus expense	Tracks the incurred cost of bonuses paid or payable to employees
4210	Commission expense	Tracks the incurred cost of commissions paid or payable to employees
4220	Wage expense	Tracks the incurred labor expense associated with administrative and selling activities
4230	Payroll taxes expense	Tracks the incurred cost of payroll taxes paid or payable to the government
4240	Medical insurance expense	Tracks the incurred cost of medical insurance paid or payable to suppliers
4250	Dental insurance expense	Tracks the incurred cost of dental insurance paid or payable to suppliers
4260	Disability insurance expense	Tracks the incurred cost of disability insurance paid or payable to suppliers
4270	Life insurance expense	Tracks the cost of life insurance paid or payable to suppliers

Tip: When constructing a chart of accounts, always leave gaps in the numbering between accounts, which makes it easier to add accounts later, as the business expands and its information storage needs grow.

The General Ledger

The general ledger is the master set of accounts that summarize all transactions occurring within an entity. The general ledger contains all accounts currently being used in a company's chart of accounts, and it is sorted by account number. Either individual transactions or summary-level postings from subsidiary-level journals (such as the payroll journal) are listed within each account, sorted by transaction date. Each entry in the general ledger includes a reference number that states the source of the information. The source may be a subsidiary ledger, such as the payroll journal, or it may be a journal entry.

The Payroll Journal

A payroll journal is a detailed record of accounting transactions related to payroll. Smaller organizations may record their payroll transactions directly in the general ledger, but larger companies will find that the sheer volume of these transactions will clog the general ledger; instead, they record day-to-day payroll-related transactions, especially those arising from the various payrolls, in the payroll journal, and then just record a single summary-level entry in the general ledger that reflects all of the transactions recorded in the payroll journal.

If there is a need to investigate a specific payroll transaction and an employer is using a payroll journal, it will be necessary to conduct research within the payroll journal, since the detail-level information will not be available in the general ledger.

In some software accounting packages, the payroll journal may be invisible, since the database is structured so that one can simply enter transactions, without being concerned about the specific journal within which they are recorded.

> **Note:** It is possible to make handwritten entries into a payroll journal or use an accounting computer system to keypunch entries into a database version of a payroll journal. In both cases, the information is then summarized in the payroll journal and transferred to the summary in the general ledger.

Where to Record Payroll Transactions

We have just described the chart of accounts, payroll journal, and general ledger. How are they used to record accounting transactions? The following table reveals the differences between these three items:

Item	Description
Chart of accounts	This is a list of valid account numbers that can be used to record accounting transactions. It is used as an index of available accounts. It is not an accounting record, and so cannot be used to store information.
Payroll journal	Contains individual payroll transactions that are periodically summarized and forwarded (posted) to the general ledger. For example, the contents of a weekly payroll appear in the payroll journal.
General ledger	Accepts summary-level payroll entries from the payroll journal, as well as journal entries. This is the source document for the financial statements.

Thus, when a payroll is created, the accounting software stores the detailed results of the payroll in the payroll journal. When additional payroll-related entries are created, such as a bonus or commission accrual, record these journal entries in the appropriate general ledger account.

The following general ledger report is a sample extract from the wages expense account of a company's general ledger. The report illustrates where payroll transactions are recorded. Note the following:

- Journal entries flow directly through the general ledger. Thus, the reversal of the wage accrual from the prior period, as well as the wage accrual for the current period, are both shown in the report. The references for these entries contain the journal entry numbers from which they are derived (JE 704 and JE 727, respectively).

- The total wage expense from each individual payroll is brought forward into the account from the payroll journal. The report shows that there were two payrolls during the month, occurring on 2/14 and 2/28. The references for these entries are listed as "PJ," denoting the payroll journal from which they are derived.

General Ledger Report

Account 4220 – Wages Expense

Date	Description	Source	Debit	Credit	Balance
	Beginning balance				287,500
2/1	Reverse wage accrual	JE 704		15,000	272,500
2/14	Payroll	PJ	136,500		409,000
2/28	Payroll	PJ	138,200		547,200
2/28	Wage accrual	JE 727	18,000		565,200
	Ending balance				565,200

Types of Payroll Journal Entries

There are several types of journal entries that involve the recordation of compensation. The primary entry is for the initial recordation of a payroll. This entry records the gross wages earned by employees, as well as all withholdings from their pay, and any additional taxes owed by the company. There may also be an accrued wages entry that is recorded at the end of each accounting period, and which is intended to record the amount of wages owed to employees but not yet paid. Under some circumstances, it may also be prudent to accrue a portion of the bonus that an employee may be paid at the end of a period if he or she meets certain performance criteria. A more common entry is for the accrual of commissions earned by the sales staff, but which have not yet been paid. Each of these types of compensation is based on different source documents and requires separate calculations and journal entries.

There are also a number of other payroll-related journal entries that a payroll staff must deal with on a regular basis. They include:

- Benefit payments
- Accrued benefits
- Stock subscriptions
- Manual paychecks
- Employee advances
- Accrued vacation pay
- Tax deposits

All of these journal entries are described in the following sections.

Primary Payroll Journal Entry

The primary journal entry for payroll is the summary-level entry that is compiled from the payroll register, and which is recorded in either the payroll journal or the general ledger. This entry usually includes debits for the direct labor expense, wages, and the company's portion of payroll taxes. There will also be credits to a number of other accounts, each one detailing the liability for payroll taxes that have not been paid, as well as for the amount of cash already paid to employees for their net pay. The basic entry (assuming no further breakdown of debits by individual department) is:

	Debit	Credit
Direct labor expense	xxx	
Wages expense	xxx	
Payroll taxes expense	xxx	
Cash		xxx
Federal withholding taxes payable		xxx
Social security taxes payable		xxx
Medicare taxes payable		xxx
Federal unemployment taxes payable		xxx
State unemployment taxes payable		xxx
Garnishments payable		xxx

Note: The reason for the payroll taxes expense line item in this journal entry is that the company incurs the cost of matching the social security and Medicare amounts paid by employees, and directly incurs the cost of unemployment insurance. The employee-paid portions of the social security and Medicare taxes are not recorded as expenses; instead, they are liabilities for which the company has an obligation to remit cash to the taxing government entity.

A key point with this journal entry is that the direct labor expense and salaries expense contain employee gross pay, while the amount actually paid to employees through the cash account is their net pay. The difference between the two figures (which can be substantial) is the amount of deductions from their pay, such as payroll taxes and withholdings to pay for benefits.

There may be a number of additional employee deductions to include in this journal entry. For example, there may be deductions for 401(k) pension plans, health insurance, life insurance, vision insurance, and for the repayment of advances.

When withheld taxes and company portion of payroll taxes are paid at a later date, use the following entry to reduce the balance in the cash account, and eliminate the balances in the liability accounts:

	Debit	Credit
Federal withholding taxes payable	xxx	
Social security taxes payable	xxx	
Medicare taxes payable	xxx	
Federal unemployment taxes payable	xxx	
State withholding taxes payable	xxx	
State unemployment taxes payable	xxx	
Garnishments payable	xxx	
Cash		xxx

Thus, when a company initially deducts taxes and other items from an employee's pay, the company incurs a liability to pay the taxes to a third party. This liability only disappears from the company's accounting records when it pays the related funds to the entity to which they are owed.

> **Note:** If the payroll system is tightly integrated into the accounting system, it is not necessary to create the entries just described. Instead, the software will automatically transfer detailed payroll information into the payroll journal, which will eventually be transferred to the general ledger.

Accrued Wages

It is quite common to have some amount of unpaid wages at the end of an accounting period, so accrue this expense (if it is material). The accrual entry, as shown next, is simpler than the comprehensive payroll entry already shown, because an employer typically clumps all payroll taxes into a single expense account and offsetting liability account. After recording this entry, reverse it at the beginning of the following accounting period, and then record the actual payroll expense whenever it occurs.

	Debit	Credit
Direct labor expense	xxx	
Wages expense	xxx	
Accrued salaries and wages		xxx
Accrued payroll taxes		xxx

Companies with predominantly salaried staffs frequently avoid making the accrued wages entry, on the grounds that the wages due to a small number of hourly personnel at the end of the reporting period have a minimal impact on reported financial results.

The information for the wage accrual entry is most easily derived from a spreadsheet that itemizes all employees to whom the calculation applies, the amount of unpaid time, and the standard pay rate for each person. It is not necessary to also calculate the cost of overtime hours earned during an accrual period if the amount of such hours is relatively small. A sample spreadsheet for calculating accrued wages is:

Hourly Employees	Unpaid Days	Hourly Rate	Pay Accrual
Anthem, Jill	4	$20.00	$640
Bingley, Adam	4	18.25	584
Chesterton, Elvis	4	17.50	560
Davis, Ethel	4	23.00	736
Ellings, Humphrey	4	21.50	688
Fogarty, Miriam	4	16.00	512
		Total	$3,720

Accrued Bonuses

Accrue a bonus expense whenever there is an expectation that the financial or operational performance of a company at least equals the performance levels required in any active bonus plans.

The decision to accrue a bonus calls for judgment, for the entire period of performance may encompass many future months, during which time a person may *not* continue to achieve his bonus plan objectives, in which case any prior bonus accrual should be reversed. Here are some alternative ways to treat a bonus accrual during the earlier stages of a bonus period:

- Accrue no expense at all until there is a reasonable probability that the bonus will be achieved.
- Accrue a smaller expense early in a performance period to reflect the higher risk of performance failure, and accrue a larger expense later if the probability of success improves.

One thing *not* to do is accrue a significant bonus expense in a situation where the probability that the bonus will be awarded is low; such an accrual is essentially earnings management, since it creates a false expense that is later reversed when the performance period is complete.

EXAMPLE

The management team of High Noon Armaments will earn a year-end group bonus of $240,000 if profits exceed 12 percent of revenues. There is a reasonable probability that the team will earn this bonus, so the controller records the following accrual in each month of the performance year:

	Debit	Credit
Bonus expense	20,000	
Accrued bonus liability		20,000

The management team does not quite meet the profit criteria required under the bonus plan, so the group instead receives a $150,000 bonus. This results in the following entry to eliminate the liability and pay out the bonus:

	Debit	Credit
Accrued bonus liability	240,000	
Bonus expense		90,000
Cash		150,000

The actual payout of $150,000 would be reduced by any social security and Medicare taxes applicable to each person in the management group being paid.

Tip: Employee performance plans are usually maintained by the human resources department. The payroll manager should summarize these plans into a format that the payroll staff can consult when calculating its estimates of bonus accruals.

Accrued Commissions

Accrue an expense for a commission in the same period when the accounting staff records the sale generated by a salesperson, *and* when one can calculate the amount of the commission. This is a debit to the commission expense account and a credit to a commission liability account. The commission expense can be classified as part of the cost of goods sold, since it directly relates to the sale of goods or services. It is also acceptable to classify a commission as part of the expenses of the sales department.

EXAMPLE

Wes Smith sells a $1,000 item for High Noon Armaments. Under the terms of his commission agreement, he receives a 5% commission on the revenue generated by the transaction, and will be paid on the 15th day of the following month. At the end of the accounting period in which Mr. Smith generates the sale, High Noon creates the following entry to record its liability for the commission:

	Debit	Credit
Commission expense	50	
Accrued commissions (liability)		50

High Noon then reverses the entry at the beginning of the following accounting period, because it is going to record the actual payment on the 15th of the month. Thus, the reversing entry is:

	Debit	Credit
Accrued commissions (liability)	50	
Commission expense		50

On the 15th of the month, High Noon pays Mr. Smith his commission and records this entry:

	Debit	Credit
Commission expense	50	
Cash		50

Benefit Payments

Benefits are paid through the accounts payable system, while the employee-paid portion of benefits is deducted from their pay through the payroll system. Thus, two different systems are required to process benefits, on the assumption that employees are paying for a portion or all of the benefits.

A company enrolls an employee in a benefit plan with a supplier, and is usually billed in advance for benefits, with payment due to the supplier by the beginning of the month in which the benefits are to be incurred. This early payment means that the proper recordation of such a benefit is as a prepaid expense, which is classified as a current asset. The entry is:

	Debit	Credit
Prepaid expenses (asset)	xxx	
Accounts payable		xxx

At the beginning of the next month, which is the month to which the benefits apply, shift the amount in the prepaid expenses account to the applicable benefits expense account. A sample entry for medical benefits would be:

	Debit	Credit
Medical benefits expense	xxx	
Prepaid expenses (asset)		xxx

Any deductions taken from employee pay are then recorded as credits to the applicable benefits expense account, thereby reducing the amount of the expense borne by the company.

EXAMPLE

Giro Cabinetry pays $20,000 for its employee medical insurance per month. The company requires all participating employees to pay 20% of the total cost of the insurance, which is $4,000. The company pays its employees twice a month. The entries into its medical benefits expense account in May are:

Date	Description	Source	Debit	Credit	Balance
	Beginning balance				$63,900
5/1	Payment to First Medical	AP	20,000		83,900
5/15	Payroll deductions	PJ		2,000	81,900
5/31	Payroll deductions	PJ		2,000	79,900
	Ending balance				$79,900

The transaction detail reveals that Giro records the medical insurance expense at the beginning of the month, with the source document being the accounts payable journal. The payroll deductions come from the mid-month and end-of-month payrolls, and the source document in both cases is the payroll journal.

Tip: When there is a change in the cost of a benefit charged by a supplier, some portion of this cost increase is usually paid by employees through an increased pay deduction. However, there may be a disconnect between a change in a benefit cost and the related deduction, resulting in deductions being too low, and the company paying all of the cost increase. To avoid this problem, schedule a periodic internal audit of employee deductions, where the auditors are specifically verifying that deduction amounts are correct.

Accrued Benefits

The proper way to account for the accrual of employee benefits is to use a journal entry template to record the amount of any benefits that have been consumed by employees, and for which a supplier billing has not yet arrived.

Certain types of insurance may be billed after the fact, when the insurer has sufficient information about employees to create an invoice. For example, an employer might send employee information to its insurer at the end of each month, so that the insurer can devise an accurate billing that is issued in the next month, but which applies to the preceding month. In this case, the company accrues the estimated cost of the insurance in the current month, and sets the entry to automatically reverse in the next month, when the insurer's invoice arrives.

A sample of this transaction is:

	Debit	Credit
Medical insurance expense	xxx	
Dental insurance expense	xxx	
Disability insurance expense	xxx	
Life insurance expense	xxx	
Accrued benefits liability		xxx

Most benefit providers issue billings in advance of a reporting period, so there may be few benefit accruals to record. Also, if a proposed accrual is a small one, it may make little sense to record it, on the grounds that it has no material impact on the financial statements, requires accounting labor, and introduces the risk of incorrectly recording or reversing the transaction.

Stock Subscriptions

A publicly-held company can create a stock subscription arrangement, where employees pay for shares in the company by having a standard amount deducted from their pay. Under this arrangement, a receivable is set up for the full amount expected from employees, with an offset to a common stock account and the additional paid-in capital account (for the par value of the subscribed shares). When the cash is collected and the stock is issued, the funds are deducted from these accounts and shifted to the common stock account.

EXAMPLE

High Noon Armaments sets up a stock subscription system for its employees. They choose to purchase 10,000 shares of common stock with a par value of $1 for a total of $52,000. Employees are paying $1,000 per week through payroll deductions. The company has a weekly payroll. The initial entry is:

	Debit	Credit
Stock subscriptions receivable	52,000	
Common stock subscribed		42,000
Additional paid-in capital		10,000

When High Noon receives a cash payment, it offsets the stock subscriptions receivable account and shifts funds stored in the common stock subscribed account to the common stock account. The following entry shows the processing of a typical $1,000 payment arising from the deductions in one of the weekly payrolls:

	Debit	Credit
Cash	1,000	
Stock subscriptions receivable		1,000
Common stock subscribed	1,000	
Common stock		1,000

Manual Paycheck Entry

It is all too common to create a manual paycheck, either because an employee was short-paid in a prior payroll, or because the company is laying off or firing an employee, and so is obligated to pay that person before the next regularly scheduled payroll. This check may be paid through the corporate accounts payable bank account, rather than its payroll account, so it may be necessary to make this entry through the accounts payable system. If it is recorded directly into the general ledger or the payroll journal, use the same line items already noted for the primary payroll journal entry.

EXAMPLE

High Noon Armaments lays off Mr. Jones. High Noon owes Mr. Jones $5,000 of wages at the time of the layoff. The payroll staff calculates that it must withhold $382.50 from Mr. Jones' pay to cover the employee-paid portions of social security and Medicare taxes. Mr. Jones has claimed a large enough number of withholding allowances that there is no income tax withholding. Thus, the company pays Mr. Jones $4,617.50. The journal entry it uses is:

	Debit	Credit
Wage expense	5,000	
Social security taxes payable		310.00
Medicare taxes payable		72.50
Cash		4,617.50

At the next regularly-scheduled payroll, the payroll staff records this payment as a notation in the payroll system, so that it will properly compile the correct amount of wages for Mr. Jones for his year-end Form W-2. In addition, the payroll system calculates that High Noon must pay a matching amount of social security and Medicare taxes (though no unemployment taxes, since Mr. Jones already exceeded his wage cap for these taxes). Accordingly, an additional liability of $382.50 is recorded in the payroll journal entry for that payroll. High Noon pays these matching amounts as part of its normal tax remittances associated with the payroll.

Employee Advances

When an employee asks for an advance, this is recorded as a current asset in the company's balance sheet. There may not be a separate account in which to store advances, especially if employee advances are infrequent; possible asset accounts that can be used are:

- Employee advances (for high-volume situations)
- Other assets (probably sufficient for smaller companies that record few assets other than trade receivables, inventory, and fixed assets)
- Other receivables (useful if management is tracking a number of different types of assets, and wants to segregate receivables in one account)

EXAMPLE

High Noon Armaments issues a $1,000 advance to employee Wes Smith. High Noon issues advances regularly, and so uses a separate account in which to record advances. It records the transaction as:

	Debit	Credit
Other assets	1,000	
Cash		1,000

One week later, Mr. Smith pays back half the amount of the advance, which is recorded with this entry:

	Debit	Credit
Cash	500	
Other assets		500

No matter what method is later used to repay the company – a check from the employee, or payroll deductions – the entry will be a credit to whichever asset account was used, until such time as the balance in the account has been paid off.

Employee advances require vigilance by the accounting staff, because employees who have limited financial resources will tend to use the company as their personal banks, and so will be reluctant to pay back advances unless pressed repeatedly. Thus, it is essential to continually monitor the remaining amount of advances outstanding for every employee.

Accrued Vacation Pay

Accrued vacation pay is the amount of vacation time that an employee has earned as per a company's employee benefit manual, but which he has not yet used. The calculation of accrued vacation pay for each employee is:

1. Calculate the amount of vacation time earned through the beginning of the accounting period. This should be a roll-forward balance from the preceding period.
2. Add the number of hours earned in the current accounting period.
3. Subtract the number of vacation hours used in the current period.
4. Multiply the ending number of accrued vacation hours by the employee's hourly wage to arrive at the correct accrual that should be on the company's books.
5. If the amount already accrued for the employee from the preceding period is lower than the correct accrual, record the difference as an addition to the accrued liability. If the amount already accrued from the preceding period is higher than the correct accrual, record the difference as a reduction of the accrued liability.

A sample spreadsheet follows that uses the preceding steps, and which can be used to compile accrued vacation pay:

Name	Vacation Roll-Forward Balance	+ New Hours Earned	- Hours Used	= Net Balance	× Hourly Pay	= Accrued Vacation $
Hilton, David	24.0	10	34.0	0.0	$25.00	$0.00
Idle, John	13.5	10	0.0	23.5	17.50	411.25
Jakes, Jill	120.0	10	80.0	50.0	23.50	1,175.00
Kilo, Steve	114.5	10	14.0	110.5	40.00	4,420.00
Linder, Alice	12.0	10	0.0	22.0	15.75	346.50
Mills, Jeffery	83.5	10	65.00	28.5	19.75	562.88
					Total	$6,915.63

It is not necessary to reverse the vacation pay accrual in each period if an employer chooses to instead record just incremental changes in the accrual from month to month.

EXAMPLE

There is already an existing accrued balance of 40 hours of unused vacation time for Wes Smith on the books of High Noon Armaments. In the most recent month that has just ended, Mr. Smith accrued an additional five hours of vacation time (since he is entitled to 60 hours of accrued vacation time per year, and $60 \div 12$ = five hours per month). He also used three hours of vacation time during the month. This means that, as of the end of the month, High Noon should have accrued a total of 42 hours of vacation time for him (calculated as 40 hours existing balance + 5 hours additional accrual – 3 hours used).

Mr. Smith is paid $30 per hour, so his total vacation accrual should be $1,260 (42 hours × $30/hour), so High Noon accrues an additional $60 of vacation liability.

What if a company has a "use it or lose it" policy? This means that employees must use their vacation time by a certain date (such as the end of the year), and can only carry forward a small number of hours (if any) into the next year. One issue is that this policy may be illegal, since vacation is an earned benefit that cannot be taken away (which depends on state law). If this policy is considered to be legal, it is acceptable to reduce the accrual as of the date when employees are supposed to have used their accrued vacation, thereby reflecting the reduced liability to the company as represented by the number of vacation hours that employees have lost.

What if an employee receives a pay raise? Then increase the amount of his entire vacation accrual by the incremental amount of the pay raise. This is because, if the employee were to leave the company and be paid all of his unused vacation pay, he would be paid at his most recent rate of pay.

Tax Deposits

When an employer withholds taxes from employee pay, it must deposit these funds with the government at stated intervals. The journal entry for doing so is a debit to the tax liability account being paid and a credit to the cash account, which reduces the cash balance. For example, if a company were to pay a state government for unemployment taxes, the entry would be:

	Debit	Credit
State unemployment taxes payable	xxx	
Cash		xxx

Payroll Information in the Financial Statements - Wages

When a company pays wages, the effect is a reduction in the cash balance on the balance sheet and an increase in the wages expense line item in the income statement. In addition, if there is a wage, commission, or bonus accrual to reflect an unpaid wage amount, this appears in the balance sheet as an increase in the accrued wages, commissions, or bonuses liability, and in the income statement as an increase in one of the compensation expense line items.

If expenses are categorized by line item in the income statement, the various compensation expenses may be charged to specific departments. It is particularly common to shift the cost of direct labor into the cost of goods sold line item in the income statement.

Payroll Information in the Financial Statements – Payroll Taxes

When a company incurs an obligation to pay payroll taxes to the government, a portion of it appears on the income statement, and a portion on the balance sheet.

An employer would record an expense on the income statement for the employer matching portion of any social security and Medicare taxes, as well as the entire amount of any federal and state unemployment taxes (since they are paid by the company and not the employees). In some locations, there may be additional taxes owed by the company, such as a head tax for every person employed within the boundaries of a city. All of these payroll taxes are valid expenses of the company, and so will appear on its income statement.

These taxes should be charged to expense in the period incurred. They may be charged to a single payroll taxes account, or to a payroll taxes account within each department. If the latter is the case, some part of the taxes will likely be charged to the production department, in which case there is an option to include them in an overhead cost pool, from which they are allocated to the cost of goods sold and ending inventory; this can defer the recognition of a portion of the payroll taxes until such time as the inventory is sold.

A company also incurs a liability for payroll taxes, which appears as a short-term liability on its balance sheet. This liability is comprised of all the taxes just noted (until they are paid), plus the amount of any social security and Medicare taxes that are withheld from the pay of employees. In the later situation, the company is essentially an agent for the government, and is responsible for transferring the funds to the government. Thus, the employee portion of social security and Medicare taxes are not an expense to the company, but they are a liability.

Summary

This chapter has shown a broad array of journal entries that can be used to record payroll-related transactions. Given the large number of journal entries, it is common for errors to arise in the accounting for payroll. Here are several ways to reduce payroll accounting errors:

- *Journal entry templates.* Use a standard format for each type of journal entry, to consistently use the same account numbers. This can be a simple form if there is a manual payroll system, or a template function within an accounting software package.
- *Automated reversing entries.* If it is necessary to reverse a journal entry in the next accounting period and an accounting software package is being used, employ the automated reversing feature in the software, so that the reversal occurs without any further actions from the payroll staff.
- *Integrated payroll module.* If payroll is processed in-house, do so through the payroll module provided by the supplier of the accounting software (if there is such a module). This module usually generates all journal entries related to payroll processing, and posts them to the accounting system.
- *Horizontal analysis.* Even if payroll entries are properly filled out, it is possible to have entered an incorrect wage amount, or charged it to the wrong department. A good way to spot these problems is to run a preliminary set of financial statements that show the results of each department over several consecutive periods (known as *horizontal analysis*). An incorrect payroll entry will likely result in a spike or drop in a payroll line item in comparison to the rest of the preceding periods.

The accrual journal entries recommended in this chapter are based on the assumption that an employer is using the accrual basis of accounting. If it is instead using the cash basis of accounting, where transactions are only recorded when there is a cash receipt or expenditure, no accrual entries are used.

Chapter 12
Payroll Reports

Introduction

This chapter describes the standard and government-mandated reports issued by the payroll department, including how they are structured and when they are issued. An exception is the Form 941, Employer's Quarterly Federal Tax Return, which is described in the Tax Remittances chapter. We also address several of the more common internal management reports that originate in the payroll department.

Payroll Register

The primary internal report generated by the payroll system is the payroll register. This document itemizes the calculation of wages, taxes, and deductions for each employee for each payroll. There are multiple uses for the payroll register, including:

- *Investigation.* It is the starting point for the investigation of many issues involving employee pay.
- *Journal entries.* Create journal entries to record a payroll based on the information in the register.
- *Payments.* If manual check payments are being created, the source document for these payments is the register.
- *Reports.* The information on almost any government or management report related to payroll is drawn from the register.

The format of the payroll register is built into the payroll software, and so will vary somewhat by payroll system. If payroll processing is outsourced, the supplier will issue its own version of the payroll register as part of its basic service package. The following is a typical payroll register format, with overtime and state and local taxes removed in order to compress the presentation:

Sample Payroll Register

Empl. Nbr.	Employee Name	Hours Worked	Rate/ Hour	Gross Wages	Taxes	Other Deductions	Check Nbr.	Net Pay
100	Johnson, Mark	40	18.12	724.80	55.45	28.00	5403	641.35
105	Olds, Gary	27	36.25	978.75	74.87	42.25	5404	861.63
107	Zeff, Morton	40	24.00	960.00	73.44	83.00	5405	803.56
111	Quill, Davis	40	15.00	600.00	45.90	10.10	5406	544.00
116	Pincus, Joseph	35	27.75	971.25	74.30	37.50	5407	859.45

A comprehensive payroll register will include the following fields:

- *Employee number.* This is a unique identification number for each employee. The preceding report is sorted by employee number.
- *Department number.* In larger organizations, it is an excellent idea to assign a department number to each employee, so that departmental wage information can be more easily aggregated and charged to the correct department.
- *Employee name.* This is usually presented in last name, first name format. The payroll register may be sorted by employee last name, rather than by employee number.
- *Salary/wage indicator.* There may be a flag in the report that indicates whether an employee is paid a fixed salary or an hourly wage.
- *Marriage code.* This is a flag in the report, indicating whether a person is classified as married or single. Marriage status impacts the amount of income taxes withheld.
- *Allowances number.* This is the number of allowances that a person has claimed on his or her Form W-4. The number of allowances is used to calculate the amount of income taxes withheld.
- *Total hours worked.* This is the combined total of regular and overtime hours worked, and should tie back to the hours listed in the timekeeping system.
- *Regular hours worked.* This states the total amount of regular hours worked during the payroll period, and is used to calculate gross pay.
- *Overtime hours worked.* This states the total amount of overtime hours worked during the payroll period, and is used to calculate gross pay.
- *Regular hours pay rate.* This rate is multiplied by regular hours worked to arrive at part of the gross pay figure.
- *Overtime hours pay rate.* This rate is multiplied by overtime hours worked to arrive at part of the gross pay figure.
- *Gross pay.* This combines wages paid from regular and overtime hours worked, and is the grand total from which deductions are then made to arrive at net pay.

- *Federal income tax withholding.* This is the federal-level income taxes withheld from employee gross wages.
- *Social security tax.* This is the employee-paid portion of the social security tax. It does not include the employer-matched amount of the tax.
- *Medicare tax.* This is the employee-paid portion of the Medicare tax. It does not include the employer-matched amount of the tax.
- *State income tax withholding.* This is the state income taxes withheld from employee wages.
- *Other deductions.* This can include a broad array of deductions, such as for medical insurance, life insurance, pension plan contributions, and so forth. Identify each type of deduction on the report with a unique code. Thus, deductions for medical insurance could be identified with the MED code, while deductions for life insurance could be identified with the LIFE code.
- *Net pay.* This is the amount of cash paid to each employee after all deductions have been made from gross pay.
- *Check number.* This is the unique identifying number listed on each paycheck issued, and is used by the bank to identify cleared checks (among other uses).
- *Payment type.* This is a code that states whether payment was made with a check, direct deposit, or debit card.

> **Tip:** Do *not* include employee social security numbers in the payroll register, since these reports may end up in the wrong hands, leading to inappropriate dissemination of the social security numbers.

The payroll register should also provide a variety of summary-level information that can be used to record wage and tax information in the general ledger. It should aggregate gross wages, each type of deduction, state-level taxes withheld by individual state, and the total amount of cash paid. If reporting is at the department level, the payroll register should provide this information not only in total for the entire company, but also at the department level.

If one were to create a payroll register that contained all of the items in the preceding list, it would be an exceptionally crowded report. However, packing information into the payroll register makes it a great source document when researching payroll issues. Consequently, it is better to create a near-comprehensive payroll register format, rather than one containing the minimum amount of information.

Internal Management Reports

There are two principle types of payroll reports from an internal management perspective, which are trend reports and annualized cost reports. A trend report targets sudden bumps in pay, which may call for investigation to see if overtime was authorized. The following report focuses on overtime pay in each time period:

196

Sample Overtime Trend Report

Name	Week of				
	Jan. 7	Jan. 14	Jan. 21	Jan. 28	Feb. 4
Brett, J.	$0	$30	$0	$312	$0
Horton, M.	23	19	41	230	22
Indie, J.	0	0	30	185	0
Masters, K.	7	12	0	214	0
Totals	$30	$61	$71	$941	$22

The sample report indicates two issues. First, the company is spending an inordinate amount during the last week of the month on overtime, which may indicate a variety of problems with jamming shipments into the final week of each month. Second, there is an employee (Mr. Horton) who is consistently taking a small amount of overtime every week; this amount is so small that it may be escaping the attention of his supervisor, but the amount can add up over time.

The other type of payroll report is concerned with the total cost of an employee and incorporates all expenditures related to a person. This report is more difficult to compile, and so is usually assembled only on an annual basis. The report can reveal that certain employees are much more expensive than their base pay might initially indicate. A sample employee total cost report follows.

Sample Employee Total Cost Report

Name	Base Pay	Overtime	Taxes	Pension	Medical	Phone	Total
Abrahams	$42,500	$16,000	$5,200	$4,000	$5,500	$0	$73,200
Duran	120,000	0	10,800	12,000	3,200	1,000	147,000
Neederly	29,000	0	2,600	500	0	0	32,100
Quintana	60,500	23,000	7,500	6,000	6,700	850	104,550
Totals	$252,000	$39,000	$26,100	$22,500	$15,400	$1,850	$356,850

The preceding total cost report is designed to show a typical mix of expenditure levels. In the report, there are several employees who are clearly being paid hourly wages, and who heavily supplement these wages with overtime, resulting in a much higher total compensation level than their base pay would initially indicate. There are also large differences in the expenditure level for medical insurance, ranging from zero for those not taking this option to very high expenditures for what are presumably the company-paid portions of family medical insurance.

In addition to these reports, consider assembling a set of other reports that can be used to examine the business. Possible reports are:

- *Billable hours recorded by employee.* Can reveal which employees are not generating enough billable hours for the employer to break even on the cost of their compensation.

- *Compensation history by employee.* Shows the long-term trend of compensation for an employee; when paired with the market rate of pay, it can reveal which employees are trending higher or lower than the market rate.
- *Date of last pay raise by employee.* Can highlight instances in which an employee has not received a pay adjustment for a long period of time.
- *Vacation hours accrued by employee.* If an employer has a "use it or lose it" policy for vacation time, this report can give advance warning of situations in which employees may be about to lose a large amount of vacation time.

These types of reports are extremely useful for monitoring wage levels and bringing compensation issues to the attention of management.

Form W-2

Following the end of every calendar year, and no later than January 31, an employer must issue the multi-part Form W-2, on which it itemizes the wages it paid to each employee during the year, as well as the taxes that it withheld from employee pay. It issues this form to anyone who was paid wages by the company at any time during the year, even if they no longer work for the business. This information forms the basis for the personal income tax returns completed by all employees for the federal government and the state government in which they reside. An example of the Form W-2 is shown below.

Sample Form W-2

22222	Void ☐	a Employee's social security number	For Official Use Only ▶ OMB No. 1545-0008		
b Employer identification number (EIN)				1 Wages, tips, other compensation	2 Federal income tax withheld
c Employer's name, address, and ZIP code				3 Social security wages	4 Social security tax withheld
				5 Medicare wages and tips	6 Medicare tax withheld
				7 Social security tips	8 Allocated tips
d Control number				9	10 Dependent care benefits
e Employee's first name and initial	Last name		Suff.	11 Nonqualified plans	12a See instructions for box 12
				13 Statutory employee Retirement plan Third-party sick pay	12b
				14 Other	12c
					12d
f Employee's address and ZIP code					
15 State Employer's state ID number	16 State wages, tips, etc.	17 State income tax	18 Local wages, tips, etc.	19 Local income tax	20 Locality name

Form **W-2** Wage and Tax Statement   **2016**   Department of the Treasury—Internal Revenue Service

Copy A For Social Security Administration — Send this entire page with Form W-3 to the Social Security Administration; photocopies are not acceptable.

For Privacy Act and Paperwork Reduction Act Notice, see the separate instructions.

Cat. No. 10134D

The Form W-2 contains a large number of fields, but many of them are not needed to report the compensation and tax information for a typical employee; many of the fields are only required to report unusual compensation arrangements. The payroll system prints these forms automatically after the end of the calendar year. If payroll is being outsourced, the supplier will issue them on the employer's behalf. Thus, the Form W-2 is usually not an especially difficult document to produce.

The Form W-2 is comprised of several copies, which are used as follows:

- *Copy A*. Send this copy to the Social Security Administration.
- *Copy 1*. Send this copy to the state, city, or local tax department.
- *Copy B*. The recipient sends this copy to the IRS as part of his or her federal tax return.
- *Copy C*. This copy is intended for the employee's records.
- *Copy 2*. The recipient attaches this copy to his or her state, city, or local income tax return.
- *Copy D*. This copy is intended for the employer's records.

Tip: More than one Form W-2 can be issued to an employee. For example, if it is necessary to report more items than will fit in one box on the form, do so on an additional form. If so, fill in the same identifying information in boxes "a" through "f" that were completed for the first Form W-2 for the employee.

Explanations of the key fields on the Form W-2 are:

- *Box a, Social security number*. Enter the employee's social security number. This should be the number shown on the employee's social security card.
- *Box b, Employer identification number (EIN)*. Enter the EIN assigned to the employer by the IRS.
- *Box c, Employer address*. Enter the employer's mailing address.
- *Box d, Control number*. Use this box at the employer's option to identify an individual Form W-2. The IRS does not use the information in this box.
- *Box e, Employee name*. Enter the name of the employee that is shown on his or her social security card. If the name is too long, print the full last name, and enter initials for the first and middle names. Do not include titles in the name.
- *Box f, Employee address*. Enter the mailing address of the employee. A post office box number is acceptable.
- *Box 1, Wages, tips, other compensation*. Enter the total amount of taxable compensation paid to the employee during the calendar year.
- *Box 2, Federal income tax withheld*. Enter the total amount withheld from the employee's pay for federal income taxes during the calendar year. Include the 20% excise tax on excess parachute payments (if any).
- *Box 3, Social security wages*. Enter the amount of total wages paid during the calendar year that are subject to the social security tax.

- *Box 4, Social security tax withheld.* Enter the total amount of social security taxes withheld from the employee's pay during the calendar year. Do not include the matching amount of social security tax paid by the employer.
- *Box 5, Medicare wages and tips.* Enter the amount of total wages paid during the calendar year that are subject to the Medicare tax.
- *Box 6, Medicare tax withheld.* Enter the total amount of Medicare taxes withheld from the employee's pay during the calendar year. Do not include the matching amount of Medicare tax paid by the employer.
- *Box 7, Social security tips.* Enter the amount of tips reported by the employee to the employer, even if the employer did not have sufficient employee funds to collect the social security tax related to the tips.
- *Box 8, Allocated tips.* If the employer is a food or beverage establishment, enter the amount of tips allocated to the employee.
- *Box 9.* Do not use this box.
- *Box 10, Dependent care benefits.* Enter the total dependent care benefits paid to the employee under a dependent care assistance program, or incurred on the employee's behalf by the employer.
- *Box 11, Nonqualified plans.* Enter any distributions to the employee from a nonqualified plan. Also report the amount of these distributions within the total in Box 1.
- *Box 12, Coded items.* Use the IRS codes in the following table to record the dollar amount of the indicated items. There is space within Box 12 for four coded items.
- *Box 13, Checkboxes.* Check the "Statutory employee" box if an employee is a statutory employee whose earnings are not subject to federal income tax withholding, but which are subject to social security and Medicare taxes. Check the "Retirement plan" box if the employee was an active participant in a variety of types of pension plans. Check the "Third-party sick pay" box if the entity is a third-party sick pay payer who is filing a Form W-2 for an insured party's employee, or an employer reporting sick pay payments made to an employee by a third party.
- *Box 14, Other.* If the employer included 100% of a vehicle's annual lease value in an employee's income, enter it here. One may enter other information in that box to give to an employee, such as union dues, uniform payments, and educational assistance payments.
- *Boxes 15–20, State and local income tax information.* Report state and local income tax information in these boxes. This includes the two-letter abbreviation of the name of the state, and the employer's state ID number. There is room to report wages and taxes for two states and two localities.

IRS Codes for Box 12 in the Form W-2

Code	Explanation
A	The social security tax on that portion of an employee's tips that the employer could not collect, because the employee did not have sufficient funds from which the employer could deduct it.
B	The Medicare tax on that portion of an employee's tips that the employer could not collect, because the employee did not have sufficient funds from which the employer could deduct it.
C	The taxable cost of group-term life insurance coverage exceeding $50,000 provided by the employer to the employee.
D	The amount of any elective deferrals under a section 401(k) plan.
E	The amount of any elective deferrals under a section 403(b) plan.
F	The amount of any elective deferrals under a section 408(k)(6) salary reduction simplified employee pension plan.
G	The amount of any elective deferrals and employer contributions under a section 457(b) plan.
H	The amount of any elective deferrals under a section 501(c)(18)(D) tax-exempt organization plan. Also include this amount in the entry in Box 1.
J	The amount of any sick pay that was paid by a third party, and which was not included in income because the employee contributed to the sick pay plan.
K	The 20% excise tax on excess golden parachute payments.
L	The amount the employer reimbursed an employee for business expenses using a per diem or mileage allowance, for the amount treated as substantiated under IRS rules.
M	The amount of uncollected social security tax related to the taxable cost of group-term life insurance over $50,000. This usually arises when the employer still provides the insurance to someone who is no longer an employee.
N	The amount of uncollected Medicare tax related to the taxable cost of group-term life insurance over $50,000. This usually arises when the employer still provides the insurance to someone who is no longer an employee.
P	The total moving expense reimbursements that were paid directly to an employee for deductible moving expenses.
Q	This is nontaxable combat pay.
R	This is the amount of employer contributions to an Archer MSA.
S	This is the amount of any deferrals under a section 408(p) salary reduction SIMPLE retirement account. If the SIMPLE is part of a 401(k) plan, use code D instead.
T	This is the total that paid or reimbursed for qualified adoption expenses furnished to an employee under an adoption assistance program.
V	This is the spread between the fair market value of stock over the exercise price of options granted to an employee under nonstatutory stock options.
W	This is the employer contributions to a health savings account.
Y	This is the amount of wage deferrals under a section 409(a) nonqualified deferred

Code	Explanation
	compensation plan.
Z	This is the amount deferred that is includible in income under section 409(a) because a nonqualified deferred compensation plan does not satisfy the requirements of section 409(a).
AA	This is designated Roth contributions under a section 401(k) plan.
BB	This is designated Roth contributions under a section 403(b) plan.
DD	This is the non-taxable cost of employer-sponsored health coverage.
EE	This is designated Roth contributions under a section 457(b) plan.

Note: If an employee leaves an employer, the employer does not have to wait until the end of the calendar year to issue a Form W-2 to the employee. If a departed employee requests a Form W-2, supply it to him within the later of 30 days of the request or the final wage payment.

An employer does not have to provide the Form W-2 on paper; the IRS also allows for the distribution of an electronic version to employees. To do so, the IRS requires that the employer adhere to the following guidelines:

- Each employee must consent to receive the form electronically.
- The employer must notify employees of the hardware and software required to receive the form.
- The employer must notify employees about how to withdraw their consent.
- The employer must notify employees of the procedure for updating their contact information that is used to provide an electronic Form W-2.
- The employer must notify employees of any changes to its contact information.

If an employee revokes his or her consent to receive the Form W-2 electronically, the company must instead provide the form on paper.

Note: The employer must furnish electronic Forms W-2 by the same date that the paper version of the form is due.

Form W-3

Once an employer creates Forms W-2 for its employees, it takes Copy A of these forms and aggregates selected information on them into a Form W-3, Transmittal of Wage and Tax Statements. It then submits all of the Copy A versions of the Forms W-2, as well as the Form W-3, to the government no later than February 28. An example of the Form W-3 is shown below.

Explanations of the key fields on the Form W-3 are:

- *Box a, Control number.* This box can be used to identify a Form W-3. The IRS does not use the information in this box.

- *Box b, Kind of payer.* Check the box that applies to the employer. Check only one box. The most common box to check is the "941" box, which indicates that the employer files the Form 941, Employer's Quarterly Federal Tax Return.
- *Box b, Kind of employer.* Check the box that applies to the employer. Check only one box. The most common box to check is the "None apply" box.
- *Box b, Third-party sick pay.* Check this box if the filer is a third-party sick pay payer, or is reporting sick pay payments made by a third party.
- *Box c, Total number of Forms W-2.* Enter the number of Forms W-2 that accompany this Form W-3.
- *Box d, Establishment number.* Use this box to identify different establishments within the business. It is allowable to file a separate Form W-3 for each establishment, along with accompanying Forms W-2, even if all of the establishments use the same employer identification number.
- *Box e, Employer identification number.* Enter the EIN assigned to the employer by the IRS. If the employer does not yet have an EIN when it files the Form W-3, enter "Applied for" in this box.
- *Box f, Employer's name.* Enter the name of the employer, which should be the same one used on the Form 941.
- *Box g, Employer's address.* Enter the employer's mailing address.
- *Box h, Other EIN used this year.* Enter any other employer identification number that was used during the year on Form 941 that is different from the EIN stated on this form.
- *Boxes 1-8.* Enter the wages, tax withholdings, and tip allocations in these boxes that are the totals from the corresponding Forms W-2 being submitting along with this form.
- *Box 10, Dependent care benefits.* Enter the total of the dependent care benefits reported in box 10 of the accompanying Forms W-2.
- *Box 11, Nonqualified plans.* Enter the total amount in box 11 of the accompanying Forms W-2.
- *Box 12a, Deferred compensation.* Enter the total for the following IRS codes in box 12 on the accompanying Forms W-2: codes D through H, S, Y, AA, BB, and EE. Do not enter the codes themselves.
- *Box 13, For third-party sick pay use only.* If the filer is a third-party payer of sick pay, enter the aggregate amount of third-party sick pay recap.
- *Box 14, Income tax withheld by payer of third-party sick pay.* Enter the total income tax withheld by third-party payers on sick pay payments to employees.
- *Box 15, State | Employer's state ID number.* Enter the two-letter abbreviation of the state being reported on the accompanying Forms W-2, as well as the ID number assigned to the employer by the state. If more than one state is being reported, then enter an "X" here, and do not enter a state ID number.

- *Boxes 16-19.* Enter the total amount of state/local wages and income taxes in the accompanying Forms W-2. If the Forms W-2 contain amounts for more than one state or locality, combine them into one reported amount.
- *Contact information.* Enter the name of the person most familiar with the payroll information on the report. An appropriate choice might be the payroll manager.

Sample Form W-3

33333	a Control number	For Official Use Only ▶ OMB No. 1545-0008		

b Kind of Payer (Check one)	941 ☐ Military ☐ 943 ☐ 944 ☐ CT-1 ☐ Hshld. emp. ☐ Medicare govt. emp. ☐	Kind of Employer (Check one)	None apply ☐ 501c non-govt. ☐ State/local non-501c ☐ State/local 501c ☐ Federal govt. ☐	Third-party sick pay (Check if applicable) ☐

c Total number of Forms W-2	d Establishment number	1 Wages, tips, other compensation	2 Federal income tax withheld
e Employer identification number (EIN)		3 Social security wages	4 Social security tax withheld
f Employer's name		5 Medicare wages and tips	6 Medicare tax withheld
		7 Social security tips	8 Allocated tips
		9	10 Dependent care benefits
		11 Nonqualified plans	12a Deferred compensation
g Employer's address and ZIP code			
h Other EIN used this year		13 For third-party sick pay use only	12b
15 State Employer's state ID number		14 Income tax withheld by payer of third-party sick pay	
16 State wages, tips, etc.	17 State income tax	18 Local wages, tips, etc.	19 Local income tax
Employer's contact person		Employer's telephone number	For Official Use Only
Employer's fax number		Employer's email address	

Under penalties of perjury, I declare that I have examined this return and accompanying documents and, to the best of my knowledge and belief, they are true, correct, and complete.

Signature ▶   Title ▶   Date ▶

Form **W-3** Transmittal of Wage and Tax Statements   **2017**   Department of the Treasury
Internal Revenue Service

As was the case for the Form W-2, the employer's payroll software should generate the Form W-3 automatically. If not, be sure to verify that the information on the accompanying Forms W-2 add up to the totals printed on the Form W-3. Also, verify that the totals on the Form W-3 match the aggregate of the amounts listed on all Forms 941 filed during the year.

Corrections to Forms W-2 and W-3

If a change must be made to the reported wages, social security, or Medicare taxes of an employee for a prior year, the employer must file Form W-2c, Corrected Wage and Tax Statement, as well as Form W-3c, Transmittal of Corrected Wage and Tax Statements. It is not necessary to use the Form W-3c if the correction is for the Form W-2 of just one employee, or if the corrections are only to employee names, addresses, or social security numbers. A sample Form W-2c follows.

Sample Form W-2c

	For Official Use Only ▶		c Tax year/Form corrected		d Employee's correct SSN
44444	OMB No. 1545-0008				
a Employer's name, address, and ZIP code			/ W-2		
			e Corrected SSN and/or name (Check this box and complete boxes f and/or g if incorrect on form previously filed.)		☐
			Complete boxes f and/or g only if incorrect on form **previously filed** ▶		
			f Employee's **previously reported** SSN		
b Employer's Federal EIN			g Employee's **previously reported** name		
			h Employee's first name and initial	Last name	Suff.

Note. Only complete money fields that are being corrected (exception: for corrections involving MQGE, see the General Instructions for Forms W-2 and W-3, under Specific Instructions for Form W-2c, boxes 5 and 6).

i Employee's address and ZIP code

Previously reported	Correct information	Previously reported	Correct information
1 Wages, tips, other compensation	1 Wages, tips, other compensation	2 Federal income tax withheld	2 Federal income tax withheld
3 Social security wages	3 Social security wages	4 Social security tax withheld	4 Social security tax withheld
5 Medicare wages and tips	5 Medicare wages and tips	6 Medicare tax withheld	6 Medicare tax withheld
7 Social security tips	7 Social security tips	8 Allocated tips	8 Allocated tips
9	9	10 Dependent care benefits	10 Dependent care benefits
11 Nonqualified plans	11 Nonqualified plans	12a See instructions for box 12	12a See instructions for box 12
13 Statutory employee ☐ Retirement plan ☐ Third-party sick pay ☐	13 Statutory employee ☐ Retirement plan ☐ Third-party sick pay ☐	12b	12b
14 Other (see instructions)	14 Other (see instructions)	12c	12c
		12d	12d

State Correction Information

Previously reported	Correct information	Previously reported	Correct information
15 State	15 State	15 State	15 State
Employer's state ID number	Employer's state ID number	Employer's state ID number	Employer's state ID number
16 State wages, tips, etc.	16 State wages, tips, etc.	16 State wages, tips, etc.	16 State wages, tips, etc.
17 State income tax	17 State income tax	17 State income tax	17 State income tax

Locality Correction Information

Previously reported	Correct information	Previously reported	Correct information
18 Local wages, tips, etc.	18 Local wages, tips, etc.	18 Local wages, tips, etc.	18 Local wages, tips, etc.
19 Local income tax	19 Local income tax	19 Local income tax	19 Local income tax
20 Locality name	20 Locality name	20 Locality name	20 Locality name

For Privacy Act and Paperwork Reduction Act Notice, see separate instructions.

Copy A—For Social Security Administration

Form **W-2c** (Rev. 8-2014)   **Corrected Wage and Tax Statement**   Cat. No. 61437D   Department of the Treasury Internal Revenue Service

Form 1099-MISC

An employer must file a Form 1099-MISC, Miscellaneous Income, to report payments of $600 or more to individuals who are not classified as employees (usually independent contractors) in exchange for services performed for the employer. This form must also be filed for each individual for whom an employer has withheld any federal income tax under backup withholding rules (irrespective of the amount). Thus, do *not* use this form to report compensation paid to employees (that information appears on the Form W-2). A sample Form 1099-MISC is shown below.

Sample Form 1099-MISC

An employer must send the form to recipients no later than January 31 for payments made during the preceding calendar year. Also, send a copy of the form to the IRS no later than February 28, along with a Form 1096, Annual Summary and Transmittal of U.S. Information Returns, which aggregates the information on the individual Forms 1099.

Note: It is not necessary to issue the Form 1099-MISC to corporations, except for fish purchases for cash, attorney's fees, medical services, and substitute payments in lieu of dividends or tax-exempt interest.

Explanations of the key fields on the Form 1099-MISC are:

- *Box 1, Rents.* Enter amounts of $600 or more for all types of rent payments, such as for real estate rentals and equipment rentals.
- *Box 2, Royalties.* Enter amounts of $10 or more for such items as oil and gas or mineral property royalties, as well as for patents, copyrights, and trade names.

- *Box 3, Other income.* Enter amounts in this box that do not clearly fall into one of the other categories, such as prizes and awards paid to individuals who are not employees, and punitive damages received.
- *Box 4, Federal income tax withheld.* Enter any amount of federal income tax withheld for persons who did not furnish the company with a taxpayer identification number.
- *Box 5, Fishing boat proceeds.* Enter the recipient's share of the proceeds from a catch, as well as cash payments up to $100 per trip that are contingent upon a minimum catch, and which are paid solely for extra duties (such as being the cook) for which such payments are traditional in the industry.
- *Box 6, Medical services.* Enter amounts of $600 or more made to each physician or supplier of medical services. If the payments are to a corporation, report the payments in this form.
- *Box 7, Nonemployee compensation.* Most of the reporting on the form is in this field. Consider this box to be the default location in which to report payments. Examples of such payments are professional service fees, referral fees, payments by attorneys to witnesses or experts in legal adjudication, commissions paid to non-employees, and directors' fees.
- *Box 8, Substitute payments.* Enter the total amount received by a broker for a customer in lieu of dividends or tax-exempt interest resulting from the loan of a customer's securities, if the amount is $10 or more.
- *Box 9, Consumer products.* Check this box if $5,000 or more of consumer products have been sold to a person on a buy-sell or commission basis for resale. Do not enter a monetary amount in this box.
- *Box 10, Crop insurance proceeds.* Enter crop insurance proceeds of at least $600 paid to farmers.
- *Box 13, Golden parachute payments.* Enter any amount of excess golden parachute payments. The amount is considered excess if it exceeds three times the average annual compensation for services included in an individual's gross income over the most recent five tax years.
- *Box 14, Attorney payments.* Enter amounts of $600 or more to an attorney in connection with legal services provided.
- *Box 15a, Section 409A deferrals.* Enter amounts of $600 or more deferred during the year under a nonqualified plan.
- *Box 15b, Section 409A income.* Enter all amounts deferred that are includible in income under section 409A because a nonqualified compensation plan does not satisfy the requirements of section 409A. Do not include amounts that are considered to be subject to a substantial risk of forfeiture.
- *Boxes 16-18, State and local withholdings.* It is not necessary to enter information in these fields, since they are only for internal use, and are not required by the IRS. There is room in these boxes to report payments for up to two states.

The Form 1099-MISC is comprised of several copies, which are used as follows:

- *Copy A.* To be filed by the employer with the summary-level Form 1096 with the IRS. A sample of the Form 1096 is shown below.
- *Copy 1.* To be filed by the employer with the state tax department.
- *Copy B.* To be sent to the individual ("recipient") who provided services to the employer.
- *Copy 2.* To be filed by the recipient with the recipient's state income tax return.
- *Copy C.* To be retained by the employer.

If an employer generates at least 250 Forms 1099, they must be filed electronically.

The Form 1096, Annual Summary and Transmittal of U.S. Information Returns, is a summary-level document that aggregates the information on a batch of Forms 1099. List on this form the number of accompanying Forms 1099, check off the type of Forms 1099 (there are several varieties), and enter the total amount of federal income tax withheld on the forms. A sample form is shown below.

Sample Form 1096

New Hire Reporting

The state governments require that an employer report to a state-level registry whenever it hires a new employee. This notification must be made within 20 days of an employee's start date. The state governments peruse this information to locate people who owe child support payments. The new hire information to be supplied is:

- Employee name

- Employee social security number
- Employee home address
- Employee start date with the employer
- Employer name
- Employer address
- Employer identification number

Each state government provides a separate system for reporting new hire information. If payroll processing is outsourced, the supplier usually completes the new hire reporting on the employer's behalf, and includes this service in its basic payroll package.

If the employer has employees in multiple states, one can either report this information to the state in which each employee works, or send all of the new hire reports to just one state in which any employees work. If the second option is chosen, notify the U.S. Department of Health and Human services of this decision, indicate which state will receive the reports, and the states in which employees currently work[2]. This notice should include the employer name, address, contact information, and employer identification number. Send the notice to:

> Department of Health and Human Services
> Multi-State Employer Registration
> Office of Child Support Enforcement
> P.O. Box 509
> Randallstown, MD 21133

Summary

This chapter addressed the key internal payroll report that a company uses – the payroll register – as well as the payroll reports that the federal and state governments require it to issue. It may not be necessary to alter the format of internal reports for long periods of time. However, this is not the case for government-mandated reports. Some of these government reports are replaced with updated versions at the beginning of each year, so be sure to replace older report forms with newer ones. This step can be included in the year-end closing procedure, as a reminder to the payroll staff.

---

[2] Source: http://www.acf.hhs.gov/programs/css/resource/multistate-employer-registration-form-instructions

Chapter 13
Payroll Recordkeeping

Introduction

Various legal and operational requirements of the payroll function mandate that a large number of records be maintained. The most critical government-mandated forms are explained in this chapter, along with an array of other information to consider as part of the official set of payroll records to be retained.

Related podcast episodes: Episodes 126 through 129 of the Accounting Best Practices Podcast discuss the streamlining of payroll. They are available at: **www.accountingtools.com/podcasts** or **iTunes**

The Employment Application

The first document that an employer hands to a prospective recruit is the employment application. This document is available in many formats, and can be purchased at any office supply store. The more common items found on the application are:

- *Personal information.* Includes name, social security number, phone number, and address.
- *Warning flags.* Asks for information that allows one to screen an application quickly, and possibly eliminate it from consideration. Examples of warning flags are:
  - Willingness to travel
  - Willingness to relocate
  - Criminal convictions and nature of the crime
- *Employment history.* Key issues in an employment history are the reason for leaving and the intervals between jobs, which give some indication of how long-term a recruit may be if the company elects to hire him.
- *Education.* Asks for degrees earned and dates of study, which is useful for determining how recently and the extent to which a person was trained.
- *Additional information.* Recruits may have additional skills that relate to the prospective job, so this gives them a place in which to bring it to the prospective employer's attention.
- *Referral.* It is useful to determine how a recruit heard about the position, which indicates the effectiveness of the company's recruiting efforts. This section can include check boxes for the various types of marketing that the company employs.

It is not necessary to ask for references in an employment application, since that information is only needed after interviews have been conducted.

Tip: Consider setting up the employment application for on-line data entry by recruits, so that one can more easily peruse information, forward it to other parties, and perhaps have software sort through the applications and flag the most promising ones, based on key words.

Much of the information on an employment application is duplicated in an employee's resume, but the application is still a useful document because it requires an applicant to supply information in *every* area that the employer believes is important.

The Employer Identification Number

A business can only report employment taxes or give tax statements to employees if it has an employer identification number (EIN). The EIN is a nine-digit number that is issued by the IRS. The EIN is arranged in the 00-0000000 format. Include the company EIN on all reports and other correspondence sent to the IRS and Social Security Administration.

Tip: A business should only have one EIN. If there is more than one EIN, contact the IRS and they will rule on which one to use.

To apply for an EIN, either fill out Form SS-4 (of which an example is reproduced below), or go to the www.irs.gov website and click on the Apply for an Employer Identification Number link.

Tip: A social security number cannot be used instead of an employer identification number.

Tip: If an employer has applied for an EIN but has not yet received one by the date when a tax return or remittance is due, write "Applied for" and the date when the entity applied for the EIN in the space on the form where one would normally enter the EIN.

The Social Security Number

Record each new employee's name and social security number directly from his or her social security card. Any employee who does not have a social security card should apply for one.

This requirement applies to both resident and nonresident alien employees. A person applying for a social security number for the first time must provide at least two documents that prove his or her age, identity, and U.S. citizenship or current work-authorized immigration status. To obtain a replacement card, a person must provide one document to prove his or her identity. Acceptable documents that provide proof are described in the information accompanying the application for a social security card. An example of the social security number application form is shown below.

> **Tip:** An employer cannot accept a social security card that says "Not valid for employment." Such a card does not permit employment.

An employee social security number is needed for every employee in order to enter this information on the year-end Form W-2, on which is reported the wages paid to each employee. If a social security number is not entered on the Form W-2, an employer may owe the IRS a penalty, unless there is a reasonable justification for not reporting this information.

> **Tip:** If an employee has filed for a social security number but does not yet have one, and a Form W-2 must be filed in the meantime, enter "Applied for" on the form (if creating it manually) or enter all zeros (if filing electronically). When the employee later receives the social security number, file Copy A of Form W-2c, Corrected Wage and Tax Statement, with the social security number included.

If an employee's name is not shown correctly on his or her social security card (most commonly as a result of a name change arising from a marriage or divorce), continue reporting wage information under the old name until the employee provides the employer with an updated social security card.

Application for Employer Identification Number

SS-4 Form (Rev. January 2010) Department of the Treasury Internal Revenue Service	**Application for Employer Identification Number** (For use by employers, corporations, partnerships, trusts, estates, churches, government agencies, Indian tribal entities, certain individuals, and others.) ▶ See separate instructions for each line. ▶ Keep a copy for your records.	OMB No. 1545-0003 EIN

<table>
<tr><td rowspan="12">Type or print clearly.</td><td colspan="4">1   Legal name of entity (or individual) for whom the EIN is being requested
Orion Designs</td></tr>
<tr><td colspan="2">2   Trade name of business (if different from name on line 1)</td><td colspan="2">3   Executor, administrator, trustee, "care of" name</td></tr>
<tr><td colspan="2">4a Mailing address (room, apt., suite no. and street, or P.O. box)
402 Galactic Way</td><td colspan="2">5a Street address (if different) (Do not enter a P.O. box.)</td></tr>
<tr><td colspan="2">4b City, state, and ZIP code (if foreign, see instructions)
Palomar</td><td colspan="2">5b City, state, and ZIP code (if foreign, see instructions)</td></tr>
<tr><td colspan="4">6   County and state where principal business is located
Arapahoe, CO</td></tr>
<tr><td colspan="2">7a Name of responsible party
Mr. Alvin Herschel</td><td colspan="2">7b SSN, ITIN, or EIN
43-127-7193</td></tr>
</table>

8a Is this application for a limited liability company (LLC) (or a foreign equivalent)? . . . . ☐ Yes ☑ No
8b If 8a is "Yes," enter the number of LLC members . . . . . ▶
8c If 8a is "Yes," was the LLC organized in the United States? . . . . ☐ Yes ☐ No

9a Type of entity (check only one box). Caution. If 8a is "Yes," see the instructions for the correct box to check.
- ☐ Sole proprietor (SSN) _____
- ☐ Partnership
- ☑ Corporation (enter form number to be filed) ▶ _____
- ☐ Personal service corporation
- ☐ Church or church-controlled organization
- ☐ Other nonprofit organization (specify) ▶ _____
- ☐ Other (specify) ▶
- ☐ Estate (SSN of decedent) _____
- ☐ Plan administrator (TIN) _____
- ☐ Trust (TIN of grantor) _____
- ☐ National Guard   ☐ State/local government
- ☐ Farmers' cooperative   ☐ Federal government/military
- ☐ REMIC   ☐ Indian tribal governments/enterprises

Group Exemption Number (GEN) if any ▶

9b If a corporation, name the state or foreign country (if applicable) where incorporated

State	Foreign country

10 Reason for applying (check only one box)
- ☑ Started new business (specify type) ▶ _____
- ☐ Hired employees (Check the box and see line 13.)
- ☐ Compliance with IRS withholding regulations
- ☐ Other (specify) ▶
- ☐ Banking purpose (specify purpose) ▶ _____
- ☐ Changed type of organization (specify new type) ▶ _____
- ☐ Purchased going business
- ☐ Created a trust (specify type) ▶ _____
- ☐ Created a pension plan (specify type) ▶ _____

11 Date business started or acquired (month, day, year). See instructions.
01/01/2017

12 Closing month of accounting year

13 Highest number of employees expected in the next 12 months (enter -0- if none). If no employees expected, skip line 14.

Agricultural	Household	Other
		50

14 If you expect your employment tax liability to be $1,000 or less in a full calendar year and want to file Form 944 annually instead of Forms 941 quarterly, check here. (Your employment tax liability generally will be $1,000 or less if you expect to pay $4,000 or less in total wages.) If you do not check this box, you must file Form 941 for every quarter. ☐

15 First date wages or annuities were paid (month, day, year). Note. If applicant is a withholding agent, enter date income will first be paid to nonresident alien (month, day, year) . . . . ▶

16 Check one box that best describes the principal activity of your business.
- ☐ Construction   ☐ Rental & leasing   ☐ Transportation & warehousing
- ☐ Real estate   ☐ Manufacturing   ☐ Finance & insurance
- ☐ Health care & social assistance   ☐ Wholesale-agent/broker
- ☐ Accommodation & food service   ☐ Wholesale-other   ☐ Retail
- ☑ Other (specify) ▶ Architectural Design

17 Indicate principal line of merchandise sold, specific construction work done, products produced, or services provided.
Architectural design

18 Has the applicant entity shown on line 1 ever applied for and received an EIN? ☐ Yes ☑ No
If "Yes," write previous EIN here ▶

Third Party Designee	Complete this section only if you want to authorize the named individual to receive the entity's EIN and answer questions about the completion of this form.	Designee's telephone number (include area code)
	Designee's name	
	Address and ZIP code	Designee's fax number (include area code)

Under penalties of perjury, I declare that I have examined this application, and to the best of my knowledge and belief, it is true, correct, and complete.

Name and title (type or print clearly) ▶

Applicant's telephone number (include area code)

Signature ▶   Date ▶

Applicant's fax number (include area code)

For Privacy Act and Paperwork Reduction Act Notice, see separate instructions.   Cat. No. 16055N   Form **SS-4** (Rev. 1-2010)

> **Tip:** Do not accept an individual taxpayer identification number (ITIN) instead of a social security number. The ITIN is only used by aliens who are not eligible for employment in the United States. The ITIN is a nine-digit number that always begins with "9" and which has either a "7" or an "8" as the fourth digit. Thus, the format is 9NN-7N-NNNN.

It is possible to verify employee social security numbers online at www.socialsecurity.gov/employer/ssnv.htm. One can verify up to 10 names and numbers per screen with immediate feedback of the results, or upload batch files of as many as 250,000 names and numbers, with results reported the next business day.

To register for this service, go to www.ssa.gov/employer and click on the Business Services Online link.

Employment Eligibility Verification

The Immigration Reform and Control Act of 1986 required the use of the Form I-9. The Act contains a number of clauses; the most relevant one for this discussion requires employers to attest to the immigration status of their employees. The employer must verify that every new employee is legally eligible to work in the United States. This verification involves having each employee complete Section 1 of the Form I-9, Employment Eligibility Verification, no later than the beginning of employment. The employer must complete Section 2 of the form within three business days of the beginning of employment. In the form, the employee presents appropriate types of identification, and the employer verifies these documents. The employer may also need to complete Section 3 of the form in cases where an employee's previous grant of work authorization has expired, and new evidence of work authorization is therefore required. It is also acceptable for the employer to require an entirely new Form I-9, rather than completing Section 3 of an existing form.

An example of the Form I-9 is provided next, along with a listing of the types of documents that are considered acceptable evidence. In essence, an employee can present a single document that proves both identity and employment authorization (such as a U.S. passport or a permanent resident card) or two documents, one proving identity (such as a driver's license) and the other proving employment authorization (such as a social security card).

The employer does not file a completed Form I-9 with any government agency. Instead, it must retain these forms and make them available for inspection by U.S. government officials.

It is not necessary to complete a Form I-9 under the following circumstances:

- The person is employed for casual domestic work in a private home on an intermittent basis
- The person is an independent contractor
- The person is working for a contractor, who is turn is providing contract services to the business

> **Tip:** If there are a large number of employees, it may be cost-effective to store completed I-9 forms in an electronic format, along with digital signatures. This format is allowed by law.

The Withholding Allowance

Each employee should have a current Form W-4 on file. This form is explained in more detail in the Payroll Taxes chapter. Essentially, employees use it to claim a certain number of withholding allowances, which directly affect the amount of income taxes withheld from their wages. An employee may replace an existing Form W-4 with a new one that claims a different number of allowances. Retain all versions of the Form W-4, in case an employee ever questions the calculation of the income taxes deducted from his wages. A sample of the Form W-4 follows.

Application for a Social Security Card

SOCIAL SECURITY ADMINISTRATION			
Application for a Social Security Card			Form Approved OMB No. 0960-0066

		First	Full Middle Name	Last
1	**NAME** TO BE SHOWN ON CARD			
	FULL NAME AT BIRTH IF OTHER THAN ABOVE	First	Full Middle Name	Last
	OTHER NAMES USED			

2	Social Security number previously assigned to the person listed in item 1	☐☐☐ – ☐☐ – ☐☐☐☐

3	**PLACE OF BIRTH** (Do Not Abbreviate) City State or Foreign Country	Office Use Only FCI	**4**	**DATE OF BIRTH** MM/DD/YYYY

5	**CITIZENSHIP** (Check One)	☐ U.S. Citizen	☐ Legal Alien Allowed To Work	☐ Legal Alien Not Allowed To Work(See Instructions On Page 3)	☐ Other (See Instructions On Page 3)

6	**ETHNICITY** Are You Hispanic or Latino? (Your Response is Voluntary) ☐ Yes ☐ No	**7**	**RACE** Select One or More (Your Response is Voluntary)	☐ Native Hawaiian ☐ Alaska Native ☐ Asian	☐ American Indian ☐ Black/African American	☐ Other Pacific Islander ☐ White

8	**SEX**	☐ Male	☐ Female

9	**A. PARENT/ MOTHER'S NAME AT HER BIRTH**	First Full Middle Name Last	
	B. PARENT/ MOTHER'S SOCIAL SECURITY NUMBER (See instructions for 9 B on Page 3)	☐☐☐ – ☐☐ – ☐☐☐☐	☐ Unknown

10	**A. PARENT/ FATHER'S NAME**	First Full Middle Name Last	
	B. PARENT/ FATHER'S SOCIAL SECURITY NUMBER (See instructions for 10B on Page 3)	☐☐☐ – ☐☐ – ☐☐☐☐	☐ Unknown

11	Has the person listed in item 1 or anyone acting on his/her behalf ever filed for or received a Social Security number card before?
	☐ Yes (If "yes" answer questions 12-13) ☐ No ☐ Don't Know (If "don't know," skip to question 14.)

12	Name shown on the most recent Social Security card issued for the person listed in item 1	First Full Middle Name Last

13	Enter any different date of birth if used on an earlier application for a card	MM/DD/YYYY

14	**TODAY'S DATE** MM/DD/YYYY	**15**	**DAYTIME PHONE NUMBER** Area Code Number

16	**MAILING ADDRESS** (Do Not Abbreviate)	Street Address, Apt. No., PO Box, Rural Route No.		
		City	State/Foreign Country	ZIP Code

I declare under penalty of perjury that I have examined all the information on this form, and on any accompanying statements or forms, and it is true and correct to the best to my knowledge.

17	**YOUR SIGNATURE**	**18**	**YOUR RELATIONSHIP TO THE PERSON IN ITEM 1 IS:** ☐ Self ☐ Natural Or Adoptive Parent ☐ Legal Guardian ☐ Other Specify

DO NOT WRITE BELOW THIS LINE (FOR SSA USE ONLY)				
NPN	DOC	NTI	CAN	ITV
PBC	EVI	EVA	EVC	PRA	NWR	DNR	UNIT
EVIDENCE SUBMITTED			SIGNATURE AND TITLE OF EMPLOYEE(S) REVIEWING EVIDENCE AND/OR CONDUCTING INTERVIEW	
				DATE
			DCL	DATE

Form SS-5 (08-2011) ef (08-2011)   Destroy Prior Editions   Page 5

Form I-9, Employment Eligibility Verification (page one)

Employment Eligibility Verification

Department of Homeland Security
U.S. Citizenship and Immigration Services

USCIS
Form I-9
OMB No. 1615-0047
Expires 03/31/2016

►**START HERE.** **Read instructions carefully before completing this form. The instructions must be available during completion of this form.**
ANTI-DISCRIMINATION NOTICE: It is illegal to discriminate against work-authorized individuals. Employers **CANNOT** specify which document(s) they will accept from an employee. The refusal to hire an individual because the documentation presented has a future expiration date may also constitute illegal discrimination.

Section 1. Employee Information and Attestation *(Employees must complete and sign Section 1 of Form I-9 no later than the **first day of employment**, but not before accepting a job offer.)*

Last Name *(Family Name)*	First Name *(Given Name)*	Middle Initial	Other Names Used *(if any)*
Smith	John	Q.	

Address *(Street Number and Name)*	Apt. Number	City or Town	State	Zip Code
123 Maple Street		Central City	CO ▼	80123

Date of Birth *(mm/dd/yyyy)*	U.S. Social Security Number	E-mail Address	Telephone Number
06/06/1995	4 2 2 - 5 4 - 6 9 1 3	smith.john@gmail.com	

I am aware that federal law provides for imprisonment and/or fines for false statements or use of false documents in connection with the completion of this form.

I attest, under penalty of perjury, that I am (check one of the following):

[X] A citizen of the United States

[ ] A noncitizen national of the United States *(See instructions)*

[ ] A lawful permanent resident (Alien Registration Number/USCIS Number): _____

[ ] An alien authorized to work until (expiration date, if applicable, mm/dd/yyyy) _____ . Some aliens may write "N/A" in this field.
(See instructions)

*For aliens authorized to work, provide your Alien Registration Number/USCIS Number **OR** Form I-94 Admission Number:*

1. Alien Registration Number/USCIS Number: _____

OR

2. Form I-94 Admission Number: _____

If you obtained your admission number from CBP in connection with your arrival in the United States, include the following:

Foreign Passport Number: _____

Country of Issuance: _____

Some aliens may write "N/A" on the Foreign Passport Number and Country of Issuance fields. *(See instructions)*

3-D Barcode
Do Not Write in This Space

Signature of Employee:	Date *(mm/dd/yyyy)*:

Preparer and/or Translator Certification *(To be completed and signed if Section 1 is prepared by a person other than the employee.)*

I attest, under penalty of perjury, that I have assisted in the completion of this form and that to the best of my knowledge the information is true and correct.

Signature of Preparer or Translator:	Date *(mm/dd/yyyy)*:

Last Name *(Family Name)*	First Name *(Given Name)*		

Address *(Street Number and Name)*	City or Town	State	Zip Code
		▼	

Form I-9, Employment Eligibility Verification (page two)

Section 2. Employer or Authorized Representative Review and Verification

(Employers or their authorized representative must complete and sign Section 2 within 3 business days of the employee's first day of employment. You must physically examine one document from List A OR examine a combination of one document from List B and one document from List C as listed on the "Lists of Acceptable Documents" on the next page of this form. For each document you review, record the following information: document title, issuing authority, document number, and expiration date, if any.)

Employee Last Name, First Name and Middle Initial from Section 1:

List A — Identity and Employment Authorization	OR	List B — Identity	AND	List C — Employment Authorization
Document Title: Passport		Document Title:		Document Title:
Issuing Authority: Natl Passport Authority		Issuing Authority:		Issuing Authority:
Document Number: 0123456789		Document Number:		Document Number:
Expiration Date (if any)(mm/dd/yyyy): 12/25/2022		Expiration Date (if any)(mm/dd/yyyy):		Expiration Date (if any)(mm/dd/yyyy):

Document Title:
Issuing Authority:
Document Number:
Expiration Date (if any)(mm/dd/yyyy):

Document Title:
Issuing Authority:
Document Number:
Expiration Date (if any)(mm/dd/yyyy):

3-D Barcode Do Not Write in This Space

Certification

I attest, under penalty of perjury, that (1) I have examined the document(s) presented by the above-named employee, (2) the above-listed document(s) appear to be genuine and to relate to the employee named, and (3) to the best of my knowledge the employee is authorized to work in the United States.

The employee's first day of employment (mm/dd/yyyy): 01/05/2016 (See instructions for exemptions.)

Signature of Employer or Authorized Representative	Date (mm/dd/yyyy): 01/05/2016	Title of Employer or Authorized Representative: HR Director
Last Name (Family Name): Emilio	First Name (Given Name): Joe	Employer's Business or Organization Name: Orion Designs

Employer's Business or Organization Address (Street Number and Name): 42 Center Street	City or Town: Arvada	State: CO	Zip Code: 80007

Section 3. Reverification and Rehires *(To be completed and signed by employer or authorized representative.)*

A. New Name (if applicable) Last Name (Family Name) First Name (Given Name)	Middle Initial	B. Date of Rehire (if applicable) (mm/dd/yyyy):

C. If employee's previous grant of employment authorization has expired, provide the information for the document from List A or List C the employee presented that establishes current employment authorization in the space provided below.

Document Title:	Document Number:	Expiration Date (if any)(mm/dd/yyyy):

I attest, under penalty of perjury, that to the best of my knowledge, this employee is authorized to work in the United States, and if the employee presented document(s), the document(s) I have examined appear to be genuine and to relate to the individual.

Signature of Employer or Authorized Representative:	Date (mm/dd/yyyy):	Print Name of Employer or Authorized Representative:

List of Acceptable Form I-9 Documents

LISTS OF ACCEPTABLE DOCUMENTS
All documents must be UNEXPIRED

Employees may present one selection from List A
or a combination of one selection from List B and one selection from List C.

LIST A Documents that Establish Both Identity and Employment Authorization	OR	LIST B Documents that Establish Identity	AND	LIST C Documents that Establish Employment Authorization

1. U.S. Passport or U.S. Passport Card
 	
2. Permanent Resident Card or Alien Registration Receipt Card (Form I-551)
 	
3. Foreign passport that contains a temporary I-551 stamp or temporary I-551 printed notation on a machine-readable immigrant visa
 	
4. Employment Authorization Document that contains a photograph (Form I-766)
 	
5. For a nonimmigrant alien authorized to work for a specific employer because of his or her status:
  a. Foreign passport; and
  b. Form I-94 or Form I-94A that has the following:
    (1) The same name as the passport; and
    (2) An endorsement of the alien's nonimmigrant status as long as that period of endorsement has not yet expired and the proposed employment is not in conflict with any restrictions or limitations identified on the form.
 	
6. Passport from the Federated States of Micronesia (FSM) or the Republic of the Marshall Islands (RMI) with Form I-94 or Form I-94A indicating nonimmigrant admission under the Compact of Free Association Between the United States and the FSM or RMI
	OR	1. Driver's license or ID card issued by a State or outlying possession of the United States provided it contains a photograph or information such as name, date of birth, gender, height, eye color, and address
		
		2. ID card issued by federal, state or local government agencies or entities, provided it contains a photograph or information such as name, date of birth, gender, height, eye color, and address
		
		3. School ID card with a photograph
		
		4. Voter's registration card
		
		5. U.S. Military card or draft record
		
		6. Military dependent's ID card
		
		7. U.S. Coast Guard Merchant Mariner Card
		
		8. Native American tribal document
		
		9. Driver's license issued by a Canadian government authority
		
		For persons under age 18 who are unable to present a document listed above:
		
		10. School record or report card
		
		11. Clinic, doctor, or hospital record
		
		12. Day-care or nursery school record
			AND	1. A Social Security Account Number card, unless the card includes one of the following restrictions:
				  (1) NOT VALID FOR EMPLOYMENT
				  (2) VALID FOR WORK ONLY WITH INS AUTHORIZATION
				  (3) VALID FOR WORK ONLY WITH DHS AUTHORIZATION
				
				2. Certification of Birth Abroad issued by the Department of State (Form FS-545)
				
				3. Certification of Report of Birth issued by the Department of State (Form DS-1350)
				
				4. Original or certified copy of birth certificate issued by a State, county, municipal authority, or territory of the United States bearing an official seal
				
				5. Native American tribal document
				
				6. U.S. Citizen ID Card (Form I-197)
				
				7. Identification Card for Use of Resident Citizen in the United States (Form I-179)
				
				8. Employment authorization document issued by the Department of Homeland Security

Form W-4, Employee's Withholding Allowance Certificate

Form **W-4**	**Employee's Withholding Allowance Certificate**	OMB No. 1545-0074
Department of the Treasury Internal Revenue Service	▶ Whether you are entitled to claim a certain number of allowances or exemption from withholding is subject to review by the IRS. Your employer may be required to send a copy of this form to the IRS.	**2016**

1 Your first name and middle initial	Last name	2 Your social security number
Evan	Chase	012-34-5678

Home address (number and street or rural route)
213 Main Street

3 ☐ Single ☐ Married ☐ Married, but withhold at higher Single rate.
Note: If married, but legally separated, or spouse is a nonresident alien, check the "Single" box.

City or town, state, and ZIP code
Overton, CO 80001

4 If your last name differs from that shown on your social security card, check here. You must call 1-800-772-1213 for a replacement card. ▶ ☐

5 Total number of allowances you are claiming (from line H above or from the applicable worksheet on page 2) ... **5** | 2
6 Additional amount, if any, you want withheld from each paycheck ... **6** $ | 50
7 I claim exemption from withholding for 2016, and I certify that I meet **both** of the following conditions for exemption.
• Last year I had a right to a refund of **all** federal income tax withheld because I had **no** tax liability, **and**
• This year I expect a refund of **all** federal income tax withheld because I expect to have **no** tax liability.
If you meet both conditions, write "Exempt" here ... ▶ **7**

Under penalties of perjury, I declare that I have examined this certificate and, to the best of my knowledge and belief, it is true, correct, and complete.

Employee's signature
(This form is not valid unless you sign it.) ▶ _____ Date ▶

8 Employer's name and address (Employer: Complete lines 8 and 10 only if sending to the IRS.)
Big Widget Company | 9 Office code (optional) | 10 Employer identification number (EIN) 84-1234567

For Privacy Act and Paperwork Reduction Act Notice, see page 2. | Cat. No. 10220Q | Form **W-4** (2016)

The Personnel File

Once a person is hired, create a personnel file in which can be stored a large amount of information related to that individual. This file may contain the following items:

- Job application
- Resume
- Form I-9
- Results of drug tests
- Commentary from interviewers
- Form W-4 (may be multiple versions submitted over time)
- Veteran status
- Garnishment notices and related wage deduction records
- Manager reviews
- Requests for changes in benefit deductions
- Address change notifications
- Requests by managers for pay rate changes

Under the dictates of the Family and Medical Leave Act, an employer must retain the following information:

- If an employee takes leave for less than a day, the hours taken
- If an employee takes leave for more than a day, the days taken
- The employee's signed notification of leave
- Documentation of any disputes regarding designation of the leave
- Payments made by the company for employee benefits while they are on leave

Timekeeping information is *not* stored in the personnel file, since timekeeping information is far too voluminous.

After a person leaves the company, also include the results of an exit interview, and place the file on inactive status in long-term storage.

In a small company, the payroll clerk maintains all personnel files, since there is no human resources department, and the payroll clerk is the person most likely to need the information in the files to process payroll. In a larger firm, this recordkeeping responsibility shifts to the human resources staff.

Mandated Document Retention

A variety of legislation has mandated the minimum periods over which payroll records must be maintained. The following table states these intervals and the minimum employer size for which the storage requirement is mandated.

Payroll Records Retention Schedule

Record Type	Retention Period	Minimum Employer Size
Benefit payments	3 years	20+ employees
Compensation records	3 years	20+ employees
Deductions from pay	2 years	No minimum
I-9 Form	Later of 3 years or 1 year after employment	4+ employees
Records of hours worked	3 years	20+ employees
Salary calculations	3 years	No minimum
Tax deductions	3 years	20+ employees

State and local laws may mandate longer retention intervals, so periodically check local regulations to see if they override the intervals noted here. Also, these retention periods are only the minimums. It may make sense to retain records for longer periods of time to ensure that the company has an adequate defense in case a lawsuit is filed prior to the expiration of any applicable statute of limitations.

In addition, the IRS requires that an employer retain all records of employment taxes for at least four years. These records should include:

- Employer identification number
- Amounts and dates of all wage, annuity, and pension payments
- Amounts of tips reported to the company by its employees
- Records of allocated tips
- The fair market value of in-kind wages paid
- The names, addresses, social security numbers, and occupations of employees and recipients
- Employee copies of Forms W-2 and W-2c that were returned to the company as undeliverable
- Date of employment for each employee

- Periods for which employees and recipients were paid while absent due to sickness or injury, and the amount and weekly rate of payments made to them
- Copies of employees' and recipients' income tax withholding allowance certificates
- Dates and amounts of tax deposits made by the company and acknowledgement numbers for deposits made by EFTPS
- Copies of returns filed and the related confirmation numbers
- Records of fringe benefits and expense reimbursements provided to employees, including substantiation

If the employer destroys these records prior to the end of the minimum four-year retention period, it is subject to government-imposed penalties. Consequently, adopt a document destruction policy and sign-off form that:

- Specifies which documents are to be destroyed
- States whether the holding period for the documents has been exceeded
- Requires the signature of the manager responsible for document retention

An employer must also retain documents for four years that support the information in its annual federal unemployment tax return. This information should include:

- Total wages paid during the calendar year
- Total wages paid during the calendar year that are subject to FUTA taxes
- Unemployment tax payments paid to the various state unemployment funds

Summary

We have assumed that the recordkeeping requirements in this chapter will be largely the responsibility of the payroll staff. In a larger firm, the human resources department is responsible for many of the items, rather than the payroll staff. If this is the case, the payroll staff may want to consider maintaining duplicates of some key documents that they need to process payroll, or (better yet) recording as many records as possible in a document management system, so that they can be accessed online by any authorized person.

Tip: A number of forms have been described in this chapter, many of which are updated by the IRS every year. This is a potential problem, because the IRS forms must be replenished whenever the IRS provides an updated version. The best method for doing so is to link to the PDF versions of the IRS forms on the IRS website, and make these links easily accessible to employees, perhaps through an online newsletter or a page on the company website. The same approach can be applied to company-specific forms, such as a sign-up form for a cafeteria plan.

Chapter 14
Payroll Procedures

Introduction

This chapter shows how to complete the most common activities within the payroll department, which center on payroll processing. The procedures in this chapter assume that an employer is using an in-house payroll software package to process payroll, as well as timecards or timesheets to accumulate information about hours worked. These forms and procedures will not exactly mirror the payroll operations of any company, since there are always a variety of organizational, best practices, and information systems differences that will require some modification of these basic procedures. Nonetheless, consider them a starting point for the construction of procedures that are more precisely tailored to a specific entity's needs.

Forms: The Timecard

A timecard is usually printed on heavier-weight paper and is stored in a central timecard rack. Employees can fill it out by hand, or they can insert it into a punch clock, which stamps the time on it. There are separate columns for the beginning and ending times when regular hours and overtime hours are worked. There is also a small block next to each day of regular and overtime hours, in which the payroll staff enters the total time worked for that day. They then accumulate these daily totals into overtime and regular time totals at the bottom of the timecard. Both the employee and his or her supervisor should sign the card. A sample timecard is shown next.

Sample Timecard

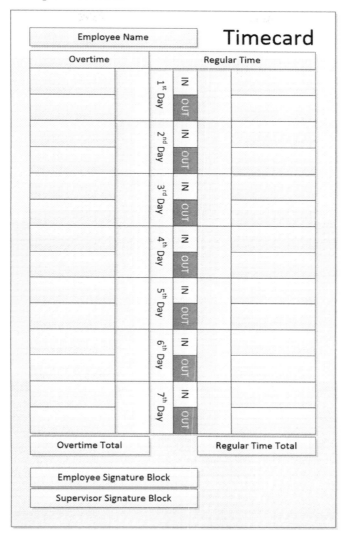

The timesheet differs from the timecard in that there is no provision for a time stamp by a punch clock. Instead, employees are expected to fill out the timesheet by hand. This is a relatively simple document, as illustrated in the following sample. Employees state the time period worked and the number and types of hours worked. There is also space for supervisory approval of the document. The name of the supervisor is stated near the top of the form, in case the payroll staff wants to contact that person with a question about information on the timesheet.

Sample Weekly Timesheet

Weekly Timesheet

Employee Name

Supervisor Name

Week of ____ to ____

Day	Regular	Overtime	Vacation	Sick	Holiday	Leave	Other	Total
Monday								
Tuesday								
Wednesday								
Thursday								
Friday								
Saturday								
Sunday								
Total Hours								

Employee Signature

Supervisor Signature

In some organizations, time tracking is only intended for hours that can be billed to customers. In this situation, the timesheet is structured so that the employee can enter the name of the client, the project, and the task. This information is not used for paying employees (unless they are only paid for billed hours) but rather for creating customer invoices. A sample billing timesheet is shown next.

Sample Billing Timesheet

Billing Timesheet

| Employee Name |
| Supervisor Name |
| Week of _____ to _____ |

Billing Information			Hours							
Client	Project	Task	Mon	Tue	Wed	Thu	Fri	Sat	Sun	Total
		Total Hours								

| Employee Signature |
| Supervisor Signature |

Forms: The Paycheck and Remittance Advice

If a company pays its employees with checks, it should issue not only the paycheck, but also a remittance advice that details the calculation of the payment. A sample paycheck and remittance advice is shown next. The presented format can be altered to include additional information, such as the remaining amount of earned vacation time.

Sample Paycheck and Remittance Advice

		Check Number
Employer Name Employer Address		Check Date

Pay to the order of: [text of amount paid]	$____.__

Employee Name Employee Address	Signature Block

Employee Number	Employee Name	Pay Period	Deductions		
			Deduction Type	Deduction this Period	Deduction YTD

Earnings

Hours Worked	Pay Rate	Pay this Period	Pay YTD			
				Total Deductions		
	Gross Pay			Net Pay		

The paycheck and remittance advice shown here can also be adapted to direct deposit payments. The paycheck part of the document is stated as being non-negotiable, and that the payment was made by direct deposit. In all other respects, the document is the same.

Procedure: Add an Employee

Use the following procedure to add an employee to the payroll system:

1. Verify the employee's authorization to work in the United States, and complete the Form I-9, Employment Eligibility Verification.
2. Have the employee fill out a Form W-4, Employee's Withholding Allowance Certificate.
3. Verify the authorization signature on the employee offer sheet.
4. Create a record for the employee in the payroll system and enter the following information:
   - Employee name
   - Employee address
   - Employee social security number
   - Employee marriage status
   - Number of withholding allowances claimed
   - Start date
   - Department code
   - Base wage or salary

- Shift worked
- Shift differential
- Banking information (for direct deposit)

5. Create an employee folder, insert all related documents in it, and store it in a locked storage area.

Procedure: Timecard Data Collection

If timecards are used to collect information about hours worked, use the following procedure:

1. Issue a reminder to employees a few days in advance to make sure their timecards are up-to-date.
2. Print a list of all employees who are supposed to submit timecards.
3. Sort all timecards received by employee last name.
4. Compare the timecards to the employee list, and note which employees have not yet submitted their timecards.
5. Compare the employee list to the schedule of employees who are on vacation, and cross off the names of those employees who did not submit timecards and who are on vacation.
6. Notify management of the remaining employees who have not submitted timecards.
7. Review all timecards for errors, such as missing beginning and ending times, and vacation used that has not been earned, and return them to employees for correction.
8. Forward all timecards containing overtime hours to management for approval.
9. Verify that all timecards returned for correction or approval have been returned.
10. Add up the time worked on each card and note the total hours worked at the top of the card.
11. Forward the approved and summarized timecards to the payroll clerk for entry into the payroll processing system.

Procedure: Commission Calculation

If commissions are paid to employees, use the following procedure to calculate the amount of commission due to them, which is based on invoices issued to customers:

1. Obtain a summary of invoices issued during the calculation period, sorted by salesperson.
2. Transfer report totals by salesperson to a spreadsheet.
3. Adjust the spreadsheet for:
    - Commission splits
    - Additional bonuses issued during the period
    - Commission increases caused by target levels being met
    - Subtractions for unpaid customer invoices more than ___ days old

228

- Different commissions for specific products or services sold
4. Send the completed spreadsheets to the sales manager for review.
5. Adjust the spreadsheets as indicated by the sales manager, and obtain approval of the spreadsheets.
6. Forward the approved commission spreadsheets to the payroll clerk for entry into the payroll processing system.

This procedure can vary considerably, given the multitude of commission plans that an employer may use.

Procedure: Process Payroll

Use the following procedure to process payroll. In the procedure, we assume that in-house payroll software is being used, though data entry into an outsourced payroll processing system would be similar.
1. Update the employee master file with the following changes, if any:
   - Change of employee name
   - Change of employee address
   - Change of employee pay rate
   - Change of employee marriage status and/or withholding allowance
   - Change of employee payment method
   - Change of shift worked
   - Change of employee status to inactive
2. Verify that the payroll module is set for the correct pay period.
3. Enter the amount of regular and overtime hours worked by each employee.
4. Verify that the hours of all wage-earning employees have been entered.
5. Enter the amounts of any manual paychecks that have not yet been recorded in the payroll system.
6. Manually calculate the amount payable to any employee who has left the company, including their unused vacation time and severance pay.
7. Enter any changes to the standard deductions from employee pay, including the following:
   - Cafeteria plan
   - Charitable contributions
   - Dental insurance
   - Disability insurance
   - Garnishments
   - Life insurance
   - Medical insurance
   - Pension plans
8. Have the software process all pay calculations for the period.
9. Print the following reports and review the underlying transactions for errors. Process payroll again until these issues have been corrected.
   - Negative deductions report

- Negative taxes report
- Preliminary payroll register
- Sorted list of wages paid
- Trend line of payroll expense by department

10. Issue payments to employees (see next procedure)
11. Issue payroll reports to management.
12. Back up the payroll database.
13. Lock down the payroll period in the payroll module for the period just completed, to prevent unauthorized changes.
14. Deposit payroll taxes and verify their transmission to the government.
15. Investigate all transaction errors encountered, and initiate changes to mitigate their continuing occurrence.

Procedure: Issue Payments to Employees

Use the following procedure to issue payments to employees. In the procedure, we assume the use of both paychecks and direct deposit.

1. Print the preliminary payroll register and review it for errors. Adjust transactions as necessary to correct errors, and re-process payroll as needed.
2. Have the payroll manager review and initial the final version of this preliminary report.
3. Remove check stock from the locked storage cabinet.
4. Print paychecks for those employees receiving paychecks.
5. Review the paychecks and reprint them if necessary.
6. Accept the printed batch in the payroll software.
7. Print remittance advices for those employees receiving direct deposit payments.
8. Review the advices and reprint them if necessary.
9. Accept the printed batch in the payroll software.
10. Return any remaining unused checks to the locked storage area, and log the range of check numbers that were used.
11. Print the final payroll register.
12. Store the final payroll register in the payroll archives area.
13. Export the direct deposit payments file to the direct deposit processor, and verify receipt of the file by the processor. Correct any direct deposit failures that arise.
14. Have an authorized check signer sign all paychecks.
15. Stuff the checks and remittance advices into envelopes.
16. Deliver the paychecks and remittance advices to supervisors for delivery to employees.
17. For off-site locations, send paychecks and remittance advices by overnight delivery service.

Summary

The five procedures described in this chapter address the core functions of the payroll department. One can certainly expand the number of procedures to address a variety of other special situations, such as the filing of new employee reports with the state government, issuing payroll cards to employees, and archiving payroll documents. These procedures will be useful as training documents, as well as evidence to show auditors that the department is following a rigidly-defined process. However, it is also possible to go too far and document every conceivable payroll function with a procedure. Doing so inserts excessive bureaucracy into the payroll department. Consequently, if an activity only arises occasionally and there is little risk associated with it, there is probably no need to document it in detail.

Chapter 15
Payroll Controls

Introduction

The payroll function is a prime source of fraud, since it is designed to disburse considerable amounts of money, and there are many ways to "game" the system to pay out funds that exceed the amounts actually earned by employees. This chapter describes a broad array of controls to consider installing in a payroll system to mitigate losses due to fraud.

Given the large transaction volume associated with a payroll system, there is also a strong likelihood that errors will arise at various points in the process that yield incorrect payment amounts. Some controls can prevent these errors from occurring, or detect them after the fact.

When reviewing the controls in this chapter to determine which ones to install, be aware that there are two types of controls, and one type is much more effective than the other. They are:

- *Detective controls*, which detect problems after they have occurred.
- *Preventive controls*, which keep problems from occurring.

Create a control system that incorporates a large proportion of preventive controls, since these controls can significantly reduce the payroll transaction error rate and reduce the occurrence of fraud. However, there should also be some detective controls, since they can spot issues not addressed by the suite of detective controls, and for which it may be necessary to install new detective controls.

The remaining sections of this chapter describe the controls that can be installed within a payroll system.

> **Related podcast episode:** Episode 14 of the Accounting Best Practices Podcast discusses payroll controls. It is available at: **www.accountingtools.com/podcasts** or **iTunes**

General Controls

Consider using a selection of the following controls for nearly all payroll systems, irrespective of how timekeeping information is accumulated or how employees are paid:

- *Audit*. Have either internal or external auditors conduct a periodic audit of the payroll function to verify whether payroll payments are being calculated correctly, employees being paid are still working for the company, time records are being accumulated properly, and so forth. If employees know that these reviews will be conducted, they will also be less likely to engage in fraudulent activities.

- *Change authorizations.* Only allow a change to an employee's marital status, withholding allowances, or deductions if the employee has submitted a written and signed request for the company to do so. Otherwise, there is no proof that the employee wanted a change to be made. The same control applies for any pay rate changes requested by a manager.
- *Change passwords.* There is a risk that someone could obtain a password that permits access to the payroll software, and use it to alter payment amounts. To reduce this risk, mandate a relatively frequent password change, such as on a quarterly basis.
- *Change tracking log.* If payroll is processed in-house with a computerized payroll module, activate the change tracking log and make sure that access to it is only available through a password-protected interface. This log will track all changes made to the payroll system, which is very useful for tracking down erroneous or fraudulent entries. The log may also record the user identification number under which the changes were made. This control is most useful if the log is examined at regular intervals, so that issues are spotted soon after they occur.
- *Error-checking reports.* Some types of payroll errors can be spotted by running reports that only show items that fall outside of the normal distribution of payroll results. These may not all indicate certain errors, but the probability of underlying errors is higher for the reported items. The payroll manager or a third party not involved in payroll activities should run and review these reports. Examples of error-checking reports are:
  - o *Activity for terminated employees.* Shows payments being made to an employee who has left the company or is on leave; may indicate a case of fraud, or that the status of the employee should be changed to active.
  - o *Negative deductions.* Shows employees being paid through a negative deduction; usually indicates either a data entry error or fraud.
  - o *Negative accrued vacation.* Shows employees being paid for vacation time they have not accrued; should require supervisory approval in these cases.
  - o *Net pay exceeds boundary.* Flags any net pay that exceeds a predetermined trigger point; may indicate a data entry error or fraud.
  - o *No payments.* Shows active employees who received no pay; may indicate missing timesheets.
  - o *Pay rate exceeds boundary.* Flags any pay rate that exceeds a predetermined trigger point; may indicate a data entry error or fraud.
- *Expense trend lines.* Look for fluctuations in payroll-related expenses in the financial statements, and investigate the reasons for the fluctuations. This analysis involves creating financial statements that list the results of multiple periods side-by-side (known as *horizontal analysis*), and doing so at the department level, to spot fluctuations at the most granular level of detail. An

alternative approach is to conduct this same analysis, but at the individual general ledger account level. The difference between account-level and financial statement line-item analysis is that several accounts may be clustered into a single financial statement line item, resulting in a more aggregate level of analysis.

- *Issue payment report to supervisors.* Send a list of payments to employees to each department supervisor, with a request to review it for correct payment amounts and unfamiliar names. They may identify payments being made to employees who no longer work for the company.

- *Restrict access to records.* Lock up employee files and payroll records at all times when they are not in use, to prevent unauthorized access. Use password protection if these records are stored on line. This precaution is not just to keep someone from accessing the records of another employee, but also to prevent unauthorized changes to records (such as a pay rate).

- *Review payments without deductions.* If a payment has no tax deductions or other types of withholdings, there is an enhanced risk that this is a payment issued to a ghost employee, since these items would reduce the amount paid. A ghost employee is a fake employee record to which payments are fraudulently made. It could be an entirely fabricated person, or else a former employee whose record still indicates that he is an active employee. Thus, one should run a report that searches for these payments and investigate them.

- *Separation of duties.* Have one person prepare the payroll, another authorize it, and another create payments, thereby reducing the risk of fraud unless multiple people collude in doing so. In smaller companies where there are not enough personnel for a proper separation of duties, at least insist on having someone review and authorize the payroll before payments are sent to employees.

Payroll Calculation Controls

Without even considering the challenges posed by fraudulent payroll transactions, it is sufficiently hard enough to calculate payroll to insist on installing a number of controls – just to spot errors. The following list of possible controls address such issues as missing timesheets, incorrect time worked, and incorrect pay calculations. They are:

- *Automated timekeeping systems.* Depending on the circumstances, consider installing a computerized time clock. These clocks have a number of built-in controls, such as only allowing employees to clock in or out for their designated shifts, not allowing overtime without a supervisory override, and (for biometric clocks) eliminating the risk of buddy punching. Also, send any exception reports generated by these clocks to supervisors for review.

- *Calculation verification.* If payroll is being calculated manually, have a second person verify all calculations, including hours worked, pay rates used, tax deductions, and withholdings. A second person is more likely to conduct a careful examination than the person who originated the calculations. This control is especially useful if the primary payroll clerk is relatively new to the job or is inexperienced.

- *Hours worked verification.* Always have a supervisor approve hours worked by employees, to prevent employees from charging more time than they actually worked. This can be a weak control if a supervisor has many employees, since it is difficult to keep track of hours worked.
- *Match payroll register to supporting documents.* The payroll register shows gross wages, deductions, and net pay, and so is a good summary document from which to trace back to the supporting documents for verification purposes. This is hardly a good control for *every* payroll, since it is vastly time-consuming, but use it occasionally as a deterrent to anyone intending to commit payroll fraud.
- *Match timecards to employee list.* There is a risk that an employee will not turn in a timesheet in a timely manner, and so will not be paid. To avoid this problem, print a list of active employees at the beginning of payroll processing, and check off the names on the list when their timesheets are received. A variation is to maintain a list of those employees who are habitually late in submitting timesheets, and using that as the basis for a review.
- *Negative deduction approval.* When an employee receives a negative deduction through the payroll system, it means that he or she is receiving additional cash. While a negative deduction can be used to correct an excessively large deduction in a prior period, it can also be used to fraudulently increase wages. Consequently, either require supervisory approval for negative deductions, or at least run a report that highlights these items.
- *Overtime worked verification.* Even if supervisors are not required to approve the hours worked by employees, at least have supervisors approve overtime hours worked. There is a pay premium associated with these hours, so the cost to the company is higher, as is the temptation for employees to claim them. It can also be useful to issue a report to supervisors that shows the trend line of overtime hours taken, by employee, so that employees habitually working overtime are clearly evident.
- *Pay change approval.* Consider requiring not just one approval signature for an employee pay change, but two signatures – one by the employee's supervisor, and another by the next-higher level of supervisor. Doing so reduces the risk of collusion in altering pay rates.
- *Verify tax remittances.* The penalties associated with a late or missing tax remittance are severe, so have someone independently verify the amount of tax to remit, and verify that the funds were actually sent to the government.

Cash Payment Controls

Cash is not only easily stolen, but also leaves fewer transactional traces than other types of payment. Thus, use at least a few controls over cash payments, such as the following:

- *Match payroll register to pay envelope.* Have a second person match the amount of cash in each pay envelope to the amount specified on the payroll register. This makes it more difficult for a payroll clerk to collude with an employee to pay him or her more cash. The second person should then initial each verified envelope, seal it, and transport all verified envelopes to the employees for distribution.
- *Receipt.* When cash is given to an employee, insist on receiving a signed receipt in exchange that states the amount paid and the date of payment. Doing so yields proof of payment, in case an employee later complains of being shortchanged or not paid at all. To make this control even more effective, insist on having each employee count the money in his or her pay envelope, rather than just signing off on the receipt without looking.
- *Use ink on pay envelope.* Use ink to note the pay amount on the outside of each envelope, which makes it more difficult for someone to alter the amount to be paid.

Check Payment Controls

When employees are paid with checks, this calls for quite a large number of controls, as noted in the following bullet points. The controls are necessary, because there are risks of fraud and errors in multiple places during the storage, printing, and distribution of checks. Not *all* of the following controls will be needed, but consider a robust subset of them to provide a significant amount of protection.

- *Copy protection features.* There are a number of protection features that can be added to the payroll check stock. These include:
    - *Dollar space background.* The check includes a cluster of wavy lines in the dollar space, which makes it difficult for someone to erase the payment amount on a check and replace it with a larger number without damaging the background.
    - *Void image.* If someone tries to photocopy a check, the word "void" appears on the image.
    - *Watermark.* This is a background image that is only visible when viewed from an angle. It is very difficult to duplicate. Such checks also state that the recipient should not accept the check unless the watermark is visible.
- *Fill space.* When creating a check, be sure to fill all of the empty spaces on the payment amount line, so that no one can add to the amount of the payment. For example, this can be a line of hyphens. Also, write the numerical amount of the payment as close to the dollar sign as possible, so that no one can insert another number in front of those already recorded.

236

- *Full identification.* Use the full spelling of employee names, rather than initials. This keeps someone with a similar name from intercepting and cashing a paycheck. For example, use Steven Smith instead of S. Smith.
- *Hand checks to employees.* Where possible, hand checks directly to employees. Doing so prevents a type of fraud where a payroll clerk creates a check for a ghost employee, and pockets the check. If this is too inefficient a control, consider distributing checks manually on an occasional basis.
- *Limit access to signature stamp.* If a signature stamp is used to authorize payroll checks, lock up the stamp, and not in the same location as unused checks. Having two separate, locked locations makes it more difficult to fraudulently create payroll checks.
- *Limit access to unused checks.* Lock up all unused checks to mitigate the risk that someone could remove blank checks, fill them out, and cash the checks.
- *Lock up undistributed paychecks.* If paychecks are issued directly to employees and someone is not present, lock up their check in a secure location. The check might otherwise be stolen and cashed. It can make sense to separately maintain a list of the checks still being held in the safe, so that a missing check will be noticed.
- *Match addresses.* If the company mails checks to its employees, match the addresses on the checks to employee addresses. If more than one check is going to the same address, it may be because a payroll clerk is routing illicit payments for ghost employees to his or her address.
- *Match check total to calculations.* If paychecks are being manually created, have a second person compare the amount on the checks to the net pay amounts indicated in the check register. The person who writes the checks is less likely to be thorough in matching these numbers.
- *Payroll checking account.* Pay employees from a separate checking account, and fund this account only in the amount of the checks paid out. Doing so prevents someone from fraudulently increasing the amount on an existing paycheck or creating an entirely new one, since the funds in the account will not be sufficient to pay for the altered check.
- *Positive pay.* This is a procedure under which a company sends its bank a list of all the checks it has issued that day, and which the bank compares to all checks presented. The bank only issues funds for those checks on the list. This approach essentially eliminates the risk of unauthorized checks being cashed, but does require a company to issue notifications to the bank for *all* the checks it creates, which can be troublesome in the case of manual checks.
- *Pre-numbered checks.* Using pre-numbered checks makes it easier to keep track of unused checks, to notice if someone removes a check. This control only works if a log of used checks is kept.
- *Reconcile the checking account.* Conduct a monthly reconciliation of the bank account to detect any unauthorized transactions and undocumented

bank charges. The person who creates the reconciliation should not be the same person who prepares or signs the checks. Better yet, if there is on-line access to the bank's account information, consider conducting a daily reconciliation, which will more quickly spot problems and lead to faster corrective action.

- *Review uncashed checks*. Do not treat an uncashed check as simply an unexpected source of funds! It may also mean that a flaw in the payroll process created a check that was sent to an incorrect address or a nonexistent employee. Instead, periodically investigate the reasons for any uncashed checks.
- *Segregation of duties*. The person who signs paychecks should not be the person who prepares the paychecks. Doing so gives the check signer an opportunity to review paychecks for problems.
- *Two signatures*. Create check stock on which a second signature is required for paychecks exceeding a certain amount. The second signature introduces a third person to the paycheck creation process for larger checks. This is a weak control, since banks do not always detect situations where a second signature should have been used.
- *Update signature cards*. When an authorized check signer leaves the company, strike his name from the authorized check signer list at once, to eliminate the risk of that person gaining access to and signing any payroll checks. Further, review the official check signer list at least once a year.
- *Use ink*. If handwritten paychecks are prepared, always do so in ink, since anything written with a pencil can be erased and replaced with a larger amount. Using ink means that any error will require the issuer to void a check and start over with a new check.
- *Voided check mutilation*. When a check is voided, do so not only in the accounting software, but also on the check itself, so that no one will attempt to cash it again. This involves writing "VOID" across the face of the check and cutting away or tearing the signature line.

Direct Deposit Controls

The number of controls required for direct deposit are substantially fewer (and less intrusive) than those needed for check payments, largely because the authorization to pay cash (e.g., the check) has been removed from the payment process. Still, there are a few controls to consider, mostly involving the accuracy and security of bank account information. The controls are:

- *Authorization signature*. Have employees sign a form, stating their authorization for the company to pay them by direct deposit, to which is stapled a copy of a cancelled check for the designated account. This makes it more difficult for someone to fraudulently alter the bank account information.
- *Identify simultaneous deposits to the same account*. If an employee has created multiple ghost employees and pays them by direct deposit, it is like-

ly that the payments will all be sent to the same bank account. Create a custom report that searches for this evidence of fraud.

- *Lock up direct deposit information.* Since direct deposit authorization forms include an employee's bank account information, lock them in a secure location, probably with the employee personnel folders.
- *Require a cancelled check.* Employees must submit a cancelled check, from which is extracted the bank routing number and account number. This is a key point, for many employees find it easier to simply submit a deposit slip instead – but the information on a deposit slip does not always match the information on a check.

Self-Service Controls

If a company allows employees or their managers to alter certain information in their pay records through on-line access, there is a possibility that they will enter incorrect information that will hinder the proper processing of wages. To avoid these problems, consider using the following controls:

- *Confirm changes.* The system should send a confirming e-mail to the person who made changes to an employee record, describing the changes made. A fraudulent record modification can be flagged by this control, since an authorized person will receive an e-mail that a record was changed.
- *Limit checks.* The system should either not allow excessively large pay rate changes, or route them to a more senior supervisor for review and approval.
- *Notify of pre-note failures.* If an employee enters new bank account information for a direct deposit payment and the pre-notification fails, the system should send a notification of the failure by e-mail to the employee.

Garnishment Controls

A cause for concern is garnishments, since a company is liable for garnishments if the payroll staff does not deduct garnished amounts from employee pay as required by court orders. To mitigate this risk, consider the following controls:

- *Garnishment tracking log.* Maintain a tracking log that itemizes which garnishments have been received, the amount to be deducted, and the start and termination dates of the garnishment. The payroll manager should periodically compare this log to the payroll register to ensure that required garnishments are being acted upon.
- *Deduction to payables matching.* In addition to the control just noted, the payroll manager should periodically compare the garnishment deductions from the payroll system to the checks issued through the accounts payable system to the garnishing entity, to ensure that deductions are being forwarded in the correct amounts and by the required dates.

Employee Advances Controls

Those employees who are short on funds may ask for an advance on their pay. This transaction can be lost in a poorly-organized payroll department, so that an employee receiving an advance effectively receives additional pay, and does not even pay taxes on it. Here are several controls to combat the problem:

- *Approval requirement.* Never pay an advance without the approval of the manager of the person requesting the advance. This is needed, since an advance is essentially a transfer of company assets to a third party, and if it is not paid back, the manager's department is charged the amount of the unrecovered funds.
- *Periodic advances review.* Require that all advances be recorded in a designated asset account, and have someone review the contents of the account regularly and follow up on outstanding amounts. If advances are large, the status of this account could be shared with the controller each month, who may then choose to take action to obtain repayment.
- *Repayment policy.* Have a corporate policy that all advances are to be repaid as part of the next scheduled payroll. Doing so cuts down on the risk of any advances remaining on the books for a long time, and also reduces the attractiveness of advances to employees.

Vacation Pay Controls

One area of the payroll department that tends to produce an inordinate number of errors is the calculation of accrued and used vacation pay. This is a particular problem when a person changes to a different accrual rate when they reach a work anniversary date, such as increasing from two to three weeks per year when they reach their fifth anniversary with the company. Another problematic area is year-end vacation roll-forward calculations, where employees are only allowed to roll forward a certain number of hours. Here are several controls to consider that may alleviate the situation:

- *Error checking.* Have a second person review the vacation roll-forward calculations at the end of each year. A second person is more likely to spot errors than the person who originated the calculations.
- *Scheduled review.* Schedule at least a quarterly review of all vacation calculations, during which one should verify calculations that have changed recently, such as new vacation accruals for those employees reaching anniversaries that trigger new vacation rates.
- *Standard policy.* Managers may be tempted to offer new hires unusual vacation terms in order to sweeten an employment offer. This causes monumental calculation problems for the payroll staff, so adopt and enforce a standard vacation rate schedule for all new hires. At worst, allow some variation for the first year of employment, after which everyone reverts to the standard corporate vacation policy.

Summary

It may seem prudent to install every control itemized in this chapter. However, doing so may interfere with the efficient processing of payroll, and introduce an unnecessary amount of costs into the payroll department. Consequently, evaluate the probability of loss reduction associated with each control, and decide if it is worthwhile to install the control based on its offsetting cost and impact on departmental efficiencies. A basic set of recommended controls are shown after this summary for both a manual and computerized payroll system.

Also, some controls may buttress each other, so that there are overlapping effects resulting from multiple controls. In these cases, it may be possible to safely eliminate a few controls, knowing that other controls will still mitigate the risk of loss.

The specific business conditions under which a company operates may call for controls that would not normally be necessary. Consider the following situations:

- A company employs day laborers, and pays them in cash at the end of each day. This situation calls for stronger controls over cash than would normally be the case.
- A company employs a large proportion of immigrants whose English skills are suspect. They are more likely to make errors on handwritten timesheets because of their language skills, so a computerized time clock may be a better control in this situation.
- A company has experienced problems with buddy punching in the past. This may call for the use of a biometric time keeping system to eliminate a known problem.

Finally, it is worthwhile to occasionally review the existing set of controls to see if any of them can be eliminated. This is a particularly worthwhile activity under the following circumstances:

- The payroll process flow has changed, rendering a control irrelevant.
- Experience shows that a control is ineffective in preventing or identifying problems.
- The control acts as a backup for another, more robust control.
- The control significantly degrades the performance of a process, and other controls can replace it that have a reduced impact on the process.
- The control is inordinately expensive in comparison to the value of the errors it prevents or fraud risk that it mitigates.

Basic Set of Payroll System Controls

For Manual System

1. Collect time information

Match timecards to employee list

Verify hours worked

2. Data entry

Require change authorizations

Verify aggregations

3. Calculate gross and net pay

Review pay calculations

Review payroll register

4. Payment

Split check printing and signing

Match check total to calculations

Sign checks

5. Remit taxes

Verify tax remittances

For Computerized System

1. Collect time information

Install automated timekeeping

Verify hours worked

Confirm self-service changes

2. Data entry

Require change authorizations

Verify pre-noting

3. Calculate gross and net pay

Review preliminary payroll register

Manager approves payroll register

4. Payment

Split check printing and signing

5. Remit taxes

Verify tax remittances

Chapter 16
Payroll Measurements

Introduction

The measurements described in this chapter fall into two distinct categories – cost and efficiency ratios and human resources ratios. The first group of ratios will be of the most use from a purely payroll management perspective. The latter group may be requested of the payroll department by management, so know how to calculate them.

> **Related podcast episode:** Episode 26 of the Accounting Best Practices Podcast discusses payroll measurements. It is available at: **www.accountingtools.com/ podcasts** or **iTunes**

Payroll Entries to Headcount Ratio

In some companies there may be a broad array of payroll deductions, goal entries such as targets for annual pension deductions, and memo entries regarding the amount of vacation or sick time remaining. If these entries are entered manually as part of every payroll, the payroll department is facing not only a major efficiency problem, but also a high risk of data entry errors. These problems will likely result in a major degradation of the efficiency of the payroll department. Consequently, the payroll manager should be keenly aware of the number of payroll entries being made, particularly in proportion to the number of employees.

The calculation of the number of payroll entries to headcount is:

$$\frac{\text{Total deductions} + \text{Total goal entries} + \text{Total memo entries}}{\text{Average number of full-time equivalents}}$$

A full-time equivalent (FTE) is the number of 40-hour per week positions that would be filled if all of the hours worked in a company were aggregated and divided by 40 hours. It is intended to provide a common headcount measure when there is a large proportion of part-time employees. Thus, if 10 employees work a total of 320 hours, this is a full-time equivalent of 8 employees, which is calculated as 320 hours divided by 40 hours

In a reasonably automated payroll department, many deductions are automatically recurring, while goal entries may only be entered once a year. Consequently, the level of automation drives the need for this measurement.

EXAMPLE

The extremely detail-oriented payroll manager of Milford Sound has retired. Her replacement knows that the department has been burdened with an immense amount of data entry work for years, primarily because the former payroll manager wanted to carefully track all possible information about employees. The replacement manager compiles the following information about the various payroll entries being made in each of Milford's biweekly payrolls:

Type of Payroll Entry	Description	Number of Entries
Deduction	Medical insurance	240
Deduction	Dental insurance	224
Deduction	Long-term disability	183
Deduction	Short-term disability	172
Deduction	Cafeteria plan – child care	36
Deduction	Cafeteria plan – medical	92
Memo	Vacation time remaining	270
Memo	Sick time remaining	270
	Total entries	1,487

$$\frac{1{,}487 \text{ Payroll entries}}{270 \text{ FTEs}} = 5.5 \text{ Entries to headcount ratio}$$

The preceding information reveals that the payroll department is making an average of 5 ½ payroll entries per person, per payroll. The new payroll manager takes immediate steps to consolidate and automate the entries.

There are several action items that may arise from the use of this measurement, including:

- The automation of as many payroll entries as possible
- Using recurring payroll entries that automatically populate the next payroll
- Consolidating deductions (such as one deduction for the entire package of employee benefits)
- Having the company pay for *all* of a benefit, so there is no employee-paid portion

Payroll Transaction Error Rate

A massive amount of raw data must be organized by the payroll department and translated into a payroll, with the volume of data being highly dependent upon the number of employees who are paid on an hourly basis. If there is an error in this data stream, it takes time for an experienced payroll person to track down and correct it. If there are many such errors, the payroll staff will be perpetually buried by the sheer volume of corrections. Consequently, it makes sense to track not only the proportion of payroll errors, but also the types of errors.

To calculate the payroll transaction error rate, divide all errors detected by the total number of payroll entries made. Use in the denominator the total amount of all entries made, such as hours worked, deductions, memo entries, and goal entries, since errors can occur in all of these areas.

EXAMPLE

Milagro Corporation employs a large staff of hourly production workers to assemble its signature home espresso machines. Milagro's payroll department is being overwhelmed by a large number of payroll transaction errors. The payroll manager summarizes the payroll errors from the past month into the following table:

Transaction Type	Total Entries	Total Errors	Error Rate
Hours entry	1,440	180	12.5%
Salary change entry	36	1	2.8%
Deductions entry	150	4	2.7%
Address change	14	--	0.0%
Direct deposit	60	6	10.0%
Exemptions entry	24	2	8.3%
Totals	1,724	193	11.2%

The information in the table reveals that there is a significant error rate in its hours entry, both on a proportional basis and in terms of the gross number of errors. The payroll manager realizes that fixing the underlying problem will nearly obliterate her transactional errors, and so targets this area for correction.

Of particular concern to the payroll manager is the proportion of *recurring* payroll errors, rather than the stray errors that arise in small numbers on an occasional basis. Recurring errors should be the focus of an intense amount of corrective action. By making such corrections, entire layers of transaction errors can be eliminated.

Form W-2c to Form W-2 Ratio

When a payroll department makes mistakes in its calculation and recording of employee pay, the information rolls into the annual wage and tax withholding information contained in the Form W-2, which a company issues to its employees and the government. If anyone spots an error in a Form W-2, the company must issue a corrected version on the Form W-2c. It is important to track the proportion of

Forms W-2c to the total number of Forms W-2 issued, since it is an indicator of the transactional errors being made by the payroll staff.

The calculation of the Form W-2c to Form W-2 ratio is a simple one:

$$\frac{\text{Total Forms W-2c issued}}{\text{Total Forms W-2 issued}}$$

Calculate this measurement well after the initial issuance of all Forms W-2, in order to give sufficient time for all errors to be located and Forms W-2c to be issued.

EXAMPLE

Milford Sound issues a Form W-2 to each of its 412 employees following the end of the calendar year. During the following few weeks, 38 employees point out that the pay totals listed on their forms are incorrect. Milford issues 38 Forms W-2c to replace the incorrect Forms W-2. The resulting ratio of Forms W-2c to Forms W-2 is calculated as:

$$\frac{38 \text{ Forms W-2c issued}}{412 \text{ Forms W-2 issued}} = 9.2\% \text{ Ratio of W-2c to W-2}$$

This ratio does not represent a sufficient amount of information for corrective action to be taken, so accompany it with a detailed report that itemizes the underlying transaction errors.

Proportion of Manual Checks

Manual payroll checks are usually cut because there was an error in the normal payroll process that resulted in an under-payment to an employee. When there are a significant number of manual checks, it can be an indicator of persistent data collection or pay calculation problems somewhere within the payroll system.

The presence of manual checks can be measured as a simple total of these checks cut, or it can be compared to the total number of payments (both direct deposit and checks) issued to employees. In many cases, the payroll manager will want to investigate *every* manual check, irrespective of the relative proportion of these payments issued, in order to delve into the reasons for payroll errors.

If using this measurement, be aware that a manual payroll check could also be issued to an employee as an advance, which is not indicative of an error. This exception can be eliminated from the payroll system either by imposing a no-advances policy or by issuing the payments through the accounts payable system, rather than the payroll system.

Outsourced Payroll Cost per Employee

It is extremely common for a company to outsource its payroll processing to a supplier, since doing so eliminates a great deal of payroll calculation, payment, and tax remittance work. However, once outsourced, management tends not to closely track the cost of this activity. The cost of outsourcing commonly balloons over time, since suppliers typically bid low to obtain a company's business, and then escalate or add to the fees. These fees can involve special charges for garnishments, direct deposit, sealing checks inside envelopes, tracking vacation as a memo item, and so forth.

When calculating the outsourced transaction fees per employee, the simplest approach is to add up the supplier's invoices for the measurement period and divide by the number of employees paid during that period. Supplier invoices tend to contain a mixture of per-person charges and fixed fees; for the purposes of this measurement, it does not matter if a cost is variable or fixed. Instead, obtain the gross supplier cost and divide it by the headcount paid. Thus, the calculation is:

$$\frac{\text{Total payroll cost billed by supplier during the measurement period}}{\text{Total number of employees paid}}$$

EXAMPLE

Kelvin Corporation produces a variety of thermometers. The payroll director feels his temperature rise when he reads the latest supplier invoice for processing the company's payroll. He runs a comparison of the outsourced payroll cost for the most recent month and for the same period one year ago, which results in this summary table:

	February 20X1	February 20X2
Monthly payroll fee	$1,900	$3,045
Employees paid	380	420
Cost per employee	$5.00/person	$7.25/person

The payroll director compares the supplier billings from the two periods and discovers the following three issues:

- The supplier implemented a 6% price increase, which accounts for $0.30 of the increase.
- The company authorized overnight delivery by the supplier of check payments to 14 company locations twice a month, which accounts for $0.80 of the increase.
- The human resources department authorized activation of the supplier's on-line human resources package, which enables employees to update their own records on-line. This purchase accounts for $1.00 of the increase.

Several minor items account for the remaining $0.15 of the cost increase. Based on this information, the payroll director has the cost of the human resources package charged to the human resources department, and arranges to have the payroll supplier use the company's own overnight delivery billing code to pay for the check deliveries.

This measurement gives valuable insights into cost escalations over time. Though it may not persuade management to shift payroll processing in-house, it may at least initiate some management discussion of how to minimize supplier fees.

Annualized Compensation per Employee

Some pay structures are quite complex, with employees being paid bonuses, stock, overtime, and other forms of compensation. It is quite useful to aggregate all forms of compensation on an individual employee basis, in order to fully understand pay levels. This information can be used to determine the amount of additional pay raises, as well as for comparing a company's pay levels to those in the industry. It is also useful when compiling annualized wages for a specific job title or position, and comparing that average compensation level to industry standards.

If annualized pay is compiled for one person, the calculation is to add together the following amounts for the past 12 months:

+	Fixed base pay
+	Wages
+	Commissions
+	Overtime
+	Bonuses
+	Stock
+	Other pay
=	Total annualized compensation

If this information is being compiled for a group of employees, one would compile the same information for the entire group for the past 12 months, and then divide it by the number of full-time equivalents to arrive at the average annual compensation for that group.

EXAMPLE

Colossal Furniture manufactures chairs for its oversized customers. The company's repair department has been overwhelmed with work recently, as the company finds that its customers are so large that they are crushing its chairs, which must be reinforced with metal support struts. Colossal's president compiles the following information about the annual compensation being paid to the repair department employees:

$$\frac{\$600,000 \text{ Wages} + \$250,000 \text{ Overtime} + \$50,000 \text{ Bonuses}}{10 \text{ FTEs}} = \$90,000/\text{FTE}$$

Clearly, the repair staff is being paid a princely amount, largely because of the overtime they are working to keep up with their repair queue. The president decides that it is time to redesign the company's chairs to handle a heavier load.

248

It is extremely useful to track annualized total compensation for each employee on a trend line, to see compensation changes over the course of a person's employment.

Net Benefits Cost per Employee

Management tends to spend a great deal of time observing the wage and salary cost of company employees, but has a much lower awareness of the cost of net benefits per employee. This can be a major failing, especially when a company has adopted a disparate group of benefits whose total cost is difficult to discern. In many cases, the net cost of benefits may be much higher than expected, which can cut deeply into profits.

Measure the net benefit cost on a per-person or departmental basis, rather than as an average figure for all employees, since employees make differing use of benefits. For example, some employees may elect to take advantage of a company 401(k) plan that requires matching funds from the company, while others will not.

To calculate the net benefits cost per employee at the company level, follow these steps:

1. Summarize the cost of all benefits. Examples of the more common benefits are the cost of medical insurance, dental insurance, life insurance, and disability insurance, as well as pension matching funds. Less-common benefits are reimbursement for health club or country club memberships, and the leases on company cars.
2. Subtract employee deductions. If the company is deducting the cost of a portion of benefits from employee pay, compile this amount and subtract it from the total derived in the first step.
3. Calculate the average number of full-time equivalents during the measurement period, and divide this number into the net benefit cost derived in the first two steps.

Thus, the calculation of the net benefit cost per employee is:

$$\frac{\text{Insurance cost} + \text{Pension matching cost} + \text{Other benefits} - \text{Employee deductions}}{\text{Average number of full-time equivalents}}$$

To calculate the net benefit cost for an individual employee, run the same calculation using the benefit costs and deductions specific to that employee, and skip the third calculation step.

EXAMPLE

Alien Battles Corporation (ABC) creates digital space battles for science fiction movies. To stay ahead of its competitors, ABC offers a first-rate benefits package to its software developers. The president of ABC wants to know the net benefits cost per employee, which the accounting staff derives from the following information:

Benefit Item	Gross Cost	Employee Deductions	Net Cost
Medical insurance	$420,000	$(85,000)	$335,000
Dental insurance	35,000	(7,000)	28,000
Pension matching	85,000	--	85,000
Long-term disability	15,000	--	15,000
Short-term disability	48,000	--	48,000
Other	39,000	--	39,000
Totals	$642,000	$(92,000)	$550,000

ABC had an average of 40 full-time equivalent employees during the one-year measurement period. Thus, the net benefits cost per employee is $13,750, which is calculated as the net cost of $550,000 divided by 40 FTEs.

It is not always wise to use the information provided by this measurement to cut back on the total cost of benefits, especially when employees are particularly sensitive about benefit levels. However, a close examination of the various benefit components may allow management to reconfigure the benefit package to provide the largest amount of those benefits that are of the greatest value to employees, while paring back less necessary benefits.

Sales per Person

In some industries, there is a direct relationship between the efficiency and effectiveness of a company's employees and its resulting sales. This relationship is particularly true in industries where employees bill customers for their time. In such industries, the sales per person measurement is closely watched.

To calculate sales per person, divide the total sales for the preceding 12 months by the average number of full-time equivalents during that period. The calculation is:

$$\frac{\text{Revenues (trailing 12 months)}}{(\text{Beginning FTEs} + \text{Ending FTEs}) / 2}$$

EXAMPLE

Pulsed Laser Drilling Corporation (PLD) manufactures lasers that use a pulsed laser beam to drill through rock. Its products are used in such applications as drilling for oil and gas, water wells, and laying subsurface fiber optic cables. The company only employs full-time technicians who assemble and field service its complex laser products. Headcount tends to closely follow sales levels, since a great deal of the manufacturing process is by hand. During the past year, PLD had revenues of $18 million and 90 full-time equivalents. The calculation of its sales per person is:

$$\frac{\$18,000,000 \text{ Sales}}{90 \text{ Full-time equivalents}} = \$200,000 \text{ Sales per employee}$$

The sales per person measurement is not useful, and may even be misleading, in the following situations:

- *Product based.* If a company derives its sales from standardized manufactured goods, there may not be a causal relationship between sales and headcount, especially when production activities are highly automated.
- *Step headcount.* It is possible that a company may be able to use a fixed number of employees to generate an increasing amount of sales, until it reaches a "step" point where the company must hire a number of additional employees to support the next incremental block of sales. This situation arises when sales are supported by a single facility that requires a certain minimum amount of staffing.

The sales per person measurement is a popular one, but it only focuses on top-line sales. A company may have an astoundingly high sales per person measurement, and still lose money. A more focused measurement is the profit per employee measurement, which is covered next.

Profit per Employee

In a service-intensive industry, there is a direct relationship between employees and the amount of profits generated. This is particularly true in such service areas as equipment field servicing, management consulting, and auditing. In these situations, it makes sense to track profit per employee, not only for the company as a whole, but also for those individual employees who are billable.

Payroll Measurements

To calculate profit per employee, divide the company's operating profit by the average number of full-time equivalent employees. Do *not* use net after-tax profits for this measurement, since doing so would include such financing line items as interest expense and interest income, which have nothing to do with employee performance. The calculation is:

$$\frac{\text{Operating profit}}{(\text{Beginning FTEs} + \text{Ending FTEs}) / 2}$$

EXAMPLE

Maid Marian is a nationwide maid service that is run by friars within the Franciscan Order. The friars want to introduce a bonus system that encourages part-time maids to work additional hours, and needs to determine the existing profit per employee, so that it can determine how large a bonus pool to create.

During the past 12-month period, employees of Maid Marian worked a total of 832,000 hours, which is an FTE equivalent of 400 employees. This equivalent is calculated as 832,000 hours divided by the 2,080 hours worked by a full-employee in one year (52 weeks × 40 hours/week). During that period, the service generated an operating profit of $3 million, which is a profit per employee of:

$$\frac{\$3,000,000 \text{ Operating profit}}{400 \text{ Full-time equivalents}} = \$7,500 \text{ Profit per employee}$$

The friars want to create a bonus pool that is 20% of operating profits, which is a $600,000 pool. Based on the 400 FTEs in Maid Marian, this works out to a potential bonus per FTE per year of $1,500.

There are three caveats to the use of the profit per employee measurement, which are:

- *Industry-specific*. The profit per employee measurement is least useful in industries where there is a large investment in fixed assets and a proportionally smaller number of employees, such as heavy industry. In these situations, there is not such a direct linkage between the quality or quantity of employees, which makes the profit per employee measurement less relevant.
- *Minimal profits*. There is no point in measuring profit per employee when the operating profit is near zero, since it divulges no relevant information.
- *Manipulation*. The measurement is subject to manipulation by shifting work to suppliers. Doing so reduces headcount, which drives up the profit per employee.

Despite the caveats just noted, profit per employee is an excellent measurement in many services industries.

Employee Turnover

When an employee leaves a company, the cost of replacing that person is extremely high. An employer must pay for recruiting and training, and also endure a period of reduced efficiency before the replacement person is as efficient as the person who departed. For these reasons, a close examination of employee turnover is a key management task in almost any company.

To calculate employee turnover, obtain the number of full-time equivalent employees who left the business during the measurement period, and divide it by the average number of employees on the company payroll during that period. The calculation is:

$$\frac{\text{Number of departed FTE employees}}{(\text{Beginning FTEs} + \text{Ending FTEs}) / 2}$$

An issue to consider is the time period over which employee turnover is measured. In a larger company with thousands of employees, a single month may be an adequate time period. However, in a smaller firm, it may be necessary to use the preceding 12 months on a rolling basis in order to collect sufficient information to derive a measurement.

EXAMPLE

Crosswind Tours employs a number of part-time pilots for its tours of the Alaskan back country, which originate from multiple airstrips located near the ports where cruise ships stop during their travels through the Inside Passage. Other than a small full-time administrative staff, everyone in the company works on a part-time basis, mostly during the May through September cruise ship season. The president of Crosswinds suspects that employee turnover may be specific to the geographic location of the pilots, so he asks the payroll manager to calculate employee turnover for the past year at each of the company's locations. The results are:

	Ketchikan	Skagway	Sitka	Wrangell
FTE resignations	1.0	4.5	0.8	0.5
Average FTEs	7.2	8.0	12.0	9.5
Turnover	14%	56%	7%	5%

The employee turnover calculation clearly shows that there is a major problem with the Skagway flight operation, which experienced 56% turnover in the past year. The president personally interviews all of the pilots who left the Skagway operation, and finds that they had trouble with the local flight scheduler. He promptly replaces the Skagway flight scheduler, and works on hiring back the departed employees.

There will always be some employee turnover due to issues that are beyond the control of a company, such as a spouse being hired in another city, caring for parents, and so forth. It can also be difficult to retain employees in a tight job market where they have skills that are in high demand. Consequently, there will always be a certain amount of unavoidable employee turnover. Thus, the proper use of the employee turnover measurement is to know when turnover is exceeding a normal baseline level, which requires a deep knowledge of the precise reasons why employees are leaving.

The employee turnover metric can be manipulated by shifting work to outside contractors who fall outside of the parameters of this measurement. Consequently, if a large amount of work is outsourced, this may not be a useful measurement.

Summary

Of the purely payroll-related measurements described in this chapter, the most important is the payroll transaction error rate, especially when delving into the specific transactions that caused the errors. If the causes of these errors are investigated and corrected, one can substantially improve the efficiency of the payroll department.

Of the later measurements related to human resources, the most important is employee turnover. Turnover is extremely expensive, in terms of both the lost expertise of a departed employee and the time required before a new employee is fully functional. Accordingly, if the reasons for turnover are investigated and reported to management, it may lead to a reduced level of turnover.

Chapter 17
The Outsourcing Option

Introduction

A typical in-house payroll department has many concerns. Besides the task of issuing paychecks, it may have to do so for many company locations where tax rates differ, employees are paid on different dates, and tax reporting to the various state governments must be made on a number of different forms. Worst of all is the tax remittance, which involves a heavy penalty if it is paid even one day late. All of these problems and costs can be avoided by handing over the payroll processing function to an outside supplier.

This chapter describes what is involved in the outsourcing of payroll, why an employer should and should not do it, and how to manage an outsourced payroll function.

Overview of Payroll Outsourcing

When payroll is outsourced, this rarely means that the entire payroll function is physically transferred away from the company. Instead, only the payroll calculation, tax remittance, and employee payment functions are shifted to a third party. The employer is still responsible for collecting information about hours worked, as well as inputting information about employees. The splitting of responsibilities between the employer and its payroll supplier are roughly as follows:

Employer responsibilities:

- Collect hours worked
- Collect employee allowance, deduction, and personal information
- Input the preceding information into the payroll system maintained by the supplier
- Distribute paychecks and remittance advices forwarded by the supplier
- Record payroll transactions based on reports issued by the supplier

Supplier responsibilities:

- Calculate wages based on hours worked
- Calculate tax deductions and withholdings
- Create paychecks, initiate direct deposit payments, and forward cash to payroll debit cards
- Remit taxes and withholdings to government entities
- Issue standard reports to clients

- Issue W-2 forms to employees following the end of the calendar year

The reason for this split is that payroll suppliers are focusing on the data processing aspects of payroll, where they use mainframe-based computers to handle the payroll processing for large numbers of clients. The fixed cost of these systems is high, but suppliers can achieve considerable profitability if they have many clients using their systems. What a payroll supplier wants to avoid is the low value-added and highly error-prone tasks of collecting information about employees and entering it into the payroll system. Thus, payroll suppliers are narrowly focused on the highest value-added portion of the tasks handled by the payroll department.

Reasons to Outsource Payroll

Payroll is one of the most commonly outsourced company functions. There are several good reasons for this, which are:

- *Backups.* Suppliers backup a company's payroll information continually, and should have off-site storage of the backups, as well.
- *Check stuffing.* All payroll suppliers will stuff paychecks into envelopes, which eliminates a low-end clerical task that the payroll staff would otherwise have to perform.
- *Direct deposit.* Most payroll suppliers have the capability to issue payments to employees by direct deposit. Companies that process their payroll in-house can also do this, but only through the services of a third party that handles direct deposit.
- *Expert staff.* Suppliers have a core of highly-trained staff who not only know their systems and payroll regulations quite well, but who also provide training to clients, as well as advice over the phone.
- *Multi-location processing.* Larger payroll suppliers have locations in most major cities, and so can directly deliver paychecks to most urban locations. They send paychecks to more remote locations by overnight delivery service.
- *New hire reporting.* Each state government requires a company to report the hiring of new employees to them, so that they can determine if there are any garnishments outstanding against these individuals. Payroll suppliers usually offer this reporting service free of charge.
- *Pay cards.* Larger payroll suppliers offer payroll debit cards as a payment option. This is a good alternative to direct deposit for those employees who do not have bank accounts.
- *Pension plan linkage.* Some payroll suppliers either operate their own 401(k) pension plans or are linked to such plans offered by third parties. These suppliers can link pension deductions in the payroll system to their plans, so no separate pension remittances are required.
- *Reporting.* Suppliers have a standard set of "canned" payroll reports, and usually offer report writing software that allows a user to extract information and present it in formats that are specific to an employer.

- *Software updates.* The employer no longer has to maintain any payroll software in-house, and so is no longer concerned with software updates. The supplier is responsible for all updates to its own software.
- *Tax remittances.* A supplier calculates all payroll taxes and remits them to the government without the company having to be involved. The savings from avoided tax remittance penalties may pay for the entire cost of the supplier.
- *Tax tables.* Suppliers maintain the most up-to-date records of tax rates charged by all government entities, and so can accurately calculate taxes payable to cities, counties, states, the federal government, and other special entities throughout the country.
- *Unemployment claims.* Large payroll suppliers will respond to unemployment claims on behalf of the company. This involves the complete range of activities from initial claims filings through final disposition of the claims. Suppliers typically provide summaries of all claims on a secure website, which the payroll manager can access to obtain the latest status of claims. This is not a cost-effective service for smaller firms that only deal with a few claims per year.
- *W-2 forms.* All suppliers provide W-2 forms to employees after the end of each calendar year. Many also store this information on-line, so that employees can access their forms from previous years.
- *Other services.* Some suppliers offer additional services related to payroll, such as pension plans, benefits administration, and timekeeping systems.

Thus, there are a broad range of services available to a company that is willing to outsource its payroll function. The key factors are enhanced convenience and the elimination of any risk associated with not remitting payroll taxes on a timely basis.

Reasons not to Outsource Payroll

There are some situations where using a payroll supplier is not viable or is not cost-effective. These situations are:

- *Cost.* Despite what the payroll suppliers may say, outsourcing payroll is more expensive than processing it in-house, because the supplier has marketing costs and a profit requirement that an in-house payroll department does not have. Suppliers give the appearance of having low-cost services by selling a basic bundle of services at a low cost, and then adding high fees for additional services.
- *Database linkage.* Outsourcing payroll shifts the payroll database to the supplier. This can be a problem when a company is maintaining a large, integrated database of information (as is the case with an enterprise resources planning system) and needs to have this information in-house. Some larger payroll suppliers may be willing to create an interface that extracts the needed payroll information from a company's ERP system, thereby keeping information on-site.

These two factors are less critical for smaller businesses, which therefore form the core group that outsource payroll. Larger companies are more likely to retain payroll in-house, since they can process payroll at lower cost than suppliers, and can retain payroll information within their computer systems.

The Outsourced Payroll Contract

When negotiating a contract with a payroll supplier, a smaller company will generally have very little room to maneuver. The reason is that payroll suppliers are usually very large organizations with thousands of clients, and so it is not cost-effective for them to allow and subsequently monitor any customized changes to an outsourcing contract.

However, there is still some leeway on pricing. It may be possible to negotiate price reductions for a short period of time, such as one year, after which the supplier's normal pricing structure will take effect. Possible pricing options are a reduction in specific itemized costs, or a percentage reduction in the total cost of the supplier's services for a specific period of time – the exact type of discount negotiated will likely be driven by the types of discounts allowed by the supplier's computer system.

A larger company will have more negotiating power on prices, since a supplier's potential revenue from it will be potentially higher than for a small company with just a few people on its payroll. However, a smaller company may successfully obtain a small discount if the person pushing for the switch to outsourcing has dealt with the supplier before – this level of loyalty to a specific supplier may be sufficient grounds for a discount.

The key point to remember with pricing negotiations is that many payroll supplier costs are fixed; the supplier will incur few additional costs (if any) if it adds a new client, so it certainly has room in its internal cost structure to absorb a price reduction.

The Transition to Payroll Outsourcing

The conversion to payroll processing by a supplier is almost always conducted as of the first day of a calendar year, so that wage information is accumulated by the supplier that exactly matches IRS requirements for the social security wage base, federal and state unemployment wage bases, Form W-2 total wages paid, and so forth.

The payroll staff should meet with the supplier at least one month prior to the conversion date (and quite a bit sooner for a larger company) to address the key conversion dates prior to the year-end conversion and who is responsible for which task.

If the conversion appears to be a complex one, consider converting only the most important items first, and adopt the remaining items as soon thereafter as possible. For example, if the payroll supplier is also taking on the company's 401(k) pension plan, one could implement the pension plan shortly after the main payroll conversion has been completed.

A central problem with the transition is allowing not only enough time for the initial data entry of all required employee information into the supplier's payroll system, but also additional time to thoroughly review the entered information for errors. If the company has a large number of employee records to enter, it may be possible to arrange for the transfer of a data file to the supplier, which is then automatically imported into the supplier's system with a custom interface. Even in this case, however, budget a substantial amount of time to review the transferred information for accuracy; an incorrect interface may shift data into the wrong fields in the supplier system.

Managing Outsourced Payroll

Even if payroll is being processed by a supplier, retain a payroll clerk or manager in the accounting department who not only oversees this function, but who also inputs payroll data into the supplier's system. This person is the point of contact with his or her counterparts at the supplier.

The key management issues involving a payroll supplier involve the transition to new payroll services, training for any company employees who are designated to deal with the supplier, and answering questions about specific payroll issues and how they are handled through the supplier's payroll system. These are all important issues, but are also very much more tactical than strategic in nature, and so are best assigned to a lower-level manager who has a detailed knowledge of payroll. Once senior management makes the decision to shift payroll processing to a payroll supplier, there is little additional need for interaction by senior managers with the supplier.

From the perspective of the person required to manage a payroll supplier, the primary issue will likely be any errors found by employees in their pay. Realistically, most or all of these issues will originate in the data entry function that still resides at the employer. The supplier is merely providing a platform for calculating pay and distributing payments, and as long as the company inputs the correct information into the supplier's payroll system, the supplier should be able to produce accurate payments and related reports. Thus, a large part of managing a payroll supplier *really* involves the accuracy and proper inputting of the information that the company sends to the supplier.

Depending upon the complexity of the relationship with the supplier, consider installing either or both of the following controls to assist in managing the supplier:

- *Audit transactions*. Schedule a periodic internal audit of the payroll function. This audit should include a rotating set of objectives, such as veri-fying whether payroll taxes have been remitted, garnishment payments were sent to the appropriate entities, supplier fees match the amounts noted in the contract, and so forth.
- *Regular meetings*. Schedule a periodic meeting with the department's counterpart at the supplier. This should not be a salesperson, but rather

someone deeply involved in the supplier's operations. The goal is to discuss with this person the results of any audits, problems that have arisen since the last meeting, any new feature implementations, and so forth. If these meetings are contentious, consider documenting them with meeting minutes, and sending copies to all participants to confirm who is responsible for which action items, and the dates by which tasks are to be completed.

For companies with modest payroll outsourcing needs and minor supplier billings, there will be little need for formal audits or ongoing meetings. Instead, a short annual meeting may be sufficient to manage the relationship.

Measuring Outsourced Payroll

Payroll suppliers are highly regimented organizations that are exceptionally good at processing payroll in a timely manner and remitting withheld taxes to the correct government entities by the mandated dates. Thus, there is little need to measure these issues. However, suppliers routinely increase their fees, and sometime charge exorbitant amounts for special reports or functions. Consequently, consider routinely tracking several measurements related to the cost of their services. These measurements are:

- *Payroll fees per person.* A payroll supplier typically charges a broad array of fees, including a fixed fee for each payroll and a per-unit fee for checks created, envelopes stuffed, direct deposits initiated, and so forth. Though some of the fees are not directly related to headcount, it is useful to formulate a metric that calculates the payroll fee per person. The basic calculation is to divide the total supplier billing per month by the number of employees paid through the supplier's payroll system during the month. If only variable charges are to be associated with employees, then instead divide the employee-specific variable charges per month by the number of employees paid through the supplier's payroll system during the month.
- *Proportion of non-standard fees.* When a payroll supplier initially issues a quote for services to be provided, the quote contains their most competitive prices for a basic package of payroll services. After they gain an employer's business, they typically charge much higher fees for a variety of add-on services. It is useful to periodically (perhaps annually) calculate the proportion of these non-standard fees to the total amount billed by the supplier. If the proportion becomes excessively high, it may be time to prune back the extra services, discuss a price reduction with the supplier, or shop the payroll business with competitors to see if a better pricing package is available.

If an employer has multiple locations, another useful metric is the percentage of payrolls that are not delivered to the correct locations, or which are not delivered by the correct pay date. Such situations should be rare, but it is a major concern to those receiving paychecks, and so may be worthy of a tracking system. The calculation is to divide all payroll deliveries that were in error by the total number of payroll deliveries.

Terminating an Outsourcing Arrangement

Payroll outsourcing contracts usually allow for a relatively easy notification to the supplier in order to terminate the service arrangement. However, there are three reasons why outsourcing arrangements tend to be somewhat more difficult to terminate from a practical perspective. They are:

- *Data accumulators.* A payroll supplier usually commits to issue an accurate Form W-2 to all employees following the end of each calendar year, but only if all payroll transactions during the year have been run through its system. If an outsourcing contract is terminated prior to the end of the year, the supplier will issue the W-2 at year-end, but only for the payroll that it processed; the employer must issue another W-2 for any additional wages and related tax deductions that occurred after the termination.
- *Data entry.* Payroll data is retained in the supplier's database, so the employer must find a way to export the data and re-enter it into whichever system it intends to use to replace the supplier's system. This can be a significant problem for larger firms that have many employees.
- *Pension plan.* If a company is using a 401(k) pension plan that is administered by its payroll supplier, it will likely want to shift to a different pension plan at some point, though this can possibly be delayed until after the payroll processing has been shifted elsewhere.

Of the termination issues noted here, the key one for the smaller companies that are the primary users of payroll suppliers is data accumulators. If at all possible, only terminate a payroll outsourcing arrangement at the end of a calendar year, so that the supplier will issue complete W-2 forms to employees. This allows one to start with new data accumulators at the beginning of the next calendar year, and issue a single Form W-2 to employees for that year.

Summary

There are many good reasons for a company to outsource its payroll function to a qualified supplier. The only companies that should *not* do so are those that are either highly sensitive to the cost of payroll processing or those that must link their payroll data to other company databases. In most other cases (generally involving smaller businesses), the convenience of payroll outsourcing makes it an excellent choice for those company managers who want to devote their time to the operation of other aspects of their businesses – rather than the nuts and bolts of processing payroll.

Appendix A
2016 Federal Payroll Tax Calendar

The following table describes the dates on which certain forms are to be filed with the federal government. Filings are with the Internal Revenue Service, unless otherwise noted. If any of the following dates fall on a Saturday, Sunday, or federal holiday, use the next business day instead.

**Due
Date**

January

10   *Form 4070.* Any employees who received cash tips of at least $20 in the preceding month must report them to the company on Form 4070, Employee's Report of Tips to Employer.

15   *EFTPS.* Electronically transfer FICA taxes and withheld federal income taxes for the preceding month.

31   *Form W-2.* Furnish each employee a completed Form W-2, Wage and Tax Statement.

      Form 1099. Furnish each payee a completed Form 1099.

      Form 945. File a Form 945, Annual Return of Withheld Federal Income Tax, to report any non-payroll income tax withheld in the preceding year. If the company deposited all taxes when due, there are 10 additional calendar days in which to file.

      Form 940. File a Form 940, Employer's Annual Federal Unemployment Tax Return. If the company deposited all taxes when due, there are 10 additional calendar days in which to file.

      FUTA taxes. Deposit federal unemployment taxes if the amount due exceeds $500.

      Form 941. File Form 941, Employer's Quarterly Federal Tax Return, for the fourth quarter of the preceding calendar year and deposit any undeposited income, social security, and Medicare taxes. If all taxes were deposited when due, there are 10 additional calendar days in which to file.

February

10   *Form 4070.* Any employees who received cash tips of at least $20 in the preceding month must report them to the company on Form 4070, Employee's Report of Tips to Employer.

15   *Form W-4.* Ask employees to submit a new Form W-4, Employee's Withholding Allowance Certificate, if they claimed exemption from income tax withholding last year.

Due
Date

    EFTPS. Electronically transfer FICA taxes and withheld federal income taxes for the preceding month.

16   This is the expiration date for any Forms W-4 used to file for exemption from withholding in the preceding year.

28   *Forms 1099 and 1096.* File Copy A of all paper Forms 1099 with Form 1096, Annual Summary and Transmittal of U.S. Information Returns. These Forms should contain the aggregate prior year compensation of at least $600 paid to non-employees.

    Forms W-2 and W-3. File Copy A of all paper Forms W-2 with Form W-3, Transmittal of Wage and Tax Statements, with the Social Security Administration.

    Form 8027. File a Form 8027, Employer's Annual Information Return of Tip Income and Allocated Tips, if there is tip income to report.

March

10   *Form 4070.* Any employees who received cash tips of at least $20 in the preceding month must report them to the company on Form 4070, Employee's Report of Tips to Employer.

15   *EFTPS.* Electronically transfer FICA taxes and withheld federal income taxes for the preceding month.

31   *Form 1099.* File any electronic Forms 1099.

    Form W-2. File any electronic Forms W-2 with the Social Security Administration.

April

10   *Form 4070.* Any employees who received cash tips of at least $20 in the preceding month must report them to the company on Form 4070, Employee's Report of Tips to Employer.

15   *EFTPS.* Electronically transfer FICA taxes and withheld federal income taxes for the preceding month.

30   *FUTA taxes.* Deposit federal unemployment taxes if the amount due exceeds $500.

    Form 941. File Form 941, Employer's Quarterly Federal Tax Return, for the first quarter of the calendar year and deposit any undeposited income, social security, and Medicare taxes (if the total tax liability for the quarter is less than $2,500). If all taxes were deposited when due, there are 10 additional calendar days in which to file.

May

10   *Form 4070.* Any employees who received cash tips of at least $20 in the preceding month must report them to the company on Form 4070, Employee's Report of Tips to Employer.

Due
Date

15   *EFTPS.* Electronically transfer FICA taxes and withheld federal income taxes for the preceding month.

June

10   *Form 4070.* Any employees who received cash tips of at least $20 in the preceding month must report them to the company on Form 4070, Employee's Report of Tips to Employer.

15   *EFTPS.* Electronically transfer FICA taxes and withheld federal income taxes for the preceding month.

July

10   *Form 4070.* Any employees who received cash tips of at least $20 in the preceding month must report them to the company on Form 4070, Employee's Report of Tips to Employer.

15   *EFTPS.* Electronically transfer FICA taxes and withheld federal income taxes for the preceding month.

31   *FUTA taxes.* Deposit federal unemployment taxes if the amount due exceeds $500.

      Form 941. File Form 941, Employer's Quarterly Federal Tax Return, for the second quarter of the calendar year and deposit any undeposited income, social security, and Medicare taxes (if the total tax liability for the quarter is less than $2,500). If all taxes were deposited when due, there are 10 additional calendar days in which to file.

August

10   *Form 4070.* Any employees who received cash tips of at least $20 in the preceding month must report them to the company on Form 4070.

15   *EFTPS.* Electronically transfer FICA taxes and withheld federal income taxes for the preceding month.

September

10   *Form 4070.* Any employees who received cash tips of at least $20 in the preceding month must report them to the company on Form 4070, Employee's Report of Tips to Employer.

15   *EFTPS.* Electronically transfer FICA taxes and withheld federal income taxes for the preceding month.

October

10   *Form 4070.* Any employees who received cash tips of at least $20 in the preceding month must report them to the company on Form 4070, Employee's Report of Tips to Employer.

15   *EFTPS.* Electronically transfer FICA taxes and withheld federal income taxes for the preceding month.

31   *FUTA taxes.* Deposit federal unemployment taxes if the amount due exceeds $500.

**Due
Date**

Form 941. File Form 941, Employer's Quarterly Federal Tax Return, for the third quarter of the calendar year and deposit any undeposited income, social security, and Medicare taxes (if the total tax liability for the quarter is less than $2,500). If all taxes were deposited when due, there are 10 additional calendar days in which to file.

November

10   *Form 4070.* Any employees who received cash tips of at least $20 in the preceding month must report them to the company on Form 4070.

15   *EFTPS.* Electronically transfer FICA taxes and withheld federal income taxes for the preceding month.

30   Remind employees to submit a new Form W-4, Employee's Withholding Allowance Certificate, if their marital status or withholding allowances have already changed or are expected to change in the next year.

December

10   *Form 4070.* Any employees who received cash tips of at least $20 in the preceding month must report them to the company on Form 4070, Employee's Report of Tips to Employer.

15   *EFTPS.* Electronically transfer FICA taxes and withheld federal income taxes for the preceding month.

Glossary

A

Account. A separate, detailed record associated with a specific asset, liability, or equity item.

ACH. An electronic network for the processing of both debit and credit transactions within the United States and Canada. ACH payments include direct deposit payroll, social security payments, tax refunds, and the direct payment of business-to-business and consumer bills.

B

Backup withholding. The amount of income tax that a payer withholds from a payee who has not furnished the payer with a tax identification number.

Biweekly. An event that occurs once every two weeks.

Bonus. A payment made to an employee in recognition of services performed.

C

Calendar year. A 12-month period beginning on January 1 and ending on December 31.

COBRA. Refers to the Consolidated Omnibus Budget Reconciliation Act, under which terminated individuals have the option to continue their health insurance coverage with an employer for a period of time.

Commission. A fee paid to a salesperson in exchange for his or her services in facilitating or completing a sale transaction. The commission may be structured as a flat fee, or as a percentage of the revenue, gross margin, or profit generated by a sale.

D

De minimis. Something is too insignificant to be worthy of attention.

Debits and credits. A debit is an accounting entry that either increases an asset or expense account, or decreases a liability or equity account. It is positioned to the left in an accounting entry. A credit is an accounting entry that either decreases an asset or expense account, or increases a liability or equity account. It is positioned to the right in an accounting entry.

Deduction. An amount that an employer withholds from the earnings of an employee.

Defined contribution plan. A retirement plan whose eventual payments are based on specific payments into the plan, plus subsequent investment gains.

Disability benefit. A payment to an employee who cannot work due to illness or accident.

Glossary

E

Employee. A person who provides services to an employer in accordance with the legal definition of an employee.

Employer. A person or entity that retains the services of individuals.

Exempt employee. An individual who is paid a salary; to whom an employer is not required to pay overtime.

Experience rating. A method used by an insurer to determine the pricing of insurance for a business, based on the history of prior claims made by the business.

F

Fair market value of a benefit. The amount that an employee would be required to pay to obtain the benefit in an arm's length transaction.

FICA tax. A tax paid by employees and matched by the employer up to a certain wage limit, which is used to fund the federal social security system.

Fringe benefit. A form of payment for the performance of services. Examples of fringe benefits are the use of a car or the provision of medical or disability insurance. For the remainder of this chapter, we will refer to a fringe benefit as a *benefit.*

Full time equivalent. The total number of hours worked in a period divided by the normal number of working hours in that period. Thus, if a group of employees work 320 hours during a week, and the standard work week is 40 hours, then the full-time equivalent for that period is eight, no matter how many people actually worked.

G

Garnishment. The withholding of a specified amount from a person's wages in order to satisfy a legal claim or an obligation to a creditor.

Ghost employee. A fake employee record to which payments are fraudulently made. It could be an entirely fabricated person, or else a former employee whose record still indicates that he is an active employee.

Golden parachute payment. A payment made to an employee if there is a change in ownership or control of a company.

Gross earnings. The total amount of an employee's earnings, including regular and overtime pay, and before any deductions.

H

Health savings account. An account that is owned by a qualified individual who is either an employee or former employee. Any contributions made by a company into an HSA become the property of the individual. The balance in the account is used to pay for the medical expenses of the individual and that person's family.

Household employee. An employee who performs household work in a private home, local college club, or local fraternity or sorority chapter.

I

Idle time. Any time during which an employee performs no services.

Income tax. A tax on the earnings of employees, and which is deducted from their adjusted gross earnings.

Independent contractor. A person who works for himself or who owns a separate business, and offers services to the public.

Individual retirement account. A retirement account with tax deferral benefits, which an employee personally funds.

J

Journal entry. A formal accounting entry used to identify a business transaction. The entry itemizes accounts that are debited and credited, and should include a description of the reason for the entry.

L

Lookback period. A four-quarter period of time, beginning on July 1 of two years ago and ending on June 30 of one year ago, that is used as a baseline for determining whether an employer should be classified as a monthly or semiweekly depositor of taxes.

M

Minimum wage. The minimum amount that an employer can pay its employees on an hourly basis, as set by state and federal law.

Monthly depositor. An employer who incurred an employment tax liability of less than $50,000 during a lookback period.

N

Net pay. The amount that an employee is paid after all taxes and other deductions have been withheld from his or her pay.

Nonqualified retirement plan. A plan that does not meet the requirements of ERISA or the Internal Revenue Code. A company using a nonqualified plan can pay key employees more than other participants in the plan. If a company contributes funds into a nonqualified plan, it cannot record the payments as an expense until the funds are eventually paid out to the targeted employees, which may be years in the future. Also, a plan participant being paid through a nonqualified plan cannot roll the funds over into an IRA.

O

Overtime. A premium wage paid that is calculated as 1 ½ times the regular wage rate, multiplied by those hours classified as overtime.

P

Payroll cycle. The length of time between payrolls. Thus, if employees are paid once a month, the payroll cycle is one month.

Payroll register. A report that shows the earnings, deductions, taxes, and net pay of each employee during a pay period.

Per diem. A daily travel allowance that a company pays to its employees. For example, a company may have a per diem housing allowance of $100.

Piece rate pay. A compensation system under which employees are paid based on the number of units produced.

Q

Qualified retirement plan. A plan that meets all of the requirements of the Employee Retirement Income Security Act (ERISA), and Section 401(a) of the Internal Revenue Code. Under a qualified plan, the employer can deduct its contributions to the plan, while participants can defer their contributions to and earnings from the plan until they eventually withdraw funds from it. Participants can defer recognition even further by rolling their funds over into an Individual Retirement Account (IRA).

Quarter. Three consecutive calendar months.

R

Regular hours. The first 40 hours that an employee works in a designated work week.

Remittance advice. A document that accompanies a payment, and which gives the details of the payment being made.

S

Salary. A fixed amount paid to an employee for services performed, irrespective of the actual hours worked during a time period.

Semimonthly. An event that occurs twice a month.

Semiweekly depositor. An employer who incurred an employment tax liability of $50,000 or more during a lookback period.

Sick pay. A payment made to an employee because of injury or sickness.

Shift differential. Extra pay earned by employees who work a less than desirable shift, such as the evening, night, or weekend shifts.

Social security number. A unique number issued to an individual by the Social Security Administration.

Stated pay. The amount that an employer pays to an employee as wages prior to any additional payments by the employer for the employee's share of social security and Medicare taxes.

Supplemental wages. Wage payments to employees that are not regular wages. Examples of supplemental wages are back pay, bonuses, commissions, overtime pay, retroactive pay increases, severance pay, and sick leave pay.

T

Tax deposit. Tax payments made by an employer to the government.

Taxable wage base. The maximum amount of an employee's wages paid during a calendar year to which a tax can be applied.

Term of continuous employment. A period of time beginning on the first day that an employee begins work and earns pay, and ends on the earlier of the employee's last day of work. Alternatively, it ends on the last workday before a 30-day period, if the employee performs no services for the employer for more than 30 calendar days.

Time card. A standard form on which an employee records time worked, or on which a time clock stamps the individual's start and stop times.

Tip. A gratuity given by a customer to one or more employees to recognize services performed.

U

Unemployment insurance. A program that provides limited payments to individuals during periods of unemployment.

Unsafe conditions. When a reasonable person would consider it unsafe to walk or use public transportation at the time of day when that person commutes to work. This may be based on a history of crime in the region surrounding an employee's workplace or home.

W

Wage. An amount paid to an employee that is based on time worked or units produced.

Withholding. A portion of an employee's wages that an employer holds back and then forwards to the government as partial payment for the taxes owed by the employee.

Withholding allowance. An exemption claimed by an employee, which is used to calculate the amount of income taxes withheld from that person's wages.

Work week. A designated period of 168 consecutive hours.

Index

Made in the USA
Middletown, DE
23 August 2017